STATES OF
TERROR

STATES OF TERROR

Democracy and Political Violence

Peter Taylor

BBC BOOKS

To Susan, Ben, Sam and 'Caleb'
and the *States of Terror* team

This book is published to accompany the
television series entitled *States of Terror*
which was first broadcast in autumn 1993.

Published by BBC Books,
a division of BBC Enterprises Limited,
Woodlands, 80 Wood Lane,
London W12 0TT

First published 1993

© Peter Taylor 1993
The moral right of the author has been asserted.

ISBN 0 563 36774 1

Set in Times Roman by Create Publishing Services Ltd, Bath
Printed and bound in Great Britain by Clays Ltd., St Ives plc
Jacket printed by Belmont Press Ltd., Northampton

CONTENTS

Acknowledgements   vii

Introduction   ix

Prologue: Men of God   1

1   Munich   5

2   Vengeance   15

3   The Hunted   28

4   The Hunters   50

5   Betrayal   63

6   The Village   87

7   The Seeds of Conflict   112

8   A Tangled Web   147

9   The Agent   170

Epilogue: Today and Tomorrow   186

Notes   198

Bibliography   209

Index   211

PICTURE CREDITS

ACKNOWLEDGEMENTS

States of Terror has been a long project and it would take up much precious space to thank all of those by name who have made both this book and the series possible. Many helped on the record, not least by being interviewed and talking openly and honestly about events that were still painful. To do so required dignity and courage, qualities they displayed in abundance. Many, too, on both the state and the 'terrorist' side of the various conflicts, helped guide us both on and off the record through controversy and propaganda to some approximation of the truth. I thank them all for their confidence and trust and hope they feel it has not been misplaced. I must also record my gratitude to General Sir James Glover who first suggested a series on 'terrorism' over five years ago. Perhaps *States of Terror* is not quite what he had in mind, but I hope it is none the worse for that.

In the end, nothing would have been possible without the help, support and good humour of my BBC colleagues who commissioned and nourished the series and whose talents made it possible: to Paul Hamann, who encouraged me to persevere and maintained his legendary enthusiasm and energy when mine sometimes flagged; to Steve Hewlett, who gathered it under his 'Inside Story' wing when he already had more than enough on his plate; to my producers, Charles Furneaux, Stephen Walker and Martin Smith, who painstakingly put the flesh on the bones of each story, making each spring to life, and without whom the series could never have been made; to Neil Grant, who started out with me at the beginning of *States of Terror* and without whose tenacity, judgement and ferocious energy I would never have reached the end; to Tilman Remme, who time and again made the impossible possible in Germany and who unearthed records that no one ever dreamed still existed; to Nigel Townson, whose quiet persistence in Spain persuaded even the most reluctant to talk and who diligently checked all my Spanish spellings; to Lucy Wadham, whose charm and fluency eased stubborn doors in France; to Ranya Kadri for her unfailing persistence in the Middle East; to Alison McAllan, who found unfindable film; to Bhupinder Kohli, Ann Holland and Alexandra Harris, who kept all of us and the office in order; and to all the camera teams and editors whose creativity made *States of Terror* live. Thanks also to Robin Walsh, Controller, BBC Northern Ireland, and all his colleagues who were always ready to help and advise with problems they face every day; to Ken Kirby and Laurence Rees of *Timewatch*, who amplified my historical knowledge of the 'Troubles' by involving me in 'The Sparks that Lit the Bonfire'; to Sheila Ableman and Martha Caute of BBC Books, who steered these written endeavours with such gentle understanding and skill; to David Cottingham, who chose the pictures with such care; and to Linden Stafford, who edited the manuscript with such precision. Lastly my thanks to my family for their patience and forbearance. 'Quality' time has been in short supply and the grass has not been cut. At least I resisted the temptation to take my laptop to my son's cricket.

INTRODUCTION

This book and the BBC television series on which it is based are designed to examine how the democratic state responds to terrorism. America's humbling experience in Beirut in the earlier eighties, compounded by the subsequent holding of the hostages, epitomizes the state's dilemma in the most dramatic way. But terrorism remains a condition that affects us all, regardless of the states to which we belong. It may mean the irritation of endless security checks at airports; the disruption of journeys to work as bomb scares shut stations and close down city centres; the astronomical cost of bombing campaigns, met by the public purse; and, above all, the tragic loss of life that leaves families the world over bereft and uncomprehending as to why they should fall victim. In the course of my writing this book the IRA devastated the City of London, bombs in Bombay killed over 200 innocent people, the World Trade Centre in New York was shattered, and the Uffizi Gallery in Florence, home of one of the world's finest art collections, was ripped apart. During that time hundreds of men, women and children died in bomb and gun attacks at the hands of Republicans and Loyalists in Northern Ireland, 'narco-terrorists' in the cocaine heartland of South America, 'Shining Path' gueril003as in Peru, Islamic fundamentalist 'terrorists' of assorted varieties in Lebanon, Israel, Egypt and Algeria, Tamil separatists in Sri Lanka and other groups too numerous to mention. The issue is immediate and real. In the closing years of the twentieth century, terrorism has become a universal tool that is easy to use and difficult to counter. Confronted by the threat, democracies often seem impotent. So what does the democratic state do? This is the question I address.

The scope of *States of Terror* is limited, and deliberately so. I decided early on that it would be too ambitious to attempt to cover the world. In the end, I chose Europe and the Middle East as my theatre because for more than twenty years this arena has witnessed every aspect of terrorism and the state's response to it. The results range from success to stalemate and failure. Because the roots of most 'terrorism' are political, I have included a chapter based on my recent BBC2 *Timewatch* programme, which traced the origins of the conflict in Northern Ireland, in the hope that it may help readers understand the origins of Britain's own 'terrorist' problem. I make no apology for devoting considerable sections of the book to both the Middle East and Ireland, since they remain two of the world's most active and unresolved areas of 'terrorist' conflict.

States of Terror is not designed to be an academic treatise: a plethora of books already exists to meet that demand. I have tried to make the theme accessible by concentrating upon a particular story or human experience in each chapter to illustrate different aspects of the state's response. The focus may be the 'terrorists' or the agents of the state charged with countering them. In the process, I have endeavoured to challenge the stereotypes that frequently pervade writing and discussion on the subject. 'Terrorism' is one of the most emotive and subjective words in the English language. It is a value judgement in itself. That is why I invariably place the word 'terrorism' in quotation marks in the belief that the condition is seldom as black and white as the state would like to paint it. The cliché 'One man's terrorist is another man's freedom fighter' may be well worn but it is often true, a historical fact to which Menachem Begin, Robert Mugabe, Nelson Mandela and a host of others bear witness. What price Yasser Arafat or Gerry Adams?

What of my own position? I am against 'terrorism' as such, believing that in a democracy reason, debate and compromise are the way to solve complex political problems. However, I recognize that many of those who resort to violence do so because of injustice and a situation they have inherited from history. Governments ignore genuine political grievances at their peril. Addressing them does not necessarily mean 'giving in to terrorism' but it may mean replacing rhetoric with political courage. In human terms the price is high. Imperatives of the past or present are no consolation to the dead. I feel for the families of the 241 US Marines killed in Beirut in 1983 as I do for those of the 80 Lebanese civilian victims of the Bir al-Abed car bomb years later; for Clair Dignam reading her husband's last letter before his 'execution' by the IRA in 1992; for the loss of a father, be he Baruch Cohen of the Mossad or Ali Hassan Salameh of the PLO; for the family of 'Yoyes' who renounced 'terrorism' only to be shot down by her former ETA colleagues; for the innocents caught up in conflict, be they Mary Perry in Portadown, whose daughter was brutally murdered, or Ilse Maier-Witt in Hamburg, devastated when she discovered her step-daughter was a terrorist. In *States of Terror*, suffering is not confined to one side.

PROLOGUE: MEN OF GOD

I was awakened early, far too early, at 3.45 a.m. to be precise, by the sound of the muezzin calling the Muslim faithful to prayer. I could not understand why anyone, even the most devout, would want to roll out a prayer mat that early in the morning. But this was, after all, Baalbek, the heart of Shiite Islamic fundamentalism in Lebanon, high on the plateau of the Bekaa Valley, two hot hours' drive from Beirut. Several of the hostages had been kept here in unknown dark basements, and it was from here that many had been released and dispatched across the nearby border to Syria to face the waiting ranks of the world's press. I needed the sleep, since we had arrived late the previous evening – late and in the dark. The hotel was wonderful. It was a run-down, fading, nineteenth-century French mansion that seemed to have been run-down and fading ever since. Dusty carpets lined the walls and even dustier antiques and furniture filled the lobby and rooms. If it did not exist, set designers would have to invent it.

I summoned up the energy to go to the window and drag open the rusty shutters. Outside there was sunshine and the freshness of early morning. The view was stunning. Two hundred metres away, against a backdrop of rounded hills where, amazingly, the last snows of winter still lingered, stood the ruins of the temples of Bacchus and Jupiter – Roman, first century AD. These were not piles of old rocks, but magnificent Grecian columns and colonnades, soaring magnificently to the sky. They were reputed to be the tallest ancient columns in the world. But few tourists come here, to the chagrin of the hotel owner, who has run his increasingly empty establishment for forty years and been guide to the site for as long. Tourists do not like 'terrorists'.

Martin Smith, my producer, and I mused on civilizations long gone and the endless armies that had marched across this strategic plateau down the centuries. Two hours later, we were filming an interview with America's sworn enemy, Hussein Musawi, one of the main Shia political leaders of Islamic fundamentalism in Lebanon. Here was no stern-faced cleric, whose likeness adorns every wall and roadside in Baalbek, but a sophisticated politician in a well-cut Western suit, blue cotton open-necked shirt and polished black slip-on shoes. America, he said, was finished; her empire would wane and fall, as had that of the Soviet Union. The future, he assured me, belonged to Islam. He was not a man to be taken lightly, surrounded as he was by unsmiling bodyguards with AK-47s in their hands and pistols stuffed down the waistbands of their trousers. I asked him about the suicide bombings which, between the spring of 1983 and the autumn of 1984, had devastated America and American policy in Lebanon: a pick-up truck packed with 150 kilograms of TNT which on 18 April 1983 had collapsed the American embassy in Beirut like a pack of cards, killing sixty-three people, seventeen of them Americans including most of the CIA station; the truck loaded with 2000 pounds of TNT which, on 23 October 1983, caused the US Marines their greatest single loss of life in a day since Iwo Jima when 241 died in an avalanche of concrete masonry; and, remarkably, a third suicide attack in eighteen months, on 20 September 1984, which reduced the US embassy annexe in Beirut to rubble, leaving thirteen dead, two of them Americans.

Hussein Musawi said he had nothing to do with any of these bombs but supported the attacks. He corrected my use of language. They were not suicide bombers, he said. They were martyrs, happy to die to be closer to God. Such operations were the defence of the poor against their mighty American and Israeli aggressors. I asked what support Lebanese Shiites received from Iran, since the Sheikh Abdullah Barracks in Baalbek had once housed a contingent of Iranian Revolutionary Guards dispatched by Tehran in the wake of Israel's invasion of Lebanon in 1982. He seemed surprised that I should even ask the question. They provide us with military training, he said, and money to buy weapons. This was state-sponsored 'terrorism' without a doubt. I asked him if he was a terrorist. The question prompted not anger but mirth from both interpreter and interviewee. Of course not: America and Israel were the terrorists. But the Marines were part of a peacekeeping force, I suggested, not part of an offensive operation against the Lebanese people. He brushed the point aside with a dismissive wave of the hand: tell that to Tehran.

These events in Lebanon had traumatized Ronald Reagan's America. Where was the world in which Americans could 'walk tall'? The state seemed powerless to respond. Four months after the Marine headquarters bomb, the world's most powerful nation withdrew from Lebanon, its mission incomplete, forced out by the drivers of three trucks. As the dust settled, retaliatory options were considered. A missile strike on Baalbek directed at the Iranian paymasters in the Sheikh Abdullah Barracks was discussed but rejected in part lest it take out the Roman temples instead, not out of respect for history but for fear of a propaganda own goal. But America's embarrassment was not over. After the first embassy bomb, a top-secret undercover team, whose existence is so covert it has never been admitted, was sent to Beirut to assess the intelligence damage. It was led by a Vietnam war hero, Lieutenant-Colonel Bill Cowan of the US Marines. We brought him back to Beirut to tell us and show us what happened. Bill was Ronald Reagan in action. In the movie he would have to be played by Clint Eastwood. He stood in the ruins of the Marine headquarters, looking at what was once the graffiti-covered wall of their bar: alongside the motto 'Attack!' had been scrawled the names of dozens of Marines and their home towns. Many had never returned. Bill told us it need never have happened. In his report, he had warned of the threat to the Marines. There had been further intelligence that a huge bomb was under construction. The target was known; but the warnings were ignored. It got lost in the bureaucracies in Washington, he said bitterly, looking at the names on the wall.

After the bombing of the Marine headquarters, Cowan and his secret unit were sent back to Beirut with the names of those believed to have been implicated. The task was to find out where they were. The rest was un-spoken. Bill confirmed that, once they were located, their 'action' was to be left to others. High on his list was the name of Sheikh Hussein Fadlallah, the spiritual leader of Hizbollah, 'The Party of God', who was said by US intelligence 'assets' to have blessed the Marine corps suicide bomber prior to his mission – although this the Sheikh denies. President Reagan had authorized the CIA to train a section of the Lebanese security forces in counter-terrorist operations. On 8 March 1985, a year after the last Marine had left Lebanon, a car bomb was planted in the Hizbollah stronghold of Bir al-Abed in South Beirut. It was intended to wipe out Sheikh Fadlallah as he returned home from the mosque, but the sheikh unwittingly changed his route and escaped the blast. The bomb, stuffed with 100 kilos of high-explosive hexogen, was detonated, killing eighty-one civilians, many of them women returning from prayers. Today their photographs frame the lines of their graves in the nearby cemetery. A subsequent Hizbollah investigation pointed the finger at a covert unit set up at the request of the Americans within the Lebanese security apparatus known as the 'External Action and Analysis Branch'. The CIA denied all responsibility for in-volvement in the bomb. Bill Cowan, too, acquits the CIA of responsibility and accuses renegade elements within Lebanese intelligence. Clearly things had got out of hand. But was it not a case of America asking 'Who will rid us of this turbulent cleric?'? He agreed that it probably was.

Three months later, Lebanese Islamic fundamentalists hijacked TWA Flight 847 on its way from Athens to Rome. The gunmen demanded the release of 700 Shiite prisoners in Israel and an admission from the United States that it was responsible for the Bir al-Abed bomb. The Boeing 727 was flown to Beirut, where one of the passengers, a US navy diver called Robert Stethem, was shot through the head by one of the hijackers and dumped on the tarmac before the cameras of the world's media. The White House promised that those responsible would not go unpunished. Yet again, rhetoric was the state's response. The promise remains unfulfilled. The body of Robert Stethem, lying bleeding on the ground, symbolized the impotence of America. Terrorism triumphed.

1 · MUNICH

On 5 September 1972, Black September terrorists massacred eleven Israeli athletes at the Olympic Games. Munich was a watershed in modern terrorism and a turning-point in the state's response to it. The outrage marked the beginning of a top-secret policy in which Israel identified and eradicated those she perceived to be the leaders of the terrorist organizations ranged against her under the umbrella of the PLO, the Palestine Liberation Organization.[1] These 'hits', carried out by agents of the Mossad, the Israeli secret service, and Sayeret Matkal, the Israeli equivalent of the British SAS, took place outside her borders regardless of the political sensitivities involved. The Mossad's arm was long. No state, no capital was too distant: guns, booby traps and car bombs silenced her enemies from Norway[2] to Tunisia, from Rome and Paris to Nicosia and Beirut. Israel's policy is the most dramatic and controversial illustration of the state's response to terrorism – the state as assassin. That policy has continued.[3]

It is almost impossible to describe the impact that Munich had on Israel. The Olympics were heralded as the 'Games of Peace and Joy'. The last time the event was held on German soil was in Berlin in 1936, when a naive world was mesmerized by the seductive spectacle of Nazi propaganda. But, for Jews, Munich meant much more: it was the cradle of Nazism, the city where Adolf Hitler emerged from obscurity and penury to create the monster that spawned the concentration camps in which millions of Jews were systematically liquidated. The impact of Munich on the rest of the world was phenomenal too. There had been terrorist atrocities before and there were even more horrendous outrages to come: nearly 100 were killed when right-wing terrorists bombed Bologna railway station in 1980; 270 died as Pan Am 103 exploded over Lockerbie in 1988; and nearly 300 were slaughtered in a terrorist blitz on Bombay in 1993. But Munich was different. It was terrorism as theatre, watched by 900 million viewers in 100 different countries. The photograph of the hooded Palestinian on the balcony of the Olympic village became the symbol of international terrorism as the world suddenly woke up to a threat that had scarcely impinged on its emotions before. Plane hijackings, however spectacular their end as in 1970 at Dawson's Field in Jordan,[4] were removed from personal experience. Munich was an emotional watershed. As Dr George Habash, leader of the Popular Front for the Liberation of Palestine (PFLP), said in an interview to the Beirut newspaper, *Al-Sayad*:

> a bomb in the White House, a mine in the Vatican, the death of Mao Tse-Tung, an earthquake in Paris could not have echoed through the consciousness of every man in the world like the operation at Munich. . . . The choice of the Olympics, from the purely propagandist viewpoint, was 100 per cent successful. It was like painting the name of Palestine on a mountain that can be seen from the four corners of the earth.[5]

On the evening of 4 September, the Israeli team had gone into Munich for a performance of *Fiddler on the Roof*. They got back late and retired to their beds. At 10 p.m., while athletes and officials were enjoying Israel's favourite musical, eight Palestinians, armed with eight Kalashnikov assault rifles and ten hand-grenades, prepared to undertake 'Operation Birim and Ikrit', codenamed after two obscure Arab villages in Upper Galilee of which few Israelis in Munich or elsewhere had ever heard. The inhabitants of the villages had been forced to flee in the wake of the fighting in 1948 after the state of Israel had been declared. Israeli soldiers subsequently dynamited every house. More rubble, more anger, to intensify Arab bitterness at the loss of their homes and their land. Many other Arab villages suffered the same fate as Birim and Ikrit.[6] In all, over two million Palestinians fled, seeking refuge in the camps that were hastily slung up to receive them in neighbouring Arab countries. Nearly half a century later, most refugees are still there in the now permanent shanty towns that have long been the breeding ground of Middle Eastern 'terrorism'.[7] In such camps was Black September born. Until Munich, few in the non-Arab world were familiar with this pair of derelict Arab villages in the shadow of the Lebanese border. But to the Palestinians in that pre-Olympic summer Birim and Ikrit became symbols of the loss of their land, as Israel refused to allow some of the villages' former inhabitants to return and rebuild their homes.[8] Black September was to force an unwilling world to listen and watch.

As *Fiddler on the Roof* was building towards its finale, the eight Palestinians were writing what was alleged to be their last 'will' a few miles away.[9] They knew their chances of survival were slender and wished 'to leave a word to our comrades, our people, our nation and to the world public opinion'.[10] The document purports to be a record of a collective discussion on the purpose and impact of their mission. They were to issue a somewhat incongruous list of demands: the release of 236 Palestinians in Israeli gaols including Kozo Okamoto of the Japanese Red Army, the survivor of the recent Lod airport massacre,[11] and the release of Andreas Baader and Ulrike Meinhof, the founders of the German Red Army Faction. They wrote:

> We are not murderers or highway men. We are an oppressed people who have no land or home, no identity card or passport. . . . We have maintained silence as refugees for more than 28 years. . . . Their reaction will be violent against us. They will say we are terrorists, fascists, murderers and criminals. . . . Why does the Zionist delegation have a place at this tournament? Why is the banner of occupation, which is based on terrorism and intimidation, to be raised next to the flags of all countries of the world, and our flag be absent. . . . So, let the Games stop for a few hours.[12]

The halt in the proceedings was far longer. Around 4 a.m. on 5 September the operation began. The unit, dressed in tracksuits with their weapons concealed in sports bags, were observed climbing over the fence near the Israeli compound. No alarm was raised, since those who noticed them assumed they were athletes returning from some late-night binge. They made their way to apartment 1 which housed some of the Israeli weightlifting team. They knocked on the door. It was opened and rapidly shut. A burst of gunfire ripped through the woodwork, hitting and fatally wounding Moshe Weinberg, the wrestling coach.

One of those inside was the weightlifter, Tuvia Sokolovsky, whom I met in the mirrored hall of the huge Wingate Sports Centre in Netanya, Israel, where he watched young Olympic hopefuls straining and grunting as giant barbells clanged on the floor. Tuvia had felt uncomfortable from the moment he had landed in Munich. Memories of the Holocaust were more powerful than the 'Games of Peace and Joy'. 'All my family was exterminated in that country,' he told me. 'I am a Holocaust survivor. For me, Germans and Munich mean the extermination of six million Jews, including my father and his family. The Germans offered us training camps free of charge in order to cover up their evil deeds in the past. When I was there, I had a horrible feeling as I saw in every adult German the face of the murderers of my parents.' The details of that terrible day were still deeply upsetting, and his emotion was obvious as he described the events. 'At 4.30 a.m. I heard one of my colleagues shouting, "Run away, guys!" I jumped from the bed and saw him trying to hold an open door with his fists. I also saw a terrorist with a mask trying to push a gun into the room. At that moment I knew I had to escape. I ran towards the window. I tried to open it but couldn't. I pushed it with all my force. It fell out and I jumped from the first floor and began to run out. The Arab terrorists started shooting at me and I could hear the bullets flying near my ears. I lost my best friends there. I came back to Israel on my own. There were five of us and I was the only weightlifter who returned.'[13]

The terrorists then attacked apartment 3, which housed more weight-lifters and wrestlers. Here they met resistance. Yossef Romano lunged forward with a fruit-knife and was shot dead for his temerity. Gad Tzabari, an Israeli wrestling champion, watched in horror. He too escaped with bullets whistling round his head. Today he coaches boisterous young im-migrant Jews in a tiny underground bunker near his home in Tel Aviv. Munich scarred him too. When Gad went to do his military service, he was rejected because of his mental condition. He, too, is lucky to be alive. He had seized his moment. 'The terrorist with the nylon stocking over his head pushed the Kalashnikov in my stomach. He ordered me towards the exit. Instinctively, without thinking, I pushed the gun aside. I believe it was God's hand that guided me. I ran for my life, zigzagging to avoid the salvo of shots behind me. I could not believe that none of them hit me. It only lasted a few minutes but every minute was as long as the years in my life.'[14]

With nine hostages, the Palestinians then opened negotiations: they demanded the release of the prisoners in Israel and Germany and a plane to any Arab country except Jordan or Lebanon; if their demands were not met by nine o'clock that morning, they threatened executions by the hour. The authorities played for time. Zwicka 'Zvi' Zamir, the head of the Mossad, was flown to Munich. He could give advice but could not intervene, since the crisis was unfolding on foreign soil. He felt slighted and ignored. 'The Germans were useless, useless all the way,' he later bitterly confided.[15] Finally the German authorities agreed to supply the aircraft the Pal-estinians demanded and assured them that the prison releases in Israel were now under way. It was all a bluff. Two helicopters were provided to take the Palestinians and their hostages to Fürstenfeldbruch airport, where they were led to believe a Lufthansa Boeing was standing by to take them to Cairo. At the airport, five German snipers were in position awaiting the arrival of Black September and their hostages. The original plan was to station policemen in the Boeing to ambush the Palestinians when they came to inspect the plane, but, at the last moment, the German police pulled out because they thought the operation was 'suicide'. When Zamir saw eight Black September gunmen arriving at Fürstenfeldbruch and only five snipers, he was horrified. 'The German plan was so poor. It was so unprofessional. Some of our men could have been in place. The airport was an ideal place for a rescue operation.'[16]

As the Palestinians left the helicopter to inspect the Lufthansa Boeing, a German sniper opened fire. There was a fierce gun-battle that lasted for about 15 minutes. 'The German guns sounded like rifles to shoot pigeons and rabbits,' said Zamir scornfully.[17] There was then an agonizing half-hour of silence. German armoured cars arrived and battle erupted again. Realizing the game was up, the Palestinians lobbed a grenade into the helicopter holding the hostages, which exploded in flames. The other helicopter standing nearby also caught fire. When the shooting stopped and the smoke cleared, fifteen people were dead: nine hostages, five terrorists and one German policeman. Three Palestinians survived. The rescue operation was a catastrophe.

The knife was twisted even deeper when the three survivors were released less than two months later and flown to a heroes' welcome in Tripoli. On 29 October 1972 Black September had hijacked a Lufthansa flight from Damascus to Frankfurt and threatened to blow up the plane unless their three comrades in Munich were released. The Germans capitulated.

Israel felt humiliated and powerless, at the mercy of dark forces she was unable to control. Munich was the dramatic culmination of a wave of terror that had engulfed the nation at the beginning of the decade. Only three months before the Olympics, the PFLP had masterminded a bloody grenade and gun attack on passengers arriving at Lod, Tel Aviv's airport. The state had to respond to the seemingly endless round of atrocities, each one worse than the last. Three days after Munich, Israel struck back by bombing PLO bases in Syria and Lebanon. Some 200 people were killed, including many women and children, in an act of indiscriminate vengeance directed not against the perpetrators of Munich but at the people from whose midst they came. Israel realized, however, that blind air raids were not enough. She had to pinpoint Black September and strike at its heart. But what was the organization and who were its members?

Volumes have been written about Black September, the most notorious of all the Palestinian 'terrorist' groups. There is little doubt what it did, since its operations, like Munich, were invariably claimed under its banner and there is no dispute over the origins of its name. Following Israel's crushing victory over her Arab neighbours in the 1967 Six Day War, the Palestinian leadership was left shattered and demoralized. Over a quarter of a million more Palestinians fled their homes and camps, many for a second time.[18] Palestine seemed gone for ever as Israel, with vast American military and economic assistance, established her military supremacy in the Middle East. She confirmed her apparent invincibility by extending her 1948 frontiers to Egypt and the Suez Canal in the south, to Syria and the Golan Heights in the north and to Jordan and the West Bank in the east. In the aftermath of the 1967 war, Palestinians recognized that they could no longer look to their Arab brothers to liberate their land: if any liberating was to be done, they would have to do it themselves. Fatah and the other Palestinian organizations, whose contribution to the war had been largely rhetorical, regrouped in King Hussain's Jordan and attacked Israel and the newly occupied territories from across the Jordan river. In the first two months of 1968 the Israelis claimed there had been ninety-one incidents,[19] and, although the vast majority of Fatah infiltrators were captured or killed, Israel clearly faced a new threat along her borders.

True to tradition, she acted. After a land-mine attack on a school bus in which a doctor and a schoolboy were killed and twenty-nine children injured,[20] Israel attacked Fatah's main operational base at Karameh just across the border in Jordan. Eschewing all the cardinal rules of guerrilla warfare, Arafat ordered his men to stand and fight in the hope that the world would sit up and see that, if Arab armies fled before the might of Israel, Palestinians stood their ground. 'We will make Karameh the second Leningrad,' Arafat boasted.[21] On 21 March 1968 battle commenced. Although 98 of the 400 fedayeen were killed and their base at Karameh was reduced to rubble, the Israelis suffered far more casualties than they had anticipated: 28 dead, 69 injured and 34 tanks hit.[22] Arafat, with considerable help from the Jordanian army despite orders not to intervene, snatched a rhetorical victory from the jaws of defeat. Karameh became enshrined and embellished in PLO legend. Even Israel's head of military intelligence, General Aharon Yariv, gave credit to his enemy's performance. 'After Karameh, we understood that we had a serious movement on our hands,' he said. 'Although it was a military defeat for them, it was a moral victory.'[23] Karameh was also the moment at which the media and their cartoonists first became aware of the man who made the Keffiyeh (the traditional Arab headdress) and designer stubble famous: Yasser Arafat. The PLO now fell increasingly under the control of Fatah and Yasser Arafat. In July 1968 the Palestine National Covenant, the charter setting out the organization's aims and objectives, was rewritten to include the two clauses that came to haunt the PLO in its later quest for political respectability.

Article 9. Armed struggle is the only way to liberate Palestine and is therefore strategy not tactics. The Palestinian Arab people affirms its absolute resolution and abiding determination to pursue the armed struggle and to march forward toward the armed popular revolution to liberate its homeland and return to it. . . .

Article 19. The partitioning of Palestine in 1947 and the establishment of Israel are fundamentally null and void, whatever time has elapsed, because this was contrary to the wish of the people of Palestine.[24]

The battle of Karameh also emboldened the Palestinian resistance and gave birth, indirectly, to Black September. Despite the military setback, Fatah now had 2000 men under arms ready to strike at Israel, many of them based in Jordan. Their presence, along with that of other Palestinian groups who were both allies and rivals of Fatah, caused increasing concern to King Hussain's regime, the vast majority of whose subjects were Palestinian. The sight of guerrillas bearing arms and enforcing their own laws and punishments threatened the creation of a state within a state; indeed, one of Fatah's leaders, Abu Daoud, who commanded the 15 000-strong militia in Amman's Wahdat refugee camp,[25] advocated a *coup d'état* against the Hashemite dynasty. The king responded, first by introducing a series of restrictive laws against his menacing guests in February 1970, and then by declaring all-out war on them the following September after the declaration of martial law. This was 'Black September'. The fighting lasted for six days, ending in defeat for the Palestinians as their revolutionary Arab allies failed to come to their aid. According to Red Cross estimates, around 3000 are thought to have died. Arafat inflated the death toll to 20 000.[26] Jordan was lost as a base and, not for the first time, Fatah and Arafat were left in disarray. 'Black September' emerged from the ashes. Just over a year later, the world first heard its name. On 28 November 1971 the Jordanian Prime Minister, Wasfi al-Tal, was shot dead in the lobby of the Sheraton Hotel in Cairo where he was holding discussions with the Arab League. He had been regarded as the strongman of the regime who had encouraged King Hussain to put an end to the Palestinian challenge to his authority. The assassin who fired five shots into his body was a young Palestinian called Mansur Suleiman Khalifah, who was part of a four-man unit. In a gesture which subsequently took on legendary proportions, Khalifah is said to have knelt down to lick the Prime Minister's blood. As the assassins were seized by the Egyptian police, they are reported to have raised their fists with a defiant shout, 'We are Black September.'[27]

The clearest insight into the precise nature of Black September and its relationship with Yasser Arafat's Fatah was provided, ironically, by one of Fatah's senior commanders, Abu Daoud, whom Israel regarded as one of the Black September leaders behind the Munich massacre. Daoud later achieved international notoriety in 1977 when on an official visit to Paris he was arrested by the French security service, Direction pour la Surveillance du Territoire (DST). There were moves by Israel and the West German Justice Ministry to obtain his extradition for his part in the Munich massacre. The West Germans announced they were seeking Daoud on twelve charges of conspiracy to murder and eleven charges of helping to take hostages. Daoud's arrest acutely embarrassed the French government, which was notably sympathetic to the Palestinian cause. But France's dilemma and fear of becoming a target for Black September/Fatah reprisals were resolved when, to expressions of horror and outrage, Daoud was given a first-class air ticket and put on a flight to Algiers. He then wisely decided to steer clear of western Europe. Four years later, on 6 August 1981, he narrowly escaped an assassination attempt in the coffee shop of the Intercontinental Hotel in Warsaw. Daoud claims it was the hand of the Mossad, but it is generally thought more likely to have been the work of the rival Palestinian group of Abu Nidal.

The rare insight into Black September had been provided after Daoud's arrest in Jordan on 13 February 1973 while carrying out an operation to take the Jordanian Cabinet hostage in exchange for around forty Palestinian detainees. Daoud was sentenced to death. Following his interrogation, he made a series of remarkable 'confessions' which were then broadcast in interviews on Amman radio and television. Daoud, who was subsequently released after great pressure from Arab leaders and the United Nations, has always maintained that the 'confessions' were unreliable because he had been forced to make them under extreme torture. Nevertheless, most experts regard them as genuine. 'There is no such thing called Black September,' Daoud said on Amman radio on 24 March 1973.[28] 'Fatah announces its operations under this name so that Fatah would not appear as the direct executor of the operations.' In a previous television interview Daoud explained why Fatah had turned to what the West would regard as 'terrorism'.

> When Fatah used to fight with full strength over the occupied terri-
> tories, it did not need operations abroad, plane hijacking, etc. The
> Popular Front [PFLP] used to carry out operations abroad and we
> were against these operations. . . . When the organization [Fatah] lost
> the main arena in Jordan, it also lost effective work against the Zionist
> enemy. Fatah then found it necessary to carry out liquidation oper-
> ations, aircraft operations and other operations . . . concentration on
> such operations is a primary proof of the failure of actions against the
> occupied territory . . . this turns us into gangs dispersed here and
> there, carrying out operations described as terrorist operations rather
> than liberation operations.[29]

The admission came as no surprise to Israeli intelligence officers, who had always known this to be the case but had scarcely expected to hear the relationship made public on the lips of one of Fatah's leaders and broadcast by one of its enemies.

Daoud also went on to give details of the Munich massacre and his own role in it. The organizer, he said, was Abu Iyad (Salah Khalaf), one of Fatah's founding fathers, its intelligence chief and Arafat's number two.[30]

It was Abu Iyad who had given the go-ahead for Munich. Daoud said that he had been in Sofia in Bulgaria in August 1972 buying arms for Fatah when Abu Iyad came to his hotel:

> At the hotel Abu Iyad informed me . . . that they intended to attack the Israeli delegation to the Olympic Games in Munich, to detain the Israeli athletic delegation and to ask the German government for the release of the Arab prisoners in Israel in return for the release of the Israeli athletic team.[31] . . . The instructions did not include opening fire on the Israeli team.

Abu Iyad asked Daoud to part with his false Iraqi passport, which contained a German visa. Daoud handed it over to one of the Black September team, Fakhri al-Umari. Using this passport with the false ID, al-Umari travelled to Munich and attempted, initially unsuccessfully, to reconnoitre the Olympic village. He then obtained the Kalashnikovs and grenades and left them in a locker at the railway station in Munich where they were collected the day before the operation. Al-Umari then left for Tripoli, Beirut and Damascus. Questioned about ultimate responsibility for Munich, Daoud replied:

> these operations come under very strict secrecy. Only the proposal emerges. In the Munich operation and the operation against the Premier's office in Amman [for which Daoud was arrested], it seemed to me that Abu Iyad was behind the two operations. Whether Abu Iyad planned with others or was working on his own, I cannot say definitely. If Abu Iyad did not plan with others, the accusing finger would point at him.[32]

He went on to say that Abu Iyad did not link his operations to Black September: that attribution was made by Fatah's intelligence department run by Abu Youssef and Abu Hassan (Ali Hassan Salameh), who is the subject of chapter three, 'The Hunted', and was, the Israelis claimed, the 'mastermind' of Munich.

Miraculously, Abu Daoud is still alive today and living in Tunis despite his 'confessions' and having the dubious distinction of being on the 'hit list' of both Abu Nidal and the Mossad. Fatah accepted that the 'confessions' had been induced under torture and were therefore invalid. I met Abu Daoud on two occasions in his heavily guarded office in a quiet side street in Tunis where the PLO has its base. Young men in sweatshirts and leather jackets stood around cradling automatics and machine pistols. The security seemed excessive at first until you remembered the fate of many of Abu Daoud's colleagues. Tea was served in glass mugs with no milk and lots of sugar. Palestinian 'terrorists' are nothing if not hospitable. Abu Daoud is not the kind of person who enters any room unnoticed. He is a huge man, around 6 feet 6 inches tall, and not someone with whom you would want to argue. He moves slowly, and speaks English slowly. When I asked him about his 'confessions', he dismissed them and offered to show me the torture marks. But he did confirm the relationship between Fatah and Black September, although not in the detail he had given in Jordan. 'Fatah is a big organization,' he said. 'A lot of the body of Black September were members of Fatah. They were good officers and fighters from the bases. Anyone who knew their name would say, "This is Fatah".'[33] But he was not prepared to confirm, as he had in his 'confessions', that they were acting under Fatah's direction. However, another senior PLO figure I spoke to in another Arab capital gave what is likely to be an accurate assessment of the broad status of Black September which confirms what Abu Daoud said in Jordan. 'Fatah needed Black September,' he told me. 'We wanted the world to sit up and take notice. I just wanted the name of Palestine spelled properly. There was no "policy" as such. It was trial and error. The networks were not organized. It was simply a bunch of "friends". The leadership gave the operations its blessing.'

I asked Abu Daoud if he thought Munich was a mistake. He began with the standard answer given by 'terrorists' to explain away civilian casualties: 'Killing all innocent people is a mistake.' I pointed out that the victims of Munich were innocent athletes. Not so, argued Daoud. They were Israeli 'officers', he said, meaning they would serve in the army back home. I pointed out that all young Israeli men and women did. Abu Daoud found no problem in justifying Munich. 'I'll tell you the background. The Palestinians were suffering in South Lebanon, every day. Innocent women and children in the camps were being bombed by aircraft. Our camps were smashed and hundreds were killed. We have no aeroplanes to attack Israel with. So the young people thought out a way of revenge.' (He was referring to Black September.) 'It may not have been right. It may not have been good. But you have to ask the reason why. No one asks why our people are being killed. If one Israeli is killed, there are cameras everywhere. "Look at the blood!" they say, showing them the earth. But when hundreds of Palestinians are killed, where is the blood? I saw not one drop. The West should realize that it is we who are being killed every day. Although I condemn the killing of innocent people, I can't condemn those who did Munich because I understand the way that they felt.'

After Munich, though, Israel was not interested in splitting hairs and making fine distinctions between Fatah and Black September. She had one object in mind: to hunt down and eliminate not just those responsible for the Olympic massacre but the political and military leadership of the PLO. Israel sought vengeance.

2 · VENGEANCE

Black September's avenger could not be a more unlikely person. General Aharon Yariv, the former head of Aman, Israeli military intelligence, who paid credit to his PLO adversaries after their stand at the battle of Karameh in 1968, is a small, studious-looking man who lives surrounded by books and beautiful pictures in a quiet suburb of Tel Aviv. He is one of the elder statesman of the nation's intelligence community, held in special respect because of the vital contribution his intelligence analysis made towards Israel's victory in the Six Day War of 1967. General Yariv could easily be taken for an academic, with his silver hair, heavy spectacles and quiet intensity. He is also a fervent supporter of his former comrade-in-arms, Prime Minister Yitzak Rabin, who he believes is pragmatic and strong enough to do a deal with the PLO and negotiate the peace settlement that the majority of Palestinians and Israelis want after forty-five years of military conflict, guerrilla war and 'terrorism'. In 1966 General Yariv was the author of a report on Fatah which concluded that the only solution was political – a controversial conclusion for which he was roundly condemned by his fellow general, Ariel Sharon, who believes that force is the only language Israel's enemies understand. 'I can only quote a very dear friend of mine,' General Yariv told me. 'He said the peace agreement will not be paradise, but if there will be no peace agreement it will be hell.' Ironically, this quiet, peaceable man was the architect of the Mossad 'hit team' that exacted vengence for Munich.

I asked him about the impact of the Olympic massacre. 'I remember people coming to me and saying, "I volunteer to fight Black September." Of course, it's the fact that many people, not just one or two, advertised their preparedness to combat Black September that was important. They felt it was their responsibility to do something about it.'[1] The effect of Munich on the Israeli Prime Minister, Golda Meir, was profound. 'Golda', who regarded herself as the Grandmother of the Nation and was regarded as such by her people, felt tremendous guilt because she, as head of state, had let her children die. 'She took it very personally,' recalls Yariv, 'because she felt she was to be blamed for what happened in Munich. The Committee of Inquiry after the Munich massacre found out that there were two people to be blamed, and one belonged to the General Security Service, Shin Bet, and the other belonged to the Mossad. The two services come directly under the Prime Minister, and she felt terribly bad about it, terribly bad.'[2] In the traumatic aftermath of Munich, Prime Minister Golda Meir asked General Yariv to become her special adviser on terrorism and expressed eternal gratitude when he agreed.

Yariv had no doubt what needed to be done. He told me his deputy went for the more subtle approach, suggesting that a covert organization with a codename like 'The Firm', operating under the direction of the state, should be set up to liquidate the leaders of Israel's terrorist enemies. In the modern political parlance of Colonel Oliver North, 'The Firm' would have had 'plausible deniability'. But Yariv would have none of it. If the state was to get into the assassination business, it was going to do it properly. There were protracted discussions between the various intelligence agencies and Cabinet ministers at which Yariv's recommendations were considered and the pros and cons of such a highly controversial and risky enterprise meticulously weighed. 'It's what we call "laying it out on small plates",' he explained. 'We took a decision on this. We took a decision on that.' In the end, the various committees agreed on Yariv's plan. The general then had to persuade the Prime Minister. Today, General Yariv is chillingly honest about his proposal and the subsequent execution of it. I was surprised by the directness of his response to questions on a subject still shrouded in official secrecy and still highly sensitive in government circles despite the passage of time. When posing such questions, journalists are accustomed to a degree of prevarication and evasion. It was almost as if General Yariv wanted to clear the books for posterity. This was our exchange.

My carefully considered advice, checked with other chiefs of the security services, was to go for the leaders of the Black September.
Go for?
Yes, I mean eliminate the leaders of Black September, as much as possible, or as many as possible.
Kill them?
To be honest, yes.
To kill them where?
Wherever we can find them, wherever we could find them, and wherever our people could do this damn job. The circumstances were

not always propitious but in those cases where the circumstances were favourable and the man was clearly identified as being one of the leaders, either of the PLO or the Black September or Fatah, approval was given for an assassination operation.
Who was to carry out the killings?
The people of the Mossad.
How?
By all kinds of means. It could be by booby-trapping, could be by shooting, could be by blowing up a car. All these well-known methods.
How many people did Mossad kill during this operation?
I don't remember the exact count, but it seems to me something in the order of ten people.
So these people weren't just people who were thought by your intelligence agencies to be those responsible for Munich?
Not necessarily, not necessarily at all. Some of them were linked to Munich, some of them weren't.

The admission that not all the Mossad's victims were linked to Munich was a startling revelation. It explained why we had found it impossible to connect many of the victims of the 'hit team' with Munich, however indirectly. The reason was blindingly simple: they were *not* involved. Abu Daoud was right when he told us in Tunis that the Mossad's policy was 'to destroy the leadership of the PLO and Fatah on the grounds that, if they killed its strong leadership, they would demolish the entire organization'. Yariv's plan was not only outrageously daring but, to civil libertarians, outrageously immoral. I asked him how Golda Meir reacted to his suggestion. 'As a woman she was not very exhilarated by the idea, but I felt very strongly about it, very strongly indeed. In the end, I succeeded in convincing her. She relented.' I asked if the Prime Minister had agreed to the Mossad going out and assassinating specific Palestinians wherever they were. He insisted there was nothing random about it: each individual was meticulously targeted.

Each case, each operation, had to be approved and explained in detail. First of all we had to determine the personality whose life was at stake. We had to judge whether they had something – or have something – to do with Black September and the exact operational details. Every operation we undertook was approved.
But how could you be absolutely sure that the people that you thought were the leaders of Black September were the leaders of Black September?
Well, we couldn't always be sure. Some of them were not Black

September but were PLO and very active in the PLO, and were involved in these or other terrorist activities. And if we were not sure enough there was no operation.

Once convinced of the necessity of the plan, Golda Meir embraced it wholeheartedly. A month after Munich, she met some of the families of the slain athletes in her office at the Israeli parliament, the Knesset. One of those present was Ankie Spitzer whose husband, André, the team's fencing coach, died in the final shoot-out at the airport. Ankie, like all the families, has grieved for twenty-one years. 'It's a red thread that goes through my life,' she told me on the twentieth anniversary of the massacre. 'Look at the other families. Life finished at the same time. They stopped living twenty years ago.' Ankie will never forget Golda Meir's words at the Knesset meeting as she gave utterance to the Old Testament precept of 'an eye for an eye': 'No one who has Jewish blood on his hands for Munich will stay unpunished. We will get them all. It might take some time but we will get them.' The families sat silent. No one said no. At the memorial service for the victims a fortnight later the Prime Minister repeated her promise to the families: 'Be sure, we will not let them get away with it.'[3] As the months went by, Ankie received phone calls from people who never gave their names. She knew who they were, at least the organization to which they belonged. Identities were not important. The message they relayed was: another terrorist had been removed, another athlete avenged. I asked Ankie, an intelligent, civilized and sophisticated Dutch journalist, how she felt when she received such calls. Biblical notions of revenge seemed foreign to her character, however brutal her husband's death. And phone calls were not the only indication of vengeance at work. On occasions she was shown photographs of the 'hit team's' victims. She confessed to some confusion. 'My reaction was mixed. It would be very primitive to be jubilant, but when I saw the pictures I received some satisfaction that they were not able to enjoy their children. I'd prefer to bring them to court. But justice cannot be done in the courtroom.'

Within six weeks of Munich, the Mossad 'hit team' went to work. On 18 October 1972 Wael Zwaiter was gunned down in Rome with a dozen .22 bullets in the courtyard of the building where he lived. The two gunmen are said to have rushed to join their female colleague, disguised with a blond wig, and waiting in a green Fiat 125 outside the entrance to Zwaiter's flat.[4] On the face of it, Wael Zwaiter seemed an unlikely target. He was known as a poet and a man of letters. When he was shot, he was said to have been carrying a copy of *A Thousand and One Nights*, which he had recently translated.[5] Zwaiter had been Fatah's representative in Rome for four years and had made good contacts with the cultural and political left in Italy: it was all part of his job, to give Fatah and the PLO the political respectability they sought in Europe and the West. This, in itself, would have been a serious challenge to Israel. The problem with analysing the dozen assassinations that we believe Israel carried out lies in establishing the precise evidence that linked each of the victims with Black September in particular and 'terrorist' activities in general. A good deal has been written about the 'hit team' but, because of its sensational subject matter and the temptation it offers to authors, much is speculative and some inaccurate. Embellishment is free to run riot when no authority is inclined to deny it. My colleagues, Charles Furneaux and Neil Grant, and I made great efforts to find out what this evidence was but were constantly frustrated in our endeavours. Despite three visits to Israel, numerous meetings with senior military and political figures in the Israeli Defence Forces (IDF) and the Prime Minister's Office, and endless letters explaining the *States of Terror* project and detailing what we wished to establish with regard to Israel's response to Munich and Black September, we were not given even the most rudimentary off-the-record briefing about the individuals that Israel targeted. The reason remains a mystery.

In the end, we came to wonder if the evidence ever existed. Was Wael Zwaiter really an innocent poet assassinated because he was a prominent Palestinian? It seemed highly unlikely but we had no indication to the contrary. In Rome, my producer, Charles Furneaux, met Zwaiter's girl-friend, an Australian called Janet Venn Brown. The couple were due to be married and she was genuinely astonished at the suggestion that he might have been involved in terrorist activities and was, in Charles Furneaux's judgement, a remarkably credible witness. 'I had known him for many years,' she said. 'It is inconceivable that he could have been linked with any terrorist activity. He loved books. All his friends were intellectuals and journalists. Besides, he was far too disorganized to get it together.' Abu Daoud had also known Zwaiter and insists he was not involved in any 'operational' activities: 'Zwaiter was a philosopher, an artist. He only dealt with books. He was killed because they wanted to kill him because of his relationship with Italy and the Italians, in particular because of his friend-ship with writers like Alberto Moravia and the Italian Communist Party. They killed him because he carried books.'[6] It is, of course, possible if not likely that there was more to Wael Zwaiter than met the literary eye, but we were never in a position to find out at first hand. I put the unproven point about Wael Zwaiter to General Yariv. He seemed to confirm what Abu Daoud said. To Israel a 'terrorist' is not just a person who carries out an act of violence but anyone in support who helps make it possible. General Yariv's response was as follows:

Well, as far as I remember, there was some involvement on his part in terrorist activities – not in operations, but in terrorist activities: supplying, helping, let us say 'support' activities.
But you couldn't be assassinating people just because you think they happen to support terrorist activities, surely?
Well, you must remember the situation. Activity went on on their part and the only way we thought we could stop it – because we didn't have any interest in just going round and killing people – was to kill people in leadership roles. And it worked in the end. It worked.[7]

Two months later, the 'hit team' claimed its second victim. This time Paris was the hunting ground, and Dr Mahmoud Hamshari, the PLO representative, was the target. A more sophisticated way of removing him was devised. On 16 December 1972 he answered a telephone call at his flat. There was an explosion and Hamshari lay seriously wounded. A bomb had been triggered by an electronic signal sent down the telephone line when he lifted the receiver and gave his name. A technician was thought to have recently repaired the phone after apparent 'accidental damage' to the telephone wires while 'plumbers' were repairing pipes around his flat.[8] The engineer appeared to have fixed more than just the telephone. The bomb had been carefully placed either underneath the table on which the phone stood or in the base of the phone itself. Hamshari died of his injuries three weeks later in hospital, having lived long enough to tell French investigators of the high-pitched whine he heard just before the blast.

Charles Furneaux and Neil Grant met and talked with Dr Hamshari's French wife, Marie-Claude, in Paris. They found her a credible witness when she denied that her late husband had ever had anything to do with terrorism. 'What could he have done, anyway?' she told them. 'What could I have done to convince the Israelis that he wasn't who they said he was?' Again I put the point of Dr Hamshari's alleged innocence to General Yariv, and he responded:

I don't remember, it is quite some years ago. I don't remember any details, but to the best of my recollection Hamshari was not directly involved in Munich. No. But he was directly involved in PLO activities.
But that's very broad, PLO activities. He could have been a politician.
He could have been a writer, a thinker, a supporter.
That, yes, but he was in a leadership position.
And that justifies his murder?
In order to make them stop, yes.[9]

And so the killing went on as the Mossad 'hit team' roamed over Europe, eliminating its targets with bomb and bullet. Victim number three was Hussain al-Shir, the PLO representative in Cyprus. He too was killed by a remote-controlled bomb, detonated under his bed on 25 January 1973 at the Hotel Olympic in Nicosia. According to one of the more lurid accounts, his bloodied head was found sticking in the lavatory pan.[10] He was alleged to be the PLO's contact man with the KGB but we have no evidence that was the case. Paris was again the scene for the assassination of victim number four, Dr Basil Al-Kubaisi, a forty-year-old Iraqi professor who had taught at the American University in Beirut. He was alleged to be the PFLP officer in charge of the arsenal of firearms and explosives stored in Arab diplomatic missions throughout Europe.[11] Again we have no evidence that this was the case. He died while walking near the Eglise de la Madeleine, when two young men fired nine shots into him.

Victims five, six and seven met their ends in equally violent but very different circumstances. They died on 9 April 1973 in an attack, not in Europe, but in Beirut, where they were living. Israel believed she was striking at the heart of Black September. Few tears were shed in Jerusalem or Washington or Western capitals, since the Israeli attack came only five weeks after a Black September unit had machine-gunned to death two American ambassadors and the Belgian chargé d'affaires whom it had taken hostage in the Saudi Arabian embassy in Khartoum. The targets of Israel's dramatic incursion into Beirut were: Abu Youssef, a founder member of Fatah with Yasser Arafat, and the alleged operations and intelligence genius behind Black September;[12] Kamal Nasser, the PLO's official spokesman, and also an alleged high-ranking Black September officer; and a third alleged Black September leader, Kamal Adwan, who ran Fatah's information services and, allegedly, Fatah's cells in the West Bank and Gaza Strip.[13]

All three were living in adjacent apartment blocks in Beirut's Rue Verdun. Mossad observers reported that the Palestinians' security was lax. But Mossad did not know that at the time of the planned operation Yasser Arafat was staying just around the corner. The lack of security did show remarkable carelessness, given the fate of several of their comrades in Europe over the preceding months. This time their assailants were not the Mossad, although they would have played a crucial role in the planning of the operation, but soldiers from Sayeret Matkal, the IDF's elite SAS-style commando unit. The operation was codenamed 'Springtime of Youth' and was led by Colonel Ehud Barak, who is, at the time of writing, the Israeli Chief of Staff. It is one of the few assassination operations that Israel is prepared, indeed proud, to admit to having carried out. It was a textbook military operation in which Israel rejoices and about which heroic movies are made.

We met one of Barak's chief lieutenants, now living outside Tel Aviv. For security reasons I shall refer to him as 'Miki'. 'Miki' is a huge man with enormous hands. He said the team had practised for three months in Israel on a scale model of the buildings where their targets were living. 'It was a very sensitive and unusual mission,' he told us, while munching a cake. 'We had a high sense of morality. We knew it was blood revenge for Munich and we wanted to make absolutely sure that our targets *were* involved and sought an assurance from our superiors that they were. That assurance was given. Abu Youssef, whom I was to target, was involved in Munich and other terrorist acts; Kamal Adwan was the operations officer who organized and controlled the Olympic attack; and Kamal Nasser was the spokesman.' 'Miki' explained how they planned to surprise the three Palestinian leaders. 'We were to be dressed up as men and women. Barak was to be a woman, complete with wig and make-up (which was done in Israel), and I was to be his (or her) husband. I was dressed like a European tourist – with an Uzi [Israeli machine-gun] and a grenade on my body.' The pairing was obviously right. I could not imagine 'Miki' as a woman except, perhaps, as a pantomime dame.

The team was taken by a mother ship to a point seven miles off the coast of Beirut and then decanted, seven at a time, into dinghies which carried them ashore. 'Miki' was wearing what he described as a 'plastic suit so as not to wet my clothes'. When he reached the beach, he took off the 'suit' and buried it in the sand. Three American cars were waiting, with keys in the ignition, provided courtesy of the Mossad advance party – three cars between sixteen men. They headed for the Rue Verdun and got out. It was 1 a.m. 'Miki' and his 'wife' Barak walked arm in arm down the street, accidently brushing against a policeman. 'To our relief, he never turned a hair.' The team split into three, one for each apartment block, each with what 'Miki' described as 'a small bomb'. They had expected guards but there were none. 'Miki' led the assault on Abu Youssef's flat. Each team leader was in radio contact with the street below and, once in position outside the three respective doors, waited for the signal from below. There was a simultaneous countdown from five to zero and then the doors were blown open, all at the same time, so that no one target could alert the other two. 'Miki' rushed into his chosen victim's apartment. Abu Youssef opened the bedroom door. 'I'd been carrying his picture in my pocket for three months so I almost said "hello". He didn't understand. He didn't know what was going on. He was taken by complete surprise. I shot him dead.' Kamal Nasser and Kamal Adwan met the same fate. There was a gunfight in the street but all the Israeli attackers escaped without loss. The whole operation took less than half an hour. Other members of the unit had attacked and blown up the PFLP headquarters in Beirut and an arms factory in Sidon, by way of diversionary tactics.

'Springtime of Youth' left Fatah reeling and minus a host of vital documents that the raiders took away with them. Golda Meir was jubilant at the spectacular coup against Black September. 'We killed the murderers who planned to murder again,' she declared.[14] But 'Houdini' Arafat lived to tell the tale. 'Miki' and his men did not know he was within earshot of their attack.

In the course of the next two weeks, two more of Israel's enemies were dispatched by the roving 'hit team'. Ali Ahmed Khair, another supposed contact man for the KGB and the replacement for the liquidated PLO representative in Cyprus, met a similar end to that of his predecessor, blown to his death by another booby-trapped bomb in Nicosia. On 12 April 1973 the Mossad struck in Athens, killing Moussa Abu Zaiad, with yet another bomb planted in a hotel room. There was then a two-month silence until, on 28 June 1973, Mohammed Boudia, a member of the PFLP, was killed in Paris when his car was booby-trapped while its owner was said to be engaged in an amorous encounter. Ten were now dead. But the man who was supposed to be number one on the Mossad hit list, the alleged 'Mastermind of Munich', was still at large. He was called Ali Hassan Salameh or 'Abu Hassan'. The 'hit team' thought they had him in their sights in the Norwegian town of Lillehammer on 27 July 1973. Two of the team shot the man dead in the street. But the operation was a disaster. The victim was not Ali Hassan Salameh but an innocent Algerian waiter called Ahmed Bouchiki. The team had killed the wrong man. Nemesis struck in Norway. Lillehammer epitomized the moral dilemmas raised by Israel's decision to exact her own bloody vengeance against her enemies.

I put it to General Yariv that Israel was setting herself up as judge, jury and executioner: her victims, I pointed out, did not have a chance.

That's right. What chance, what chance did the poor guys in Munich have?
Two wrongs don't make a right.
That's right, but we had no choice; we had to make them stop. We had to make them stop, and there was no other way.
But Israel was using the methods of the terrorist against those that she perceived as terrorists.
That's true, and we are not very proud about it. But it was a question of sheer necessity. And it did bring fruit. As a matter of fact, they decided by an act of will to stop and they did.

In fact the temporary end to the activities of the 'hit team' was the result of a combination of circumstances: Israel was acutely embarrassed by the fiasco of Lillehammer; and the PLO and the various groupings within it decided that 'terrorism' had had its day and politics were the way forward, a change of direction signalled by Yasser Arafat's famous speech to the United Nations General Assembly in New York on 13 November 1974 when he declared: 'Today I have come with an olive branch and a freedom fighter's gun. Do not let the olive branch fall from my hand.'[15] Accompanying Yasser Arafat on his visit to New York was Ali Hassan Salameh, the lucky survivor of Lillehammer, who had become Arafat's most trusted aide and commander of his personal bodyguard 'Force 17', rather prosaically named after a telephone extension in Fatah's headquarters in Beirut. But Mossad still had to settle the score. The story of Salameh and the revival of the Mossad 'hit team' in the late seventies is told in the next chapter.

In the eighties, the 'hits' were different. 'Terrorism' continued but in a different form. In general, atrocities like those at Munich, Lod and Khartoum were off the agenda. Such activities ill accorded with the political path the PLO was bent on pursuing – which inevitably meant wooing, not alienating, Washington and the West. Such political moves did not, of course, preclude armed actions by Fatah and its sister organizations within the borders of Israel and the Occupied Territories. To the Palestinians, these operations were of a different order, although Israel, whose soldiers and civilians were on the receiving end, regarded any such actions as being equally committed by PLO 'terrorists'. By this stage the PLO had been seriously weakened by Israel's invasion of Lebanon in June 1982, which was intended to put an end to the organization's presence in the country next door, from which it had launched its attacks. After an eighty-eight-day siege, the PLO was driven from Beirut and forced to re-establish its headquarters in Tunis. But Israel's troubles did not end with the forced exit of her enemies. She became bogged down in Lebanon for another three years and finally withdrew to find another problem on her doorstep. In December 1987 the Intifada, the Palestinian uprising, erupted in the Occupied Territories of Gaza and the West Bank. Young Palestinians responded to twenty years of military occupation with stones and defiance. Their resistance was more powerful than the guns they did not have. Israel found it difficult to find an effective response, since opening fire on stone-throwing children, as her soldiers frequently did, gave game, set and match to the enemy in confrontations watched by the world. Israel had a huge problem and it was more than just public relations.

Although the Intifada was not originally orchestrated by the PLO – its outbreak was spontaneous – it was not long before the PLO took it over. It was too good an opportunity to miss. The West Bank and Gaza, so long quiescent under a scarcely benevolent Israeli occupation, suddenly seemed ungovernable. The Intifada had to be crushed. Israel decided to chop off its head on the grounds that the body would then die too. The head belonged to Khalil al-Wazir, 'Abu Jihad', Yasser Arafat's Chief of Staff, who was in command of military operations against Israel and the Occupied Territories. Abu Jihad was Fatah's senior military commander and even older than Fatah itself, having organized one of the earliest fedayeen guerrilla groups in Gaza in 1952. His experience and ability were respected even by his enemies. From his PLO base in Tunis, he was the man who masterminded, financed and directed the Intifada. It was there that he was struck down as he was writing a letter to the leaders of the uprising in his bedroom in the small hours of one morning.

Most visitors to the pretty seaside suburb of Sidi Bou Said, twenty kilometres outside Tunis, come to visit the ruins of ancient Carthage from which Hannibal and his elephants set out to destroy Rome and where Aeneas took advantage of Queen Dido in a cave before abandoning her to self-immolation on a funeral pyre. But on the night of 15 April 1988, almost fifteen years to the day after 'Springtime of Youth', more sinister visitors landed on the beaches of Sidi Bou Said. They were commandos of Sayeret Matkal. Silently they made their way to Abu Jihad's spacious villa down a quiet backstreet. Again, considering the fate of many of his colleagues, it was, like the apartments in the Rue Verdun in Beirut, scarcely heavily guarded. The two guards and the gardener were shot dead.

Today the pretty villa, with its white walls, blue shutters and blue-painted ironwork, is a shrine to Abu Jihad, cherished by his wife, Um Jihad, and family. His pictures are everywhere: meeting Chairman Mao in China and shaking hands with the North Vietnamese leadership in Hanoi; accepting flowers in East Germany flanked by heavily decorated generals; with Yasser Arafat behind a barricade during the siege of Beirut; with Abu Iyad and other 'martyred' leaders of Fatah; and relaxing with his wife and young children. Crouched at the bottom of the stairs in the marbled hall is a disturbingly realistic stuffed wild cat whose ears are missing. 'They were shot off by the Israelis,' Um Jihad told me. 'They thought it was real.' Abu Jihad had little chance to defend himself. His daughter, Hannan, who is now studying at the University of Geneva and married to a West Bank deportee, showed me her father's gun. She took it out of the fur hat Abu Jihad had bought in Moscow, which still rested on top of the bedroom wardrobe where the weapon used to lie hidden. 'Weapon' is perhaps too strong a word. It was a small Colt Cobra .38 Special with a wooden handle shattered by the impact of an Israeli bullet.

Mother and daughter, who had both been in the house, relived the attack. Hannan was asleep in the bedroom along the corridor from her parents. She told me her father had come home about eleven o'clock and she had gone to talk to him because she had had a bad dream about him:

> I told him my dream and he didn't say anything. He just laughed. I sat with him for a little while and then I told him that I wanted to go to sleep. I kissed him and I hugged him a lot. He insisted I stay with him that night: he said there was no school the next day. I said no, I want to sleep. It was the first time in his life that he really insisted on my staying with him. I left him at about one o'clock and I went directly to sleep.[16]

Not long afterwards, Hannan heard a loud noise and saw lights. She thought it was the garbage collectors, who often woke her up on their early rounds. Then she realized the noise was inside the house. She heard the sound of men running and shots and her mother screaming. She heard her shout, 'Stop! That's enough!' She rushed out and saw her father lying outside his bedroom. He was either dying or dead.

> He was lying on his stomach. The floor was full of blood – like a swimming pool – and he was swimming in it. You could see blood all over the room and all over the walls. They were black because of the smoke and the bullets. When I tried to touch him to see if there was life, his blood was still going out of him. At that moment I thought that he was still alive but he can't have been. Seventy-seven bullets were enough to kill ten men like him.

Hannan was composed while describing the killing. Her mother broke down as she described the almost ritual killing.

> I was sleeping and was awakened by a loud noise. Abu Jihad jumped up from behind his desk and reached for his gun. We saw four armed men and he fired at them and they retreated. He took position by the corner and pushed me away towards the wall [outside the bedroom]. One of the men fired at the hand in which he was holding the gun. Abu Jihad fell to the ground. I tried to help him but the armed man stopped me, pointing his machine-gun at my back. He forced me back to the wall and warned me not to move. A second man stepped forward and fired at my husband, then retreated. Then a third and a fourth. They entered the bedroom and I heard gunfire inside. I thought they had killed my little child. I lost control and screamed. I heard a female voice telling them in French, 'Ça y est! Ça y est! Vite! Vite!' ['That's

enough! That's enough! Quickly! Quickly!'] I took Hannan in my arms. She started to scream when she saw her father lying on the ground in a pool of blood.[17]

I asked Um Jihad why she thought her husband was a target. 'Because he was the commander of the Palestinian armed struggle and because he was the mastermind behind the Intifada,' she told me. 'They thought that by killing him they would stop the uprising but they failed. The Palestinian people are continuing their struggle to secure the right to return to their land. His death has made me more determined to promote the message in which my husband believed. Our own state. Our own flag. A peaceful life for our children in an independent and free country.' Black September perpetrators of the Munich massacre would have said the same.

I put a final question to General Aharon Yariv. Where was the morality in carrying out such operations when Israel had always prided herself on the notion of 'the purity of arms'?

> The morality lies in the situation of there being no alternative. That is to say, you have no better way, moral or physical, in which to handle the problem. That's what we did. We went back to the old biblical rule of an eye for an eye.
>
> *Do you believe that Israel is justified in continuing to carry out these attacks on her enemies and removing their leaders?*
>
> I'll tell you frankly. I approach these problems not from a moral point of view, but, hard as it may sound, from a cost-benefit point of view. I'm not sure that assassinating a leader here or there will bring us anywhere nearer to peace. But if it is a clear case that by removing this personality you can deal a mortal blow to your enemy that will bring him to the table, that's something else. But that doesn't happen very often. If I'm very hard-headed, I can say, what is the political benefit in killing this person? Will it bring us nearer to peace? Will it bring us nearer to an understanding with the Palestinians or not? In most cases I don't think it will. But in the case of Black September we had no other choice and it worked. Is it morally acceptable? One can debate that question. Is it politically vital? It was.

However, in Israel's eyes, there was one account still to settle: that meant completing the mission the 'hit team' had failed to accomplish in Lillehammer. Ali Hassan Salameh, 'one of the world's deadliest and most wanted Arab terrorists'[18] and the alleged 'Mastermind of Munich', still survived. The Mossad could not admit failure again.

3 · THE HUNTED

I never thought we would find it. It was not on the map. There were no signposts to it and hardly a trace of it. That is what Neil Grant and I were told. We had the name of the village, Kulleh, and its spelling in the original Arabic, together with some helpful intelligence that it was near a kibbutz several kilometres to the north-east of Ben-Gurion airport outside Tel Aviv. Finding the kibbutz was easy. Finding Kulleh was not. We mentioned the name to some kibbutzniks, whose expressions changed when they heard it mentioned. 'That's an Arab village,' said one suspiciously. I explained we were doing some historical research. 'There's nothing left to see.' Where was it? She waved and pointed up the road and then gestured a few kilometres to the east. We were standing more or less on the 'Green line', the dots on the map of Israel that mark the demarcation line between Arab and Jew after the war of 1948. To the east of it were Arabs: to the west were Jews.[1]

We drove up the hill where the coastal plain rises to the escarpment that slopes gently and then savagely down to the Jordan valley. Tel Aviv lay strung out behind us, thirty miles away. We found nothing. Rounding a corner, we suddenly came upon a herd of goats being driven by a man with a stick and two boys acting as flankers. We stopped and mentioned the word 'Kulleh'. He waved his stick in the direction from which we had just come. Would he like to park his goats and show us where Kulleh was? He hesitated, grinned, shouted something in Arabic to the two boys and then climbed into the back seat.

After a couple of kilometres, he pointed to a track leading off the road into a deep pine wood. Fiat Pandas were not designed for tracks like this, with rocks clanging against the undercarriage as we drove deeper into the trees. I was not convinced on the grounds that Arabs tended not to build their villages in pine groves. Then we arrived. 'Kulleh!' our obliging goatherd announced, waving his arms all around him. There was not much left.

Most of the houses had been reduced to rubble, although the occasional wall was still standing with moss and weeds growing out of the crumbling cement. This used to be Palestine. This was what Arabs meant when they talked about 'our land'. I later learned that the village had been partially destroyed in the war of 1948 and then subsequently finished off by the Israeli army, who used it as a training base, presumably for operations against the fedayeen. The destruction of Kulleh and the forced exile of its few hundred Arab inhabitants is a microcosm of the Middle East conflict.

But why the search for an obscure Arab village in the middle of nowhere? We wanted to find Kulleh because it had once been the home of the family of Ali Hassan Salameh, 'Abu Hassan', the man who, to the Israelis, was the 'Mastermind of Munich'. Abu Hassan followed in the footsteps of his father, Sheikh Hassan Salameh, who in 1936 allegedly fired the first shot when he led an early Arab attack against the British who had ruled Palestine under League of Nations mandate since 1920. In June 1936, Palestinian Arabs ambushed British troops and one of their convoys, inviting RAF air strikes in retaliation. Sheikh Hassan had become a legend, attacking convoys, cutting the army's slender lines of communication and organizing disparate, untrained Palestinian villagers into a guerrilla fighting force. The British placed a £10 000 price on his head as he darted from village to village, harassing his enemies and always evading capture. In 1948, as the British pulled out of Palestine leaving behind a partitioned state, Sheikh Hassan, as supreme commander of the Palestinian Arabs, turned his guns and his men on the Jews who had declared the birth of the state of Israel. He died of shrapnel wounds attacking an Irgun[2] position at Ras el Ein, a strategic position dominated by an old Crusader fortress on the road to Jerusalem. Eleven Israelis were killed in the assault and a score wounded. Neither the British nor the Jews were sorry to see Sheikh Hassan go, although the official Israeli military historian paid tribute to him and Abd el Kader, the other Palestinian commander who fell. The young Yasser Arafat had been one of Abd el Kader's aides.[3] 'In spite of all the cruelty they showed in harming non-combatant Jewish civilians, they fought personally at the head of their soldiers, and both perished in battle.'[4] Sheikh Hassan died at the age of thirty-seven, leaving behind his brother, Abu Tareq, who had fought alongside him in the thirties and forties, his widow, Um Ali, his two daughters, Nidal and Jihad, and his son, Abu Hassan. Abu Hassan too met a violent death at the age of thirty-seven. The father died in battle. The son never saw his killers. Few victims of the 'hit team' did.

Sheikh Hassan's widow, Um Ali, now lives in Beirut in an apartment block adjacent to that of her daughter, Nidal. Unlike countless similar blocks in that battle-scarred city, these have survived the devastation of civil war. Today Um Ali lives the life of a recluse. The loss of her son, added to the loss of her husband, was a devastating blow from which she has never recovered. At first, Um Ali refused to see me. Nidal warned that her mother hated the British because they were the root of all evil as the original occupiers of Palestine. Nidal is a gentle and kindly woman, whose husband, a Fatah commander in Beirut, has twice narrowly survived assassination attempts by rival Palestinian factions. Nidal, who adored her brother, is a remarkably apolitical member of such a fiercely political family. She politely advised me that, knowing her mother, she was sure I was wasting my time. Um Ali, however, finally relented, and I warily set foot across her threshold.

There was no electricity in the flat. It was late in the evening and the only light came from an oil lamp and a candle throwing shadows across the room from a low table. The shutters were closed. Sitting in a chair with a blanket wrapped round her was Um Ali. It was cold. The light made her look older than she was. Her face was wrinkled and lined, her mouth tight and bitter. Her features scarcely moved. The only motion came from the thumbs of the hands that lay clasped on her lap. I doubted if that haunted face had smiled for years. She welcomed me, as Nidal had warned, with a tirade against the British. My ears were no strangers to such attacks, accustomed as they were to withstanding similar diatribes from formidable Republican mothers in West Belfast. The attack was not personal and I never felt it to be so. Gradually the ice thawed. Tea was offered and Um Ali began to talk. I started the conversation by asking about her village and her family history.

> Kulleh was a small place with a small population. When we lived there, the Jews who were living in Palestine represented 10 per cent of the people. We lived in peace with them then. In those days, when my husband was alive, our country was occupied by the English. They called it the British mandate. They brought the Jews to Palestine from all over Europe without consulting us. When the mandate ended, they deceived us and handed over our country to the Jews. We, as a Palestinian people, were supposed to get possession of Palestine. The British army was supposed to hand over our country to us but we were surprised when they handed over everything to the Jews. Zionism was imposed upon us. Aren't we entitled, then, to defend our country? My husband had no choice but to fight.[5]

I asked her about the legendary Sheikh Hassan Salameh, and the eyes behind the glasses came to life.

> On one occasion, the British army came and went straight to the headman's house and demanded to see Hassan Salameh. The

headman sent a warning telling him to flee. But he didn't and went to see them at the headman's house. He told the British officers who he was and took tea with them. They were astonished to see the man with a price on his head, whom they fought and hunted everywhere, come to them of his own accord. He asked them why they were after him. They told him he was 'a troublemaker' and an enemy of the British army. He agreed and said he would remain so as long as Britain remained in his country and imposed its rule on it. The British officers left without arresting him. He was later arrested twice but on both occasions he escaped from prison.

She then talked about her son, Abu Hassan. It was clearly painful for her to do so.

I lost my husband when I was twenty-two years old and then I lost my son. He was all that I had in life. I pinned all my hopes on him. I sacrificed all I had to bring him up and make him a man. I told him a lot about his father. He loved him and read about him and was greatly influenced by his career. Ali was a Palestinian nationalist, a revolutionary and a natural leader. He had a personality larger than life. Here in Lebanon they used to call him 'the Minister of the Interior' and 'the Persuader'. Whenever there was a problem, Ali could solve it. But I didn't want my son to die. I wanted him to live. I knew that he would be killed because this is the inevitable end for whoever carries out such actions. I warned him and told him, 'Take care, Ali. You know that you are a wanted man and the Jews are after you.' He would say, 'Don't worry, Mother, they can't confront me.' I would reply, 'It's true they can't confront you because the coward doesn't confront the hero.' Since his death I feel as if I've aged fifty years. Ali was everything in my life. He was life itself. After his death I lost all hope and retreated into myself.

Um Ali pulled the blanket round her. Great pain lined her face but there was no sign of tears. Mothers of martyrs do not cry. I asked her gently if the suffering was worth it. 'Of course it is,' she said defiantly, eyes flashing. 'Of course it's worth it. Why not? We are defending our homeland and one pays a high price for that. We have to make sacrifices in order to retrieve our rights. The Israelis are the real criminals and bandits. They are the terrorists. Not us.'

Similar sentiments were expressed by Abu Hassan's uncle, Abu Tareq, who had fought alongside Sheikh Hassan in the thirties and forties. We had found him, purely by chance, living in the Shatila refugee camp in Beirut. He proudly produced a picture of his nephew, Abu Hassan, while we drank more sweet tea in a small, sparsely furnished room dominated by a television set of considerable size and vintage in the corner. Abu Tareq lives in conditions very different from those enjoyed by the rest of the family, who are either well off or well maintained by the PLO, although the days of generosity to martyrs' families are now gone since the oil states cut off funding to the PLO when Yasser Arafat sided with Saddam Hussein in the Gulf War.

Shatila and its sister camp, Sabra, are shameful reminders of the Palestinian diaspora forty-five years after the event. More recent history has given their names lasting notoriety after Christian Phalangists entered the camps on 16 September 1982 and slaughtered hundreds of Palestinian men, women and children.[6] Shatila lies on the southern fringe of Beirut under the flight path for the airport. Thirty thousand Palestinians used to live in the temporary housing first erected on land leased from the Shatila family in 1948. The entrance is beyond a checkpoint manned by the Syrian army, which is master in Lebanon now. The soldiers look bored, surrounded by sandbags and torn pictures of a half-smiling President Hafez al-Assad of Syria, whose picture seems to adorn every wall in Beirut. A Palestinian post stands a few yards down the muddy road. 'Post' is hardly the word. Once it would have been manned by Palestinian fighters in fatigues, with AK 47s slung over their shoulders, but the only guard I saw was an indifferent man in an office next door to a butcher's shop. 'Guard' is also perhaps too strong an expression. There is little left to watch over. Most of the fighters went long ago, scattered with Yasser Arafat when he was forced to leave Beirut and head for Tunis. Only the black, green and white of the Palestinian flag flutters less than defiantly over the entrance to the camp.

However familiar television may make the devastation of war, nothing prepared you for the real thing. Smashed concrete is everywhere, strewn on the ground in great shapeless lumps, with the steel rods that once bound it together now twisted and bent. Roofs and floors from high blocks of flats tumble over one another like great slices of bread awaiting the final cut that will sever them from the loaf. Every wall and building is scarred by a million bullet holes and the warheads of rockets fired like toys. Even the minaret of the mosque has not been spared, its pinnacle hanging on by the barest thread to support the crescent on top. One lucky survivor still living in the camp showed me his war wounds, removing his sunglasses to reveal a deep scar across his forehead and a dark socket where once there was an eye. He, like many, thanked Russian surgeons in Moscow for the operations that had saved his life. This was not Arab killing Jew but Arab killing Arab in what became known as 'the war of the camps' as the Syrian-backed Amal tried to finish off the Palestinians still left in the camps. Amazingly, most of the services in the camp still seemed to work. There were even signs of a rudimentary refuse collection, evidenced by a man with a broom over his shoulder who patrolled the perimeter of a pile of rubbish that had become paradise for the army of chickens and cats. Ahmed, our guide from the Red Crescent, the Islamic Red Cross, explained that Shatila was now under the control of dissidents who had split from the PLO. But the politics were meaningless. 'The people don't care,' he said. 'They just want to live.' Ahmed was clearly one of the lucky ones who had escaped and pursued an education. A fluorescent green anorak, tinged with pink and black, and ankle-high 'Nike Air' trainers bore witness to his success.

We initially found Abu Tareq by asking a group of people standing at a corner of the camp if there was anyone who had known Abu Hassan or had fought with him. To our surprise, they said there was – his uncle. They took us to his house. After taking tea, we went out into the sunshine to talk. I asked Abu Tareq about his martyred brother and nephew. 'Sheikh Hassan defended his country and his land,' he said. 'When the Jewish immigrants started to arrive in Palestine, he was opposed to their coming because the land belonged to the Palestinian people. The Jews owned nothing. Accordingly, Sheikh Hassan and his followers fought and defended their land and their country. Abu Hassan too was defending his cause as did his father and ancestors before. He wasn't a terrorist. He fought justly against the Zionist enemy.'[7] I hardly expected Abu Tareq to say anything else. Surrounded by rubble, he sat on a rock in the sunshine, composed and philosophical. He had a Watermans pen in his top jacket pocket, and he wore an astrakhan hat. I asked him if he ever expected to see Palestine again, given that Shatila was a pitiful reminder of how little progress had been made. 'I am hopeful that I will return to Palestine because I still consider it my country, no matter how long I remain in exile. If I died, my children and grandchildren would return. Palestine will be liberated, however long it takes.' Abu Tareq clearly lived with his dreams. What about the peace process in which the PLO was indirectly involved,[8] and Israel's offer of giving Palestinians on the West Bank and Gaza a measure of self-rule? 'I don't support the administrative autonomy they are promoting and I don't support the Palestinian delegation. I am for the liberation of the whole of Palestine.' Abu Tareq was a romantic, not a realist. His views would have been shared by his brother but not, I suspect, by his nephew, who was a revolutionary of the more practical school.

But what did Abu Hassan do to warrant the sobriquet 'one of the world's deadliest and most wanted terrorists'? Mythology does not necessarily accord with fact. Because he was never caught and because, metaphorically, his fingerprints and footprints were never found, there is no evidence linking him with any 'terrorist' operation. In modern-day parlance, Abu Hassan would be regarded as one of the 'godfathers' of terrorism, the strategist who planned and gave orders which others carried out. As is often the case in dealing with such figures, it is intelligence gleaned from agents and informers, not evidence that would stand up in a court of law, that points the finger.

Ali Hassan Salameh was born in 1942 in Iraq, where his father was undergoing a tank commander's course.[9] His parents had sought refuge in Baghdad because the British had put a price on his father's head. At two, Abu Hassan moved with his family to Beirut, where he spent most of his youth studying and enjoying himself, presumably pursuing those amorous adventures which subsequently branded him with the playboy image which ill accorded with the conduct expected of a Fatah leader. But he had charm and good looks, and no amount of remonstration could change him, whatever the embarrassment his conduct caused to Yasser Arafat, whose protégé and 'adopted son' he became. In 1958, during the crisis in which the US Marines invaded Lebanon,[10] the family moved from Beirut to Cairo, inhaling the heady revolutionary atmosphere generated by Egypt's president, Gamal Abdel Nasser. It was there that he married his first wife, Um Hassan. Soon after, their first son, Ali Hassan, was born.

Ali Hassan Salameh only ever gave one press interview, to a Lebanese journalist, Nadia Salti Stephan, in Beirut in 1976. He gave it on condition that Nadia handed over the tape when she had transcribed the interview. We met his son Hassan (now in his twenties) in Amman where he lives with his mother. We mentioned the tape and wondered if Hassan had been given any of his father's belongings. He said he had. He left the room and returned with his father's trunk which had been sent to him by the PLO after Abu Hassan's death in Beirut. We searched in vain for the tape. The 'trunk', a large metal camera box, contained his father's personal belongings. There were piles of photographs, most of them of family, and a couple of tapes of pop songs. Elvis Presley's 'Love me Tender' was his favourite. To our disappointment, there was no interview tape. Fortunately, a printed version of the interview survived in an English magazine published in Beirut, called *Monday Morning*. In it, Abu Hassan spoke of his early life and the burden which his father's revolutionary pedigree had placed upon him. He was six years old when his father died, and he clearly went on to live in his shadow, trying to cast aside the heroic mantle which his mother was anxious to thrust upon him. No doubt Um Ali would have been even more formidable in her youth.

The influence of my father has posed a personal problem for me. I grew up in a family that considered 'struggle' a matter of heritage which should be carried on by generation after generation ... my father was not the only one in the family to give his life for Palestine: some 12 young men in my family, mostly cousins, died in the 1940s. My upbringing was politicized. I *lived* the Palestinian cause. ... When my father fell as a martyr, Palestine was passed on to me, so to speak. ... My mother wanted me to be another Hassan Salameh. ... This had a tremendous impact on me. I wanted to be myself. ... Even as a child, I had to follow a certain pattern of behaviour. ... I was made constantly conscious of the fact that I was the son of Hassan Salameh and had to live up to that.[11]

Perhaps Abu Hassan's womanizing, and his obsession with his appearance (black was his favourite colour) and his physique – bodybuilding and karate were two of his favourite pastimes – were a reaction against the expectations that a fiercely proud and ambitious mother had of her son. In the end, he fulfilled both Um Ali's desires and his own.

In May 1964 he visited Jerusalem, setting foot on Palestinian soil for the second time when he attended a meeting of the embryo PLO, the First National (Palestinian) Assembly. (The first time was when he attended secondary school in Beir Zeit on the West Bank for a short while in 1956.) The PLO was primarily a political umbrella for the Palestinian cause, with military organizations, like Fatah, under its wing. The PLO and Fatah operated openly: Black September was their clandestine offshoot. The PLO's first gathering was a grand affair held at the Ambassador Hotel in East Jerusalem which was then under Jordanian control.[12] Its purpose was to establish the kind of representative body for the Palestinians that Gamal Abdel Nasser, the father of Arab nationalism, had long had in mind. Here the PLO was born under its first president, a middle-aged Palestinian lawyer called Ahmed Sukairy. In that heady atmosphere, there were also romantic proposals for a Palestine Liberation Army that would reclaim Arab land. Such ideas did not go down well with the leadership of Fatah, the guerrilla organization that had been founded six years earlier, in 1958, by Yasser Arafat and Khalil al-Wazir (Abud Jihad) and their close associates at a secret meeting in Kuwait.[13] Abu Jihad was present at the Jerusalem meeting, walking the corridors of the Ambassador Hotel and assessing whether the putative Palestine Liberation Army was a potential rival to Fatah or an ally. He told anyone prepared to listen that the priority was a 'people's war' and that Fatah had 300–400 Palestinian guerrillas ready to launch raids on Israel from their bases in Jordan.[14] The young Abu Hassan, who walked the corridors too as a member of the PLO, was attracted by Fatah's military credentials because he felt the PLO 'didn't provide the right framework for self expression'.[15] The moment Fatah went into action, Abu Hassan knew where his future lay. 'When Fatah undertook its first operation on New Year's Day, 1965, it came to embody my aspirations,' he said.[16] That operation was launched with more rhetoric than success. 'From among our steadfast people waiting at the borders,' Fatah's first military communiqué grandly proclaimed, 'our revolutionary vanguard has issued forth in the belief that armed revolution is our only path to Palestine and freedom.'[17]

Abu Hassan was clearly swept away by the hyperbole, since Fatah's first raiding party was arrested by the Lebanese authorities before it even set foot in Israel. He joined Fatah and fought on the Jordanian front during the June War of 1967, but not for long, as it only lasted six days. While he was working for the PLO in Kuwait he met Abu Daoud and encouraged him to join Fatah too. 'I was a young lawyer working in the Justice Ministry and we got on well together,' Abu Daoud stated in his 'confession' made during his imprisonment in Jordan in 1973. 'When he was asked to get some people together for some initial security and military training, he asked me to join him. I did and we continued together until he was killed.'[18] Daoud and Abu Hassan went to Cairo for the course which, in addition to military training, taught them how to build up a security department within Fatah. Abu Daoud came out top of the class. Abu Hassan put into practice what he had learned in Cairo and rose swiftly to a senior position within el Razd, Fatah's security department headed by Salah Khalaf (Abu Iyad). In 1970 he went into action again against King Hussain's Jordanian forces in the engagement that gave birth to Black September. When Yasser Arafat left for Cairo and then Beirut, Abu Hassan went with him, forming the bond that grew stronger until the day he died. In his interview, Abu Hassan was asked about Black September, and he all but put his name to it.

> Black September undertook several operations against the Jordanian regime, its men and its institutions – in Jordan and elsewhere. Some of these operations were associated with my name. It was natural that my name be singled out and a price put on my head. . . . Because we were part of an international conspiracy in which Israel, America and Jordan were involved, we sought to hit at Israeli interests and person-alities. At the time, we were subjected to a blackout – a terrible blackout [i.e. we were forgotten]. We *had* to overcome this blackout and we did. We did burst out on the world scene. We overcame the blackout and were able to tell the world, 'We are here!' . . . The world looked at us as terrorists. It didn't look at us as revolutionaries. Hence

it is wrong to attribute any of these operations to Abu Hassan or Abu Iyad or anyone specifically. They should be attributed to the many unknown, unidentifiable Palestinians who undertook them. The enemy concentrated on specific names and personalities in order to portray us as terrorist gangs. . . . That's why the enemy started to talk about deterring terrorism with terrorism and about assassinations . . . and I was one of the main targets. . . . They were trying to make our assassination a legitimate act. That's why the concentration was on destroying my image: on portraying me as a playboy . . . a murderer, a bloodthirsty killer who cannot sleep without seeing blood. The intention, obviously, was to pave the way for my liquidation.[19]

By this time, Abu Hassan had become director of Fatah's 'Special Operations Branch'. Because, not surprisingly, neither he nor his unit ever claimed responsibility for any specific attack, the closest we can come to an assessment of why he allegedly topped the Mossad 'hit list' comes from Abu Daoud's Jordanian 'confession'. Daoud first explained the source of Abu Hassan's power. 'Salameh gathered a group of young men around him. Most of them had a criminal record. The source of Ali Hassan Salameh's power comes from the fact that he is supported by Abu Ammar [Yasser Arafat] personally.'[20] He then listed five 'successful' Abu Hassan operations. The first was on 15 March 1971: a tank containing 16 000 tons of fuel oil went up in flames after three explosions at the Gulf Oil refinery in Rotterdam.[21] The second was on 15 December 1971: 'firing shots at the Jordanian ambassador in London'. The ambassador, Mr Zaid Rifai, survived the thirty rounds fired from a sub-machine-gun at his car with only a slight hand wound. He was only 150 yards from the embassy.[22] Black September claimed responsibility for the attack on 'one of their worst enemies' and on one of King Hussain's closest friends whom, ironically, he had sent to London for safety. The third occurred on 6 February 1972: 'killing five Jordanians in Hamburg on the pretext that they collaborated with Israeli intelligence'. The five were shot to death by a British Sterling sub-machine-gun and an automatic pistol.[23] The police suspected the killings were 'politically motivated'. In fact, Abu Daoud got the location wrong: it was near Cologne, not Hamburg. The fourth was on 4 August 1972: 'the Trieste operation – blowing up oil storage tanks in Trieste, Italy, that supply Europe and Germany with fuel'. Black September again claimed responsibility for the attack, in which 200 000 gallons of oil were set ablaze. Much of the oil went to Germany, and West Germany was a supporter of Israel. A fire officer said, 'This looks like a commando job. Very well planned and executed. But we don't know who did it or why.'[24]

The fifth occurred probably on 6 August 1972: 'the blowing up of an Israeli vessel in the United States'. We could trace no record of any such attack in America but did track down an explosion on board an Israeli cargo ship, the 3000-ton *Bar-Tiran*, in the Adriatic.

The other operation in which Abu Hassan was involved – according to informed Palestinian sources who knew him well – was the assassination of the Israeli air attaché in Washington, Colonel Yosef Alon, on 1 July 1973. He was shot in the chest several times as he stepped from his car into the driveway of his home.[25] The Voice of Palestine Radio announced that Colonel Alon had been 'executed' in retaliation for the assassination of Mohammed Boudia, who had died in the Mossad car bomb attack in Paris three days earlier.[26] But nowhere among non-Israeli sources did we find any evidence or suggestion that Abu Hassan was involved in Munich, and the refusal of the Israeli authorities to provide us with any indication of why they stigmatized him as such did not help. Certainly Abu Daoud made no reference to Abu Hassan in connection with Munich. On the contrary, he described Munich as one of the 'successful operations' of Abu Iyad.[27] If Abu Hassan had taken part in any way, there was no reason for Abu Daoud not to have mentioned it, given that he had already admitted to providing a false passport for one of the Black September Munich attackers. Perhaps the confusion, deliberate or otherwise, arose because, as Abu Daoud said in his 'confession', Abu Hassan, as head of Fatah intelligence, would put Black September's name to Abu Iyad's operations.

I asked other members of Abu Hassan's family if they believed he had been involved in Munich. Um Ali was dismissive and evaded the question. 'Okay, what about Munich?' she said. 'I want to pose you a question. How many crimes did the Jews commit before Munich? How many Palestinians did they kill? What about the leaders they killed – some of them here in Beirut. Why are they allowed to fight us and hunt us anywhere in our homes and our country? Aren't we entitled also to hunt them? We have the right to chase them wherever they are because they are the aggressors.'[28] I suspected that if Abu Hassan had told his mother he was involved in Munich it would have caused her little concern. To most Palestinians, those responsible for Munich were heroes and martyrs. It is unlikely that Um Ali would have seen them differently.

However, Abu Hassan's sister, Nidal, did not evade the question. Clearly, as the apolitical member of the family, she was disturbed by Munich and was anxious to establish that her brother had played no part in it. 'When I heard about Munich, I asked him right away. I'd heard in one way or another that he was behind it but I couldn't believe it. So I asked him, "Were you behind the Munich massacre?" He said, "No".' I suggested to Nidal that she would hardly have expected him to say 'yes'.

'Well, he would have said "yes" if he had done it, if he were behind it. But he said "no" and he was definite about it. I said to him, "Then why didn't you deny it? Why didn't you say you didn't do it?" If he'd told me, I would have kept it to myself. I wouldn't talk about it. But he was honest about it really. He would have never lied to me.'[29]

If Abu Hassan had been involved, he might well have kept it from his sister to spare her the upset. I put the same question to Um Hassan, Abu Hassan's first wife. Like Um Jihad in Tunis, Um Hassan now lives in Amman in a villa of some splendour, as befits a widow of one of the most famous martyrs of the revolution. Um Hassan was rather more circumspect. 'I asked him if he had anything to do with Munich or was involved in it,' she said. 'He denied it. He said he was against killing any civilian and didn't believe in it.'[30] I then pressed her, asking how she would have felt if he had told her he was involved. She did not wish to take the issue any further. I was treading on sensitive ground. I also met Abu Hussan's second wife, Georgina Rizak (a Lebanese Christian), in Beirut whom he married on 8 June 1977. Georgina, a former Miss Lebanon and Miss Universe, said that she, too, had asked him about Munich and he had denied involvement.

In July 1973 the Mossad 'hit team' moved into place to target Abu Hassan or 'the Red Prince' as he had become known to his enemies because of the amount of blood on his hands. Intelligence reports from Palestinian agents and informers told the Mossad that Abu Hassan had been moving around Europe and was due to make contact with someone in Scandinavia. The 'team' consisted of two sections: one prepared the ground and identified the victim; the other moved in for the kill. On 8 July, Dan Aerbel, a thirty-six-year-old Danish Jew who had been living in Israel for just over two years, was approached by a man he knew to be working for the Mossad and asked if he would be interested in taking part in a 'brief assignment' as an interpreter in Scandinavia.[31] He said he would. Two days later, he travelled to Stockholm and rented two apartments for six months, one in his own name and one in the name of his Mossad contact. Aerbel obtained six sets of keys and bedlinen for six persons for the flat in his name. A week later, Aerbel moved to Oslo where he was instructed by his Mossad contact to telephone a number of hotels in the city to discover whether an Arab by the name of Benamane was staying at any of them. Benamane was the Palestinian who the Mossad believed would lead them to Abu Hassan. Aerbel located him at the Panorama Hotel in Oslo and was instructed to check in to keep an eye on him. The other dozen or so members of the 'hit team' then flew out to join him after a secret briefing meeting in the VIP lounge at Ben-Gurion airport, Tel Aviv.[32] Those present at the meeting were Marianne Gladnikoff, Sylvia Rafael, Abraham Gehmer, Nora Hefner, a woman known as 'Tamara' and three men known as 'James', 'Raoul' and

'Mike'. Here the team was apparently told that Abu Hassan was to be its target.

When they reached Oslo they found that Benamane had disappeared from the Panorama Hotel and, mysteriously, turned up in the small town of Lillehammer about fifty miles to the north. Dan Aerbel, Nora Hefner and Sylvia Rafael promptly drove off in pursuit in a hired car and established that Benamane was staying at the Hotel Skotte. Other members of the team followed, checked into the hotel and shadowed their man by sitting next to him in the television lounge. The following day they lost him but caught up with him in a café talking to a man with a moustache. When Benamane returned to Oslo, the Mossad team tailed the man with the moustache, thinking they might have finally located their target, Abu Hassan. When he went into the Lillehammer swimming baths, Marianne Gladnikoff and Abraham Gehmer went for a swim too. Gladnikoff swam close to their quarry, who was talking to another man as they swam along. She wanted to hear what language they were speaking. It was French. Abu Hassan was multilingual. When he left the baths, he was shadowed by six of the team to his apartment, Rudgeveien 2A. The flat was then kept under constant surveillance by the team, usually two at a time in hired cars. Everywhere the target went the team was sure to go.

On the evening of Saturday, 21 July 1973, they watched him go to the cinema with a woman. The cinema was showing *Where Eagles Dare*. Three cars staked out the car park and the two exits. Each car had a walkie-talkie. After Richard Burton and Clint Eastwood had wiped out the Germans, the man and the woman left the cinema and caught a bus. As they got off at the stop in Furubakken and began to walk home, a light-coloured car came driving slowly towards them. Two men jumped out, one either side of their target, and pumped thirteen bullets into him. The man fell dying on the pavement. The scene was witnessed from another apartment in the block by a nurse called Dagny Bring. She told my colleague, Neil Grant, what she saw. 'I was sitting knitting with a friend, watching a British TV crime serial called *Bank Robbers*. I think the episode was called "Haven't We Met Before?" I looked out of the window and saw a couple crossing the road, having got off the bus. A white car pulled out of the parking lot and two men got out of the back seat. They were two or three metres away from the couple. Then there were three or four shots that sounded like a champagne cork. They went into the body of the man. I realized it was murder.' Dagny Bring recognized the victim. He was her neighbour, a Moroccan waiter called Ahmed Bouchiki. The woman with him was his pregnant wife. The 'hit team' had got the wrong man.

Six of them – Marianne Gladnikoff, Sylvia Rafael, Abraham Gehmer, Dan Aerbel, Zwi Steinberg and Michael Dorf – were arrested before they could leave the country. The rest of the team, including the two killers, escaped. The court judgement stated:

> In recent years, there have been a number of terrorist actions against Israeli citizens and interests, and organizations such as 'Black September' have assumed responsibility for these. Official quarters in Israel have stated clearly that Israel intends to combat these terrorist organizations wherever they may be and with all available means. . . . The Public Prosecutor has indicated that the real target of the group might be Ali Hassan Salameh who is assumed to be responsible for the tragedy during the Olympic Games in Munich in 1972. . . . This must have been a very attractive target to the Israelis, not only in a desire for revenge, but also because he must be regarded as a 'Black September' man who was extremely dangerous to Israel.[33]

The judgement concluded:

> the fact that the actions carried out may have been the link in a hard and bitter struggle against a possible terrorist organization allows no exemption from punishment. Guerrilla activities cannot be permitted on Norwegian territory, even though such activities may be directed against foreign authorities or organizations, and this applies no matter who stands behind such activities.

The court judged that the six accused were peripheral to the killing and had no 'decisive influence' on the plan. The decision to 'hit' the target 'would probably have to be made or at least approved by a central organization'. Nevertheless, five of the six were sent to gaol: Marianne Gladnikoff for two years six months; Sylvia Rafael for five years six months; Abraham Gehmer for five years six months; Dan Aerbel for five years; and Zwi Steinberg for one year: Michael Dorf was found not guilty and acquitted. Mrs Turil Bouchiki, the dead man's widow, has never received a word of apology from the Mossad. Israel was acutely embarrassed and the Mossad's guns were silenced – but not for good.

It was nearly six years before the 'hit team' struck again, called out of 'retirement' by the former leader of the Irgun and now Prime Minister of Israel, Menachem Begin. The target was, once again, the 'Red Prince'. This time there were to be no mistakes.

But what few know is the remarkable sub-plot: Israel had additional reasons for wanting Abu Hassan dead. As well as being a 'terrorist' he was a political threat which, in the longer term, posed a far greater challenge to Israel's security. Abu Hassan was not only a fighter but a fighter with a political brain. Yasser Arafat, his mentor, recognized that talent and put it to full use. Remarkably Abu Hassan, *before* the Munich massacre, began to make contacts with the Americans in the knowledge that the road to

Palestine, or at least part of it, ran through the White House, not the Kremlin, which had supplied the PLO and its constituent parts with weapons, finance and training over the years. These initial overtures were made with the blessing of Yasser Arafat and continued with his full support. Both men recognized that it was America alone who could put pressure on her client Israel to compromise and do business with the Palestinians. The American Central Intelligence Agency, the CIA, was the channel through which soundings were made. The dialogue between Abu Hassan and the CIA continued for ten years, surviving the Munich massacre and other bloody Black September operations. Despite the front-of-house rhetoric, America was talking to 'terrorists'. The contacts were made in the utmost secrecy, for there would have been an international outcry, orchestrated by an outraged Israel, if it had been discovered that her patron was talking to 'terrorists' behind her back while roundly condemning their actions. The outcry would have been all the greater had it been revealed that the Palestinian with whom the Americans were liaising was none other than Abu Hassan, the alleged 'Mastermind of Munich'. I put the point to one of the CIA's senior officers around the time. Was not America dealing with a 'terrorist'? He sat and thought. 'I suppose we were,' he said. 'But then we deal with all sorts of people.'

These remarkable contacts began in 1969–1970 as a result of the close relationship that evolved between Abu Hassan and Robert Ames, one of the CIA's best and brightest in Beirut. The introductions were made through a Lebanese intermediary called Mustafa Zein who enjoyed the trust of both sides. Mustafa is now a successful businessman living in America. A picture of a smiling Robert Ames hangs on his wall. Neil Grant and I spent many hours with him, listening to his remarkable story. He is 'Fuad', one of the main characters in David Ignatius's American bestseller, *Agents of Innocence*, an engrossing fictional account of the relationship between Abu Hassan and Ames, first published in 1987. Given the current delicacy of the Middle East peace process, there are obvious sensitivities in revealing the full extent of the relationship between the CIA and the PLO at the time of some of the most bloody terrorist atrocities involving US personnel, most notably Black September's machine-gunning of the two American ambassadors in Khartoum on 2 March 1973. In addition to the principle of 'know thine enemy', America's political interest in developing these contacts was twofold: the CIA not only wanted to steer Palestinians away from attacking American targets but needed the PLO to protect American officials and citizens in Beirut. What better person to ensure their survival than Abu Hassan, the chief of Fatah's security department and commander of Arafat's personal bodyguard, Force 17? The PLO was true to its word, and gave the Americans the protection they sought.

But it was not enough for the CIA to talk to Ali Hassan Salameh; it wanted to recruit him formally as one of its agents. Intelligence officers from whatever country and organization do not like dealing with spirits that are too free. In Washington I met the former CIA man who became Abu Hassan's case officer. I refer to him as 'Alan' as he did not wish to be identified. 'Alan' confirmed the broad brush of the story, although he was not *au fait* with all of the detail. It was, he said, part of the CIA's agent penetration exercise against the PLO. The Agency desperately wanted to get Abu Hassan on board. They first propositioned him at the Cavalieri Hilton hotel in Rome in late December 1970. Mustafa, with the approval of the PLO leadership, had rented adjoining suites between 18 and 21 of that month so that the parties could meet. Mustafa said that he was simply a rich Arab having a good time in Rome. The CIA contact at the hotel was not Robert Ames but one of his superiors. The meeting did not go well. The agent, who wanted to meet Abu Hassan alone, is said to have offered him $300 000 a month in return for his services. According to Mustafa, the CIA man told Abu Hassan he wished to 'co-ordinate activities between your organization and our organization'. It was only an offer. There was no suitcase stuffed full of dollar bills. But Abu Hassan felt insulted and angrily refused. He told Mustafa the CIA only wanted to recruit him and was not interested in dialogue. The following day, however, Mustafa soothed the two bruised egos over lunch. A fresh start was made and there was talk of dialogue between the US Administration and Chairman Arafat's office. However, the CIA appears not to have taken no for an answer. It apparently gave him an apt codename, 'Peacock', in anticipation of smoothing his feathers and luring him into its cage. The next proposition was made after Munich (during which time the relationship cooled) on Abu Hassan's home territory at his home in Beirut. Again the offer was made not by Robert Ames, who perhaps did not wish to jeopardize his relationship with Abu Hassan, but by another CIA officer who displayed even less tact. When the first approach was made in Rome, Abu Hassan was a rising star. When the second attempt was made, his star had risen. To have recruited Arafat's protégé would have been a tremendous coup but Abu Hassan was not for sale. His first wife, Um Hassan, was in the room when the offer was made.

I saw somebody giving him a cheque without any amount written in, telling him, 'You write in the number you want.' My husband was mad, very angry at the time, because it was very insulting to him. He threw the cheque back and left. He couldn't be an agent for anybody, not only the Americans. He used to tell me, 'Nobody in this world could give me anything my revolution is not giving me.' He didn't mean by that the money: he meant the satisfaction and the pride he got from fighting for his country.[34]

I asked Um Hassan what happened to the American agent. 'He was transferred. Removed,' she replied, without feeling the need to elaborate further.

The Americans did not try to recruit the Red Prince again. Twice bitten was enough; in any case, the existing relationship between Abu Hassan and Robert Ames adequately served the purposes of both sides. By 1973 the Americans had pushed a not unwilling Arafat and the PLO to the beginning of the political path. The administration, however, had made it clear that if it was to deal with the PLO, America had to be convinced that the PLO was recognized as the official representative of the Palestinian people. In October 1973, this assurance was given when the Arab summit meeting in Rabat, Morocco, gave the PLO the official recognition it sought and America needed in order to pursue the dialogue. Just over a year later, on 13 November, with Abu Hassan in the wings, Yasser Arafat made his famous 'olive branch' speech to the United Nations. While most of the world fêted Arafat as the hero of the hour, Abu Hassan was secretly meeting 'Alan', his CIA officer-to-be, a few minutes' taxi ride away in the PLO's suite at the Waldorf Astoria. When we were watching the young Hassan Salameh going through his father's trunk, he dug out a postcard of the hotel with an arrow pointing to the upper floors. On the back was scrawled the proud exclamation, 'The PLO at the Waldorf Astoria!' Fatah had come a long way since Black September – despite the undertaking the US administration had given to Israel that it would have no dealings with the PLO.

In 1976, Abu Hassan returned to the United States on a trip that combined business with pleasure. Apparently the PLO paid for the flights while the Americans picked up the hotel bills. Travelling with him was Georgina Rizak, the Lebanese beauty queen who became his second wife. It was an unlikely combination, the 'Red Prince' and Miss Universe. The purpose of the trip was for Abu Hassan to meet senior American officials at an hotel in New Orleans. According to Georgina, Abu Hassan saw it as a 'test'. 'They wanted to be sure that he had the temperament and ability of a man with whom they could do business,' she told me. The meeting seems to have lasted about five hours. 'Abu Hassan was pleased. He had passed the test.' The exam over, the couple flew to Hawaii for a holiday. 'Alan' went with them. Hawaii was 'a way of cementing the relationship,' he said. The relationship continued fruitfully in Beirut nourished by Mustafa and Robert Ames. In December 1978, Abu Hassan was invited to America for a further meeting, this time, he understood, with senior political people in

Washington. But it was postponed until early the following year. The meeting never took place. By then Abu Hassan was dead.

Abu Hassan's family had always had fears for his safety and by 1978 they were acute. He had always been meticulous about his security, constantly travelling with his bodyguards and constantly varying his route. He had been scornful of the lack of precautions taken by his Fatah colleagues in Beirut, Kamal Adwan, Kamal Nasser and Abu Youssef, which had led to their deaths in the Israelis' operation, 'Springtime of Youth'.

> [The enemy's] main victory – the assassination of three of our leaders in Beirut in April 1973 – was the result of complete carelessness, which is typical of the Oriental mentality, the fatalistic mentality. My home was about 50 metres from the late Abu Youssef's home. The Israeli assassins didn't come to my home for a very simple reason: it was guarded by 14 men.[35]

His family kept warning him of the danger but, having long accepted the inevitability of a violent death, Abu Hassan took no notice. There were whispers that his marriage to Georgina had made him less scrupulous: that he had, in a word, gone soft.

His superstitious sister, Nidal, had always dreaded her brother's fourth decade. She told me he had once visited a fortune teller who said he would die when he was thirty-seven – the age at which his father had been killed. She said he had laughed and told her not to panic: it was nonsense. He did not believe it but Nidal did. I pointed out it was only a fortune teller. 'Yes, but it scared me,' she said. 'He meant such a lot to me and I thought he was too great to die, too great to be killed. I though he was immortal – that it was impossible for him to die. My mother told him to take care, to put a radio or transmitter in his car, but he told her not to worry. He said he was alert and nothing would happen. He told me that, once a decision for your assassination had been taken, it was only a question of when and where. You'd never know when it would take place.'[36] I asked Um Ali if her fears were true. She said they were. 'The last time I saw him I warned him. I told him that I had a feeling that something bad would happen to him. He laughed and said not to worry: he would live another fifty years. I told him fifty years were not enough. I told him to take care, change his route and get a warning device. He said he'd ordered one and it should arrive in a couple of days. As he left, I felt I would never see him again.'[37]

Remarkably, only a few days before his death, Abu Hassan had received a warning of the Mossad's plan to assassinate him. It was delivered not by one of his allies but by one of his theoretical enemies in the Lebanese civil war, Karim Pakradouni, a member of the Christian Phalangist Party's executive committee. Despite being on opposite sides of the 'Green Line' that divides Muslim West Beirut from the Christian East, Pakradouni and his boss, the Phalangist leader, Bashir Gemayel, maintained a genuine friendship with Abu Hassan; they regarded him as an honourable enemy with whom they could, and did, do business. Their information was well sourced, as the Phalangists are the natural allies of the Mossad. Karim Pakradouni told me that Bashir Gemayel had asked him to warn Abu Hassan that his life was in imminent danger. Bashir, he said, had many friends in the Mossad. 'I think Bashir had some *crise de conscience* and wanted to inform Abu Hassan about the operation.'[38] Pakradouni duly passed on the message. I asked him why he thought Abu Hassan was a Mossad target.

> Because he was a member of Black September and because he had a relationship with the American embassy in Beirut. I think the Mossad decided to kill him, not just because he was involved in the Munich operation, but especially because he was the go-between with the Americans. The policy of Israel was to destroy any contact between the PLO and the USA, and Abu Hassan was the first and main contact man, the liaison between Yasser Arafat personally and the American embassy. So quickly the Mossad realized that Abu Hassan was not just a security threat but a *political* danger because he represented the Palestinian window on America. But he ignored the warning. He thought nobody could kick him. He thought he was very strong.

Abu Hassan apparently also knew at second hand that the Mossad were getting closer although the precise details are very difficult to substantiate. We are led to believe that Mossad asked the CIA if Abu Hassan was one of its agents: if he was, he would not be touched; if he was not, he would be a legitimate target. I suspect this was probably some time in 1978, the year before his death. The Mossad may have been particularly exercised by intelligence of the planned meeting in Washington between Abu Hassan and senior political people scheduled for December 1978. The plans for his assassination were clearly laid later that year. Robert Ames and his colleagues are said to have put the Mossad's question to Abu Hassan and asked him what reply they should give. He told them what he had always told them: Ali Hassan Salameh was working for Palestine and nobody else. The answer probably sealed his fate.

By January 1979 Abu Hassan had developed a fatal routine, spending the afternoons with Georgina, now five months pregnant, at her apartment in Snoubra, a fashionable part of West Beirut. A visit to the gym and sauna was part of his regular routine but the superiors of the Mossad agents who were now watching his every movement allegedly vetoed a plan to place a bomb in the sauna on the grounds of the likely civilian death toll.[39] For two months, the eyes of the Mossad had been fixed on their target in the unlikely person of an English cat-loving eccentric with the pseudonym Erika Chambers: at least that was the name on her British passport number 25948 issued on 30 May 1975.[40] She had arrived in Beirut in November 1978 ostensibly to carry on children's aid work with a Palestinian organization known somewhat infelicitously as 'The House of Steadfastness of the Children of Telesata'. On 10 January 1979 she rented an eighth-floor apartment in the Anis Assaf building overlooking the narrow Beka Street into which Abu Hassan often turned on his afternoon journeys from Georgina's flat. Ms Chambers rented the flat for three months with a downpayment of 3500 Lebanese pounds. A week later, she was joined by Ronald Kolberg (another pseudonym), a businessman allegedly in the catering trade travelling on a Canadian passport, number 104277. Kolberg checked into the Royal Garden Hotel, rented a Simca from the Lenna Car Company and then proceeded to offer a number of local shopkeepers pamphlets about cooking implements. There was haggling but no prices agreed. The following day, Chambers and Kolberg were joined by a third man, pseudonym Peter Schriver, who was travelling on a forged British passport, number 260886, dated 15 October 1972. Schriver checked into the Hotel Méditerranée and then rented a Volkswagen, also from the Lenna Car Company. Once again the 'hit team' was in place. The official Lebanese investigation described Chambers, Kolberg and Schriver as being present in Beirut to carry out 'terrorist activities'.

At 3.45 on the afternoon of 22 January 1979, Abu Hassan said goodbye to Georgina and got into the waiting Chevrolet station wagon with his driver and two bodyguards. His two other bodyguards climbed into the Land-Rover that was to travel behind.[41] Abu Hassan was on his way to his mother's apartment where his niece was celebrating her third birthday. Nidal had everything ready, including a cine-camera to record the event. The convoy turned right into Beka Street, where Schriver's rented VW was parked on the left-hand side. It was empty except for 5 kilograms of hexagene, the equivalent of 30 kilos of dynamite, packed inside with a wireless transmitter.[42] Erika Chambers watched from the apartment above, her finger poised over the switch of the remote control. As the Chevrolet drew parallel to the parked VW, there was a blinding explosion. This time the Mossad had not bungled.

We talked to an eyewitness, who described the scene. 'It was like hell. There was a flash, then a big bang. It was incredible. I'd never seen anything like it before, not even in Beirut. It was as if the whole of the city was on fire. So many dead people, burnt cars and young bodies littering the street. Then I saw Abu Hassan Salameh getting out of a car and falling on the ground. The people told me who he was.'[43] Ironically, Abu Daoud, the man whom

Abu Hassan had enrolled in Fatah in the sixties, saw him die. By chance he was living nearby. 'I heard the explosion and rushed down. At first I thought it was the noise of a plane, but when I came down I saw Ali Hassan Salameh. His face was badly cut. The handsome features of which he was once so proud were in terrible shape.'[44] Shortly afterwards, Abu Hassan died in hospital. The doctors could not save him. 'It was the shock of my life,' remembers Nidal, who had been waiting to welcome him at her daughter's birthday party. 'But there was not even one teardrop. Nothing. I didn't cry. I didn't scream. I was just stunned. I didn't say a word. I couldn't believe that Ali, my beloved brother whom I believed to be immortal, could be killed just like that.'[45] Um Ali rushed to the hospital. 'I was numb. I didn't feel the pain. I was almost unconscious. When I arrived there, they didn't let me see him. They said, "It's all over".'[46]

When the news broke in Tel Aviv that evening, few tears were shed. Ilana Romano, the widow of the weightlifting champion who had been slain in Munich by Black September, said she had been waiting years for this day. 'In my name, and in the name of all the other widows, I want to thank those who did it.'[47] Golda Meir had avenged her children. The 'Red Prince' was dead. An estimated 100 000 mourners came to his funeral. Ali Hassan Salameh's thirteen-year-old son Hassan knelt by his father's graveside, dressed in full fedayeen regalia, with his godfather, Yasser Arafat, at his side. Commentators said what you would expect: that Hassan would carry on his father's struggle as Abu Hassan had carried on that of his father, Sheikh Hassan.

But today nothing could be further than the truth. We did not find a mature fedayeen with Kalashnikov and keffiyeh but an immaculately tailored young international businessman, bent on success, with all his father's charm, intelligence and good looks. His only concession to his father's style of dress was a pair of polished black cowboy boots proudly worn under neatly pressed suit trousers. That does not mean that Hassan is any less committed to the Palestinian cause. The difference is that he now sees it being achieved through dialogue, discussion and mutual respect between Arab and Jew. Hassan is the 'new' Palestinian. 'I am not PLO,' he told us, although Arafat remains his godfather, and one who apparently takes his duties seriously.

My father wanted me to be brought up away from his kind of life. I have a genuine desire for peace but I have a different mentality from the fighters of the past. I now live in a different era and see the world differently. There are now even greater opportunities for peace through negotiation. The path is now paved for this. Before, nobody even knew who the Palestinians were. We have been killing each other for forty-five years. Assassinations will always occur where there is no secure peace. I am anxious to discuss these matters directly with the Israelis. I respect them. They all can't be bad. 'An eye for an eye' is not my way.[48]

It was extraordinary to hear such words coming from the son and grandson of two of Palestine's most celebrated martyrs. I had no doubt the feelings were genuinely expressed and sincerely held. The absence of bitterness, given the fate of his father, was remarkable. I wondered if we would find similar sentiments on the other side.

4 · THE HUNTERS

'It's incongruous, really,' said the Israeli archaeologist in the big Indiana Jones hat. 'Nearly 2000 years ago, this used to be a place of love. They had water orgies here. Barren women would come from Caesarea, take a dip in the healing springs of Aesculapius and return home pregnant. Fifty years ago it was a place of war, a military training base for the Etzel, the Irgun,[1] from where they launched some of their most famous attacks against the British.' He smiled mischievously, obviously preferring love to war.

Eli Shenhav, a veteran of Hadrian's Wall and Newcastle Brown Ale as he proudly told me, and his team have spent the past seven years excavating the ancient Roman site at Shuni on a pine-covered hillside overlooking the orchards and vineyards of Israel's northern coastal strip. The Roman amphitheatre is their greatest triumph, a treasure-house which yielded a wealth of coins, ancient terracotta vases and the occasional rusty Irgun weapon. The site is now a historical museum, testimony not to the wonders of Eli Shanhav's trowel but to the exploits of the young men and women of the Irgun who, within Shuni's walls, planned and executed some of their most daring operations. The memorial hall is adorned with their pictures, some young and fresh-faced, others more cynical and hardened. To the British soldiers they fought against, these faces belonged not to heroic freedom fighters struggling for the liberation of their land, but to terrorists. The most hardened face of all belonged to the young Menachem Begin, the 'terrorist' turned Prime Minister whose administration ran Israel at the time of the assassination of Abu Hassan.

We had been brought to Shuni by a former member of the Irgun, Tzadok Offir. Because of his youth, he had taken little part in their exploits in 1947–8, but had made up for any lack of adventure in those early days by subsequently becoming a Mossad agent, which he remained until his retirement in 1988. To be strictly accurate, Tzadok did briefly leave Mossad for a few years in the mid-seventies to run, of all things, a music shop, but it was a departure that offered limited excitement. Tzadok soon got bored and re-enlisted. 'Once you join, you never really leave,' he told me as we sat on stones in the sun in Shuni's Roman amphitheatre. Like most Mossad agents, he never referred to his former employer by name. Mossad is simply 'the Office', 'the Agency', 'the Service' or, to the CIA, 'the Southern Company'. Tzadok had served 'the Office' for nearly twenty years in the West Bank, Gaza, Europe and, more recently, Central America. I was curious about Central America. What was he doing there? He smiled, tightened his lips and wiped his hand across his chest in a gesture that indicated that the question was off-limits. Tzadok is not one to talk, at least not about the Mossad. But if you ask him about the Irgun and its shrine at Shuni, whose development has become his passion since his retirement, he is hard to contain.

He led me up the gentle hillside to the pine grove which shades the memorial to the dozen members of the Irgun who were killed on 4 May 1947 while freeing their comrades from the British military prison in Acre 50 kilometres away. He explained how the sixty-strong unit had set out from Shuni disguised as British soldiers in stolen British uniforms, driven to Acre in stolen British military trucks and sealed off the roads to the ancient Arab city to prevent the arrival of reinforcements. They blew up the walls and forty-one prisoners escaped. During the operation, five of the group were captured. Three were put on trial and sentenced to death. The Irgun warned the British not to execute their captives and kidnapped two army sergeants as hostages. They threatened to kill them if their comrades were hanged. The British military authorities were in no mood to submit to blackmail and sent the three young men to the gallows on 29 July 1947. The following day, the bodies of the two British army sergeants were found hanging from a tree.[2] 'We repaid our enemy in kind,' wrote Menachem Begin in his memoirs. 'We had warned him again and again and again. He had callously disregarded our warnings. He forced us to answer gallows with gallows.'[3]

'It was one of the most difficult decisions that Menachem Begin ever took,' said Tzadok, staring down at the headstones. 'After this there were no more hangings.'[4] He insisted that, unlike the PLO and other Palestinian groups, the Irgun was never a terrorist organization. 'We never targeted civilians. Of course, occasionally civilians get hurt. But that's war.' I had heard that defence more than once before on the grounds that circumstances, not military or terrorist actions, were to blame. I challenged Tzadok with the Irgun's bombing of the King David Hotel in Jerusalem on 22 July 1946 in which over seventy people were killed, two-thirds of them civilians, many of whom were staff. He looked at me with a rueful smile. 'I thought you might mention that,' he said. He explained that the King David was the headquarters of the British military command and a legitimate target for the Irgun. The bombs had been placed in the cellar and in the hotel's exclusive restaurant. A twenty-minute warning had been given. He claimed the British had refused to evacuate the hotel, saying that they were not at the beck and call of terrorists. Again, I had heard a similar defence many times before: that the authorities were to blame for their callousness or inefficiency, not those who planted the bomb. The carnage at the King David was appalling. According to Tzadok, his former comrades were so shocked and embarrassed that they claimed they were not responsible. 'Plausible deniability' has a long history.

The yellowing photos on the walls of Shuni's fledgling museum are the faces of Tzadok's heroes who fought and died to establish the state of Israel. Tzadok saw himself carrying on that fight against those pledged to destroy the state that these young men and women had helped create in 1948. His enemy was 'the terrorists', and intelligence was the most important commodity in planning their destruction. Intelligence was Tzadok's business. His greatest asset, apart from his training, was his ability to speak fluent Arab. He would charm, bribe and recruit any Palestinian who looked a likely candidate whether he hailed from the refugee camps of the Occupied Territories or the college campuses of western Europe where many Palestinians migrated to study.

Success for any state committed to defeating terrorism lies in recruiting such agents, who become the cancer in the enemy's ranks, frustrating operations, sapping morale and sowing mistrust. Intelligence gives the initiative to the state. Recruiting and running agents is the most dangerous aspect of all in the state's response to terrorism, with the lives of both handlers and informers permanently at risk, as we shall see in a later chapter. Once 'terrorists' have changed sides, they must feel that their security will never be compromised. Without this trust, they are vulnerable to being turned again by their former masters, either to work as double agents or to set up their handlers. Israel knows the rules as well as any state and looks after her collaborators. Remarkably, in a remote spot on the West Bank, there is a village called Facma where Palestinian informers have been resettled. When we first heard about Facma, we could not believe it. It was like being told that there was a place in South Armagh where Republican informers were living quite openly under the protection of the state.

Facma is not easy to find. Initially we hit upon the wrong village, another Facma a few miles away that turned out to be a Fatah stronghold. Our crew van was hastened on its way with a rock. Any romantic notion that Israel repays its collaborators with a life of luxury is immediately dispelled when you see the cluster of houses on the bleak hillside. It looks like any other Arab village, except few have an army post standing guard at the entrance; and in few Arab villages do you see men openly walking around with guns issued for their own protection. The head man of the village, Abu Ali, who entertained us with yet more sweet and welcome tea, sat incongruously beneath an Israeli flag with his machine-gun not far away. He was proud of being a defector. He told us there were 102 families in Facma, roughly half of whom were collaborators. He said he had 'tried the PLO' at the beginning of the Intifada but had found them 'not very good'. He had therefore decided to switch sides. He said we were free to wander round his village. Abu Ali introduced me to 'Jamal', who took me to his home. To describe it as sparsely furnished is to make an understatement, but this was home for Jamal, his wife and nine children. There was no furniture, no carpets, nothing – just two or three empty rooms with concrete floors and concrete walls. It was the middle of winter and it was cold. His family sat motionless in the middle of one of the rooms, huddled for warmth round the embers of fire on the cold concrete in the middle of the floor. If this was the reward for informing, it was hardly a carrot. Jamal said he had lived in Facma for a year and a half. How did he come to be there? He said he had had a family problem and gone to the Israelis. They told him they would help him if he would help them. He agreed. He pointed out the houses in his village where the leaders of the Intifada lived. There were about fifty of them. In return the Israelis gave him some money and some help. There was no sense of betrayal or shame. For Jamal it was simply a business proposition. I asked him if he felt safe in Facma. 'Half and half,' he replied.

I imagined that the collaborators who lived in Facma were not of the calibre of those who had worked for Tzadok in the West Bank and Europe. But the principles involved were no doubt the same. I asked him why Palestinians should work for Israelis. 'It is very difficult to explain,' he said. 'It is a skill which is gradually acquired. It isn't easy at the beginning. But once contact is established, and there's an atmosphere of mutual trust, it is possible to continue without too much difficulty.' Abu Daoud, who as a senior Fatah commander was always acutely sensitive to the dangers of penetration, saw the process from the other side. 'They were recruiting many of our students from Gaza and the West Bank who were studying in the European universities,' he told me. 'Most were from poor families who couldn't afford to send their sons money. They could go without for two to three months but after that they began to feel hungry. That's when the Israelis went to work. If they knew a student needed money, they would contact him and give him what he needed. Then they would take him back to the Occupied Territories and train him. They'd send him back, not to his studies, but to us – to infiltrate us.' Abu Daoud also explained another way in which the Israelis put young Palestinians under an obligation to the security services. 'There are some people abroad who want to go back to their villages but can't do so because their passports have expired – and they've no connections to help them get their documents renewed. So they go to the Israeli embassies and are told that they can have a *laissez-passer* on one condition: that they will go back to the Occupied Territories, undergo training, and then go back as a paid agent to Europe; from there they could be sent to Beirut or South Lebanon and they'd be working for the Israelis.' But, given the fine line between being an agent and a double agent, how did Tzadok Offir know when to trust the Palestinians he was handling? 'We worked in the field. We had the skill and the competence to make an initial appraisal. The final judgement was left to the professionals who were in charge of this aspect of our work.' There had, he explained, been 'un-written rules' that both sides had adhered to – that agents and their handlers in this shadow war were not to be touched. There was 'no question of personal violence'.

But at the end of 1972 the rules were broken, and what became known as 'the War of the Spooks' erupted. The first blow was struck by Fatah five days after Munich in an operation that must have been planned before and probably independently of the Olympic attack: but once the Mossad 'hit team' went into action, Fatah retaliated and the 'war' gathered pace. Fatah fired the first shots when it attempted to assassinate Tzadok Offir on 10 September 1972. Abu Daoud knew how the operation against him was planned. 'Tzadok was recruiting agents. We can't prevent people being recruited, but there's espionage and there's counter-espionage. So we sent somebody to Tzadok whose mission was to kill him.' But things did not go quite according to plan.

The Fatah double agent, who had been infiltrated into Europe from a training camp in Damascus, had been arrested in a most unheroic way, with stolen goods in the back of a car in Belgium. While in gaol, he wrote to the Israeli embassy in Brussels offering his services. Tzadok paid him a visit, listened to his story and told him he would have to wait until his release. 'We can do many things,' he told me, 'But getting people out of gaol, legally, in a foreign country is not one of them.' Even the Mossad did not have a 'Get out of Gaol Free' card. The Palestinian's story checked out. Tzadok knew the fedayeen camps he spoke of along the Jordanian side of the West Bank. He even knew some of the individuals he described, in particular one Fatah commander with a limp and a penchant for driving Jeeps as if they were stock cars. When the Mossad's potential recruit had served his time in gaol, Tzadok started to meet him on a regular basis. At such meetings Tzadok was never armed. I expressed surprise. 'Foreign governments don't like us wandering around with guns on their soil.'

LEFT The symbol of 'terrorism': a member of Black September holding Israeli hostages at the Munich Olympics, 1972.

BELOW Lieutenant-Colonel Bill Cowan in the ruins of the US Marine HQ in Beirut where 241 Marines were killed in a suicide attack in 1983. The wall of the bar survives, with the names of some of the victims inscribed on it. Cowan led the undercover unit charged with locating those responsible.

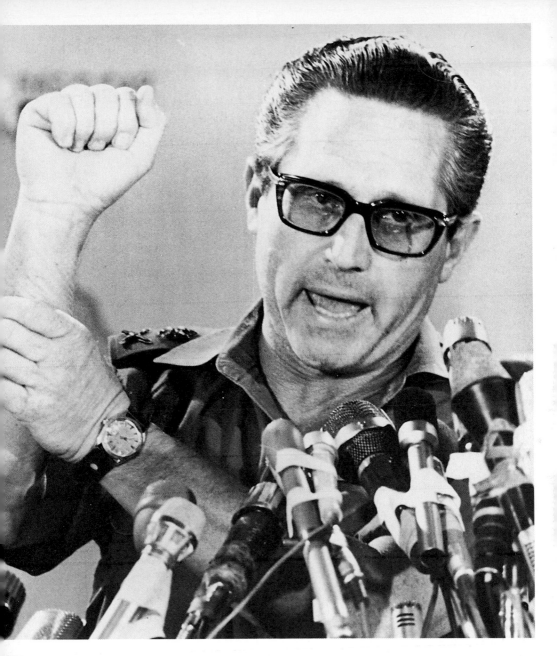

General Aharon Yariv, former head of Israeli military intelligence and architect of the Mossad 'hit' team formed after the Munich massacre to eliminate the leaders of Black September.

LEFT   Abu Daoud of the PLO: one of the former leaders of Black September.

Abu Jihad, the PLO's military chief and co-ordinator of the Intifada, assassinated in Tunis by an Israeli commando unit in 1988.

LEFT The funeral of Abu Youssef, one of the three PLO leaders assassinated in Beirut in 1973 by an Israeli undercover unit in the operation 'Springtime of Youth'.

Yasser Arafat (*left*), head of the PLO, and Abu Hassan Salameh (*right*), the alleged 'mastermind of Munich' and Arafat's heir apparent until his assassination by Mossad agents in 1979.

Robert Ames posing for a family Christmas card in Saudi Arabia in 1965. He was the CIA's star Middle East analyst and had a close relationship with Salameh, although Salameh never became a CIA agent. Ames was killed in the bombing of the US Embassy in Beirut in 1983.

RIGHT   Mossad officer Baruch Cohen (*left*) uncovering an arms cache on the West Bank. He was subsequently set up by one of his Palestinian agents and assassinated in Madrid in 1973. His killers are thought to have used this photo to identify him.

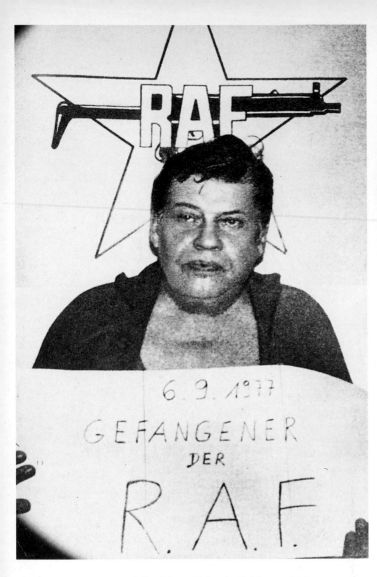

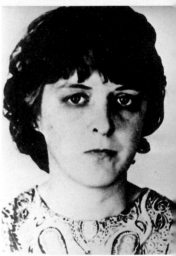

German industrialist Hanns-Martin Schleyer, kidnapped by the Red Army Faction and videotaped pleading for his release. He was 'executed' after six weeks in captivity.

RIGHT, TOP TO BOTTOM   Silke Maier-Witt as a young girl, as a wanted terrorist, and as a prisoner in 1990 after the fall of the Berlin Wall.

Then came the fateful day, five days after Munich. A meeting was arranged at the Café Prince in Brussels. The two men looked an unlikely pair, with Tzadok neatly dressed in casual clothes and his unshaven 'agent' shabbily attired in baggy jeans, trainers and an old army greatcoat. He carried a brown bag in which Tzadok assumed was the material his agent had promised to bring. They entered the coffee shop and sat down in a corner. Without warning, the agent got up and disappeared, leaving the bag at the table. Tzadok suspected the worst. A bomb? He moved as far away as possible. A minute later, the agent returned. He said he had been to the toilet. He stood a metre away from Tzadok and suddenly pulled out a long-barrelled Smith and Wesson from inside his military greatcoat and opened fire, shouting out Tzadok's codename, 'Shafiq!'

The first thing which flashed through my mind was that if I stayed here I would die. The second thing was what to do. There was a big ashtray on the table in front of me. I intended to throw it at him. I know I grabbed it. I felt two sledge-hammer blows, one to my head and one to my chest. I remember a hotchpotch of noises: shots and explosions, tables falling over, screaming women and the clatter of breaking crockery. Apparently I was moving, since I fell on my stomach about four metres away from the place where I had been sitting. Then I remember that suddenly everything became still. There was an unearthly silence. I lay down on my stomach and everything was quiet. I did not feel any pain. I did not feel that bad considering the circumstances. It felt like I was floating. I felt very light as if I were lying on a feather bed or hovering in the air. The silence was indescribable, like a whirl coming from a different planet. I opened my eyes and saw the cement joints in the floor tiles and the leg of the table. I was not sure whether I was alive but when I saw the table and the tiles on the floor I realized that I wasn't dead, as this, for sure, couldn't be heaven. I managed to hold the table leg with my left hand and started to get up. There was a lot of blood on the floor. Through the mirror, which was on the opposite wall, I saw my head and my face covered with blood. My white shirt was red. I started moving towards the barman, who was standing frozen like a waxworks dummy. Outside the coffee bar, on the pavement, there was a scene which I will never forget. I saw a sea of faces and numerous eyes which were staring blankly at the coffee bar. Nobody moved. I staggered to the counter and probably managed to utter the words 'Ambulance! Ambulance!'

Miraculously, Tzadok survived. His close friend and fellow Mossad agent, Baruch Cohen, was less fortunate. Cohen became the first Mossad agent to be killed in Europe by a Palestinian.

Baruch Cohen had an unlikely political profile for a Mossad agent. Tzadok Offir's politics were what you would expect. Baruch Cohen's were definitely not. He was a man of the left, not the right, a kibbutznik who embraced socialism and coexistence, not extreme nationalism and confrontation. He had been brought up in Haifa at a time when the northern Israeli city was predominantly Arab and when relations between the Jewish and Palestinian communities were relatively harmonious. The family lived in an apartment at 12 Ha'shomer Street on the hillside that rises steeply above the crowded harbour. Baruch's father ran a business selling leather, and most of the customers who came to his shop were Arabs who bought the material to make sandals and shoes. Most of their neighbours were Arabs too and virtually all of the children's friends were Palestinian. At home Arabic was the mother tongue. Hebrew was the language of prayer, not of day-to-day communication. 'He drank it from his mother's milk,' remembers his widow, Norit, who still lives in Haifa. 'It was second nature for him to speak Arab just like he did Hebrew. I think he loved the Arab character more than the Israeli one because the word 'honour' meant something to Arab children. If an Arab child promised to bring something to Baruch, Baruch knew that he would do it. If an Israeli child made the same offer, Baruch knew he might do it or he might not.'[5] It was Norit who introduced him to socialism and the kibbutz, to the disapproval of his brother, Meir. On the basis of his track record, it was Meir who should have become the Mossad agent, not Baruch. Meir had been a comrade of Menachem Begin's in the Irgun and had spent two and a half years in a British internment camp – testimony to his impeccable Zionist credentials. He dug out faded photographs to prove it. I suggested he had ended up there because the British regarded him as a terrorist. 'There's a very big difference between a terrorist and a liberation fighter,' he said.[6] The response had a familiar ring. I also had the same exchange with him about the King David Hotel as I had had with Tzadok Offir, with Meir pursuing the standard Irgun argument that the Hotel was a legitimate target as it housed the British Military headquarters. I pointed out that nearly two-thirds of the ninety dead were not British soldiers but Jews and Arabs, but he still refused to accept that it was a terrorist attack. Meir subsequently became Deputy Chairman of the Knesset when Menachem Begin's political party, the Likud, came to power.

Baruch Cohen did not start his career as a spy but was gradually drawn into it when his particular talents, his fluent Arabic and ability to relate to Palestinians, were recognized and then utilized by his superiors. Baruch began his service in a rather humdrum way before the June War of 1967 as a civil servant in the Department of Arab Affairs in Upper Galilee, the site of the villages of Birim and Ikrit from which Black September had drawn its codename for the Munich operation. It was here that Baruch first met Tzadok Offir when Tzadok was a soldier attached to the department. Tzadok was scrupulously reticent about what they did together. Baruch's rise was swift, as individuals with his particular abilities were rare. After the June War he was promoted from sergeant in the military reserves to captain and, remarkably, given his age and experience, appointed military governor of Nablus, the West Bank town that had become the centre of Palestinian resistance. Within a month, he is said to have almost succeeded in capturing Yasser Arafat, who was moving from town to village organizing the infrastructure for Fatah. Arafat is reported to have donned women's clothing to escape.[7]

One of their successes, however, did not remain a secret. The two friends were photographed in military uniform at the side of an arms cache that they had uncovered once Baruch had successfully extracted the information from one of the Palestinians who knew its location. The photograph was reprinted in a souvenir booklet of the Six Day War and its aftermath which would have been essential reading for Abu Hassan and his colleagues in the Razd, Fatah's intelligence department. Every photograph would have been scrutinized and every name faithfully recorded and checked. Of course, there were no names by the photographs of Baruch and Tzadok, but, inexplicably, their faces were not blotted out. It is said, although we could establish no evidence for it, that from that point on the two men became Fatah targets. Certainly Baruch was well known to Fatah because of the disruption he had caused to its infrastructure and personnel during his time on the West Bank. Norit showed us the photograph and, although she is not a bitter woman by nature, expressed strong feelings about the security lapse that had resulted in the identification of Tzadok and Baruch. She said it was wrong to have sent them to Europe. It was perhaps no coincidence that the two friends became targets. But Norit seldom worried. She knew her husband was good at his job and saw little point in living in a state of permanent anxiety. She said he did not look like a spy. He was 'Mr Average', not James Bond. He never stood out in a crowd. She gestured playfully with her hands to explain.

He was not tall, not short. Not fat, not thin. You would never give him a second look. He was like a fox. He could go out silently and respond quickly to any situation. He was like a chameleon. He could be an Israeli one minute and an Arab the next. His ears were open all the time. He knew what to get, what to throw out and what to keep. What was really important, he passed on to the Government. He was one of what we call 'the Secret Army' or 'the Shadowmen'. He fought but no one knew it. None of our neighbours were aware of who Baruch was or what he did. He was very, very clever. I don't know how he did it but I trusted him and felt confident. Once they shot at his car in Gaza and he phoned and said he was all right. I felt fine. You can't live with worry all the time. If you did, you'd become like a stone. I wanted to live and give him life. What would life be if all the time I was saying, 'Don't do it, don't go there'?[8]

At the beginning of the seventies, Baruch and Tzadok were transferred to Europe. One of their main tasks was to penetrate Black September's network. 'Black September was a murderous terrorist organization,' said Tzadok. 'Any piece of information about its members and their activities was important to us. Our job was to meet people who were ready to tell us what was going on inside these organizations.' He admitted it was dangerous work. Baruch is credited with having put the Mossad's European network in place. Abu Daoud described him to me as 'a very dangerous man'. That was perhaps an understatement, since Baruch and his colleagues probably provided much of the information that enabled the Mossad 'hit team' to operate with such devastating effect. The nerve centre of the Mossad's intelligence operation in Europe was the Israeli embassy in Brussels. This covert side of the embassy's activities had been transferred from Paris, the preferred listening post, because of General de Gaulle's pro-Arab policies. Baruch's family moved with him to the Belgian capital. Norit, who had always kept her anxieties under iron control, welcomed the move on the grounds that her husband would be more inconspicuous making his contacts in the capitals of Europe than in the shadows of Nablus, the West Bank and Gaza.

In Europe he was invisible, like air. In a city of a million people, no one recognized him. I never thought that Baruch, like Tzadok, would be a target. For me, Baruch was my husband, the father of my children. I never thought of him as a spy. In Brussels I was anonymous too. I was 'Madame Cohen'. I felt safe and felt he was safe. Of course, he worked under another name. It was only when he came home and shut the door that he was Baruch Cohen. I never asked him where he was going, whether his destination was Madrid, Vienna, London or Paris. If he was away for three weeks, I would never ask him where he had been – was it Lebanon or Italy? It was like a jigsaw. Gradually I put together the pieces and built up the picture. It was a very dangerous job, not very clean and sometimes ugly. But for me, Baruch was clean, not a hero but a man doing a job that had to be done. I hate war whether it's cold or hot and this war was cold. But it was a war.

The children enjoyed Brussels too. The family showed us their old home movies from twenty years ago that featured Baruch as a playful father fooling around in the snow, rowing the children round a boating lake and acting as guide to the famous sights of Europe. None of the children knew precisely what their father did until their suspicions were aroused by a combination of design and accident. Icki, Baruch's youngest son, found out by design. He attended school in Brussels with other Israeli children who used to boast about their fathers' guns, which since they were Israelis abroad, they had for their own protection. Some worked for Israel's state airline, El Al, others were normal staff at the embassy. 'I was amazed. I wondered how come everybody knows that his father had a gun and I didn't know anything. Then I came home one afternoon and I started to check my parents' bedroom. Finally I found the gun and I was very, very shocked.' While Icki was looking at the gun, his father came in. 'I was caught red-handed, which was embarrassing for both of us. He was very upset at my looking at his stuff. He didn't beat me or shout at me but tried to explain that I shouldn't do it. He told me he had to have this gun for what he was doing. He didn't explain any more than this. He just told me that it was a necessity and I just had to accept it. I only found out what my father really did after he died.'[9]

Icki's older brother, Adi, also did a bit of snooping and found a pair of glasses with clear lenses. 'I put them on and they made no difference. I had a flashback from the spy books I'd been reading and thought: Someone's playing at disguises.'[10] Adi's suspicions were confirmed on a family shopping trip to Amsterdam when Baruch suggested they stop off at Schipol airport for a bit. While the family was eating, Baruch excused himself and said he would be back in a few minutes. 'He got up and left,' recalls Adi. 'I don't know why but I followed him. Then I saw him talking with a young, dark guy. I didn't hear what they were talking about, but I knew that my father was talking with an Arab. This was the moment that I realized that the glasses I'd found at home and the fact that my father was speaking with an Arab added up to making him a spy. My father was a spy! When he came back I said, "Dad, I know what you are doing. You're a spy!" Then he says to me, "Sssh, this will be our little secret." OK. You know when you're a little kid and you're told, "This is our secret", it remains our secret.'

Fatah intelligence, under Abu Iyad and Abu Hassan, believed that Baruch Cohen's intelligence activities paved the way for the assassination of Wael Zwaiter in Rome on 18 October 1972 and Mahmoud Hamshari in Paris on 16 December 1972. Baruch Cohen had to be stopped. In his memoirs, Abu Iyad[11] explained why Baruch Cohen had to die.

Cohen ... had a number of passports and was often on the move among European capitals, particularly Paris, Brussels and Rome, using different identities. Everything pointed to the fact that he had important duties within the Jewish state's special services. In Spain he had set up a network of Palestinian students mainly from the West Bank and Gaza to whom he assigned duties as agents provocateurs as well as espionage tasks. ... At a later stage, Cohen started laying plans for terrorist attacks against Spanish enterprises owned by Jews or having close business relations with Israel, with the aim of discrediting Palestinians in the eyes of the Spanish and provoking their expulsion from Spain. What he didn't know was that several of the students he had recruited belonged to Black September and pretended to co-operate with him at the request of the organisation. When he began to have serious doubts about the loyalty of those who failed to carry out the tasks assigned to them on various pretexts, it was decided to execute him. His elimination became urgent when, in early January, shortly after Mahmoud Hamshari's assassination in Paris, Cohen announced that he was leaving Spain to take up other duties.[12]

Norit Cohen had a dream three days before her husband met his death. 'It was a nightmare. I dreamed that one of Baruch's senior colleagues had been murdered. I remember crying in my dream and saying to myself, "Don't cry. It's only a dream." When I woke up my pillow was wet, so I knew that I had been crying and crying all the night. When I went to work, I forgot all about the dream. But when people told me that Baruch had been killed, the dream came back. It was like something had happened that you could not stop. I think that this is the reason that I was not in shock when the people came to tell me that Baruch had been killed. I told them I knew already. I never, never cried.' Norit remembers saying goodbye to Baruch for the last time as he left on Monday morning as usual for another week away. She fetched him his suitcase, and he said he wanted to say goodbye to the children. It was early in the morning, they were sleeping, and Norit thought they should sleep for another hour or more. It was cold and there was no school that day. Baruch let the children sleep, kissed his wife goodbye and said he would be back on Thursday. On Thursday he phoned her from Madrid saying he would be a day late and back the following afternoon for the weekend. He told Norit everything was fine.

On Friday, 26 January 1973, Baruch had arranged to meet one of his agents in the La Palmera café on José Antonio Street in Madrid. According to the journalist Patrick Seale, who met and interviewed the man alleged to be the agent concerned, Baruch Cohen was set up in the same way as Tzadok Offir. Whether this is a case of Fatah cashing in on double hindsight we shall never know. Its intelligence officers are said to have baited the trap by getting a young Palestinian studying in Spain to write to his parents in the Occupied Territories saying that he was short of money, in the knowledge that the Mossad would intercept the communication. According to this account, the bait was taken and Baruch Cohen blackmailed the young student into working for him by saying that his family was in 'our power'. Baruch instructed the apparently willing student for three months, asking him towards the end to go to Beirut to infiltrate a Black September cell. The meeting at the Café La Palmera was to go over the details.[13] Baruch also apparently wanted to introduce the Palestinian to his successor, because he had said he was leaving Madrid. As he got up to leave the café, he was gunned down and fatally wounded by one of two other Palestinians who had been lying in wait. The other fired his gun in the air to create panic.[14] Baruch died in hospital several hours later, having identified the killers before he finally lost consciousness.

The effect on the Cohen family was devastating. Norit told the children their father had been shot but held back the news that he was dead. Icki was ten at the time and remembers the day as if it were yesterday. 'We went up to sleep and my brother was crying all night because he knew already that my father was in hospital and was dying. The following morning, my mother's best friend came upstairs and told me that my father had died. That specific moment is very, very clear to me. I can still see the picture of the young boy standing by the window. It was raining outside and something happened very deep inside. I felt a part of me didn't exist any more. It was as if my roots, my security had gone. Twenty years later, there's still something missing in my life.' Norit only broke the news to her youngest children once the family was back in Israel on the way to the comfort of their mother's kibbutz. The car pulled in by the wayside so the little ones could cry. Golda Meir met the family in her office in Jerusalem. She told Norit to put her head on her shoulder and cry. 'She gave me a big hug. She said, "You must cry now. You must." I said I couldn't. It was raining. The sky was crying. That was enough.' The Prime Minister told the children that she was now their aunt and, if they wanted anything, all they had to do was ask. And she made them a promise: that their father's murderers would be found and his death avenged. Their names were known. As far as we know, the promise was never fulfilled.

I asked Norit if she wanted vengeance for the death of her husband. She was adamant she did not. 'No. Never. Never. Enough blood has been spilled. I think we should talk to our enemy. Talking is better than killing. We were born with tongues to speak and with brains to understand. Animals cannot talk so they eat one another. God made us a little higher than animals and gave us the talent to speak, not fight. We'll get much further by talking and understanding each other.' I asked if she really wanted to talk to her enemies. She said she did. 'I want to know what they think about me and I can tell them what I think about them. I am sure we can sit together and drink coffee and feel not like enemies but like human beings.'

I was as surprised to hear this as I had been to hear similar thoughts expressed by Abu Hassan's son. It seemed incongruous to hear the widow of a slain Mossad agent speaking like this after so many years of bitterness and bloodshed. Adi Cohen said much the same when I discussed the future with him. Towards the end of the interview, it suddenly occurred to me to mention what Hassan had told me as I left him in Amman. There was a grim symmetry in the relationship. Hassan was the son of the alleged 'Mastermind of Munich' killed by the Mossad; Adi was the son of a Mossad agent killed by Black September. As I was saying goodbye, Hassan had shaken me by the hand and asked me to pass on his regards to the Cohen family. (We had told each family that we were talking to the other.) I passed on Hassan's regards to Adi as we were filming the interview. He looked utterly stunned and at a loss for words. 'He was being serious,' I prompted. 'It shocks me a bit,' he said, recovering. 'We don't think of our enemy as a person. An enemy is something inhuman, something evil that you have to kill. I never thought of Abu Hassan as human, I mean, as human as my father. He has a son and I am a son. I think we're even about the same age. I picture the face of Ali Hassan Salameh in my mind and I see the picture of my father, Baruch Cohen,' I asked Adi if he had any message for Hassan. 'Let's meet. Perhaps in Cyprus,' he joked. 'I can't offer him anything, except maybe my understanding. Give him my regards, if you see him again.' No doubt Baruch Cohen and Abu Hassan would have agreed and each been proud of his son.

5 · BETRAYAL

In October 1989 there was an extraordinary party held in East Berlin to celebrate the fortieth anniversary of the founding of the GDR, the East German state. It was like dancing on the *Titanic*. Two months later, the Berlin Wall came down and the state was no more. One of the guests pouring out the *Sekt*, the sparkling German champagne, was a man I shall call 'Kurt', an officer in the Ministerium für Staatssicherheit, the Ministry for State Security or 'Stasi', East Germany's notorious secret police. He was attached to Department 22, the Stasi's anti-terrorism unit. Kurt's presence at such an event would not have raised any eyebrows on the other side of the Berlin Wall; after all, the Stasi had been the instrument to which the state owed its survival. His guests, however, would have had West Germany's security services rushing to their files in astonishment. On Kurt's guest list were some of the Federal Republic's most wanted men and women, members of the Rote Armee Fraktion, the Red Army Faction or RAF, whose photographs had stared down from posters across the nation for years under the banner 'Terroristen'. In the photographs each one of them looked the part.

For nearly two decades, the RAF in its various incarnations had terrorized the West German state and its people out of all proportion to its size: the group had never been more than a handful of dedicated terrorists, but their deadly efficiency and precise targeting of the pillars of West Germany's economic, political and legal establishment had thrown the country into a virtual state of siege. Bankers, industrialists, judges and politicians had been 'executed' in the name of some notional anti-capitalist, anti-imperialist, proletarian revolution. Most of the owners of the faces on the 'wanted' posters had long disappeared from view, the authorities knew not where. Perhaps they were living in Aden with their PFLP allies or in Baghdad, Beirut, Damascus or Libya. Few suspected that for nearly ten years around a dozen had been living under the protection of the Stasi a few miles away across the border, complete with new names, new papers and new identities. Whole 'legends' had been created so that terrorists became 'new' people in more than just name, living the lives of good East German workers in the skins of citizens who had never existed. The odd sighting had been made by the occasional traveller to the East and reported back to the West, but the RAF fugitives had remained largely undetected.

Kurt had been in charge of a number of them since 1986 and had got to know them well. I met him in a coffee shop in Berlin with my colleague, Tilman Remme, who had doggedly tracked him down. Kurt was a small, nervous man, wary of talking lest he reveal his identity and former role. Rehabilitation, retraining and finding a new job in the new Germany is difficult enough for any former East German citizen, let alone a member of the Stasi. I imagined his former organization must have been made up of thousands of Kurts, all loyal Communist Party members ready to obey orders without question and accorded rank and status in return. Today that all counted for nothing. He talked about his three years as a Stasi minder to the RAF. 'From the way they looked and acted, they were in no way hard-baked terrorists who were a threat to life and limb. Basically they looked like ordinary citizens, who could have been your neighbour. They looked very inconspicuous. No one could really have expected that they were terrorists.' Kurt had his orders: to protect them and make sure no one ever found out their true identities. 'We had to do all we could to prevent this fact from becoming known. You can imagine the importance of what I had to do. If this information had become known, it would have caused immense damage. If word got out before it did, the GDR might have collapsed even earlier. The East German public would have shown no sympathy for a government that harboured terrorists. There would have been an international outcry, too, had it become known that terrorists were living under our protection. After all, the GDR was pursuing a policy which argued against terrorism.'[1]

One of Kurt's charges was a woman who had been known in East Germany as Sylvia Gersbach. The photograph on her identity card showed an attractive, dark-haired young woman. According to her records, Sylvia was born in Moscow on 18 October 1948 and her school reports indicated she had been an outstanding pupil with a talent for languages – English, French and Russian. The principal of her school, the Rathenau-Schule in Senftenberg, wrote her a glowing recommendation.

> Sylvia is an independent and intelligent worker who can easily put to good use what she has learned. She is hard-working, ambitious and always contributes in class. Outside the classroom, Sylvia has

achieved much with the youth group. She has had a positive effect on her classmates because of her committed, open and friendly attitude. General behaviour and attitude: very good. Discipline: very good. Effort: very good. Tidiness: good. Co-operation: very good.[2]

But this model pupil did not exist. Her real name and real face were familiar to the millions of West Germans who had seen the 'wanted' posters over the years. Sylvia Gersbach was, in reality, Silke Maier-Witt, who had fled to East Germany in 1979 and sought refuge there. She had never seen her family since she left Hamburg in 1977 and went underground. Silke Maier-Witt was one of Kurt's guests at the GDR's fortieth birthday party. Kurt told Silke what she already knew, her faked school report in fact being a true reflection of her intelligence and ability: the GDR was on its last legs; soon it would all be over; who knew what the future would hold? Silke had a pretty good idea. It meant arrest, trial and life imprisonment.

A few months after the Berlin Wall came down in November 1989, Silke Maier-Witt and nine other former RAF fugitives were arrested and taken into the custody of the Bundeskriminalamt, the BKA, the German equivalent of the FBI. The ten became known as the *Aussteiger*, the 'leavers'. Each *Aussteiger* was given a case officer whose job it was to drain him or her of every detail of every operation in which they had ever been involved. Presented with this unique terrorist windfall, the state was determined to bring the guilty to justice and clear the books of some of West Germany's most appalling terrorist crimes. Silke Maier-Witt's case officer was a young BKA officer called Dirk Buechner. Before he met her, he spent hours poring over the files, building up a profile of the woman he was about to encounter and use. 'She was a cool terrorist,' he told me. 'Just like you imagine a terrorist to be, with only one aim: to kill people and overthrow the government.'[3] His colleagues studying files of the other *Aussteiger* reached similar conclusions. But when Dirk met Silke he was astonished. 'She was not the cool killer I expected. She was a real, normal citizen. She had lived for ten years in East Germany without committing any crime, and she was just like me. She could have been my neighbour. My colleagues found the same and they were astonished too.' Dirk laid the options on the table. 'I told her that she had only one choice, either to talk with us and co-operate with us, or to go in gaol for life.' Co-operating meant turning state's evidence under a law passed for this specific purpose in 1989 known as the *Kronzeugenregelung*, the 'state witness ruling'. Under the new law, if terrorists were prepared to incriminate their former comrades in the witness box, the court was entitled to reward them with reduced sentences. In a word, the *Kronzeugenregelung* meant betraying your comrades.

When Dirk Buechner first laid the proposition before Silke Maier-Witt she sat and said nothing. Thirty-two meetings followed. Soon she said she would admit everything that she had done but drew the line at incriminating her colleagues. In the end, she went the whole way and told all about everybody. I asked Dirk if he thought his charge was genuinely repentant. 'I think she is,' he said. 'She said in court that she felt sorry for what she had done and I think it's a reality.' In January 1991 Silke Maier-Witt was found guilty of a string of terrorist crimes: the kidnapping and murder of Hanns-Martin Schleyer, the president of the Germany Employers' Association; the attempted murder of General Alexander Haig, NATO's Commander-in-Chief; and a bank robbery in Zurich resulting in death. The statutory sentence for such crimes was life imprisonment. Because she had turned state's evidence and expressed remorse, Silke Maier-Witt got ten years.

Initially she was sent to Stammheim prison in Stuttgart, the huge concrete fortress built in the 1970s to house Andreas Baader and Ulrike Meinhof, the leaders of the Baader–Meinhof 'gang', the founders of the RAF, and other terrorist prisoners whose bombings and selective assassinations had reduced Germany to a state of nervous panic. Today Silke Maier-Witt is still in gaol but in custody of a very different kind in Vechta women's prison an hour's drive south-west of Bremen. Vechta is a remarkable place, an amalgam of eighteenth-century monastery and Napoleonic gaol, with its warren of low, dark, subterranean corridors like a film set from Les Misérables. Both have, thankfully, been tastefully modernized, and Vechta's liberal regime is a model of its kind. Silke is now allowed out on leave and trusted to return. The director is rightly proud of his prison. He, like everyone else, finds it almost impossible to imagine Silke Maier-Witt as a terrorist, let alone one found guilty of murder. I put the point to her. She smiled the smile of one used to facing that question. 'No, I don't look like a terrorist. But who does? I mean nobody really looks the way people think terrorists are, because they are normal people, most of them – all of them.'[4]

I remember getting a similar response to a not dissimilar question, although phrased in a slightly different way, from an IRA prisoner serving a life sentence for murder in the Maze prison in Belfast. His cell was lined with books, many of them classics of English and Irish literature. I asked him, with intentional naivety, what an IRA man was doing reading Tolstoy and Hardy. He replied with a sardonic smile, 'Because an IRA man's normal just like everybody else.'[5] The myth and reality of the 'terrorist' are indeed often poles apart and most states would prefer to keep it that way. Dehumanizing the enemy is an essential part of the state's response, and many would say a legitimate one, given the atrocities committed. But the fact remains that this stereotyping is often at variance with the reality of those who use violence to achieve a political end for whatever deeply held reason. Abu Hassan, Silke Maier-Witt and their IRA counterparts looked no more like terrorists than Baruch Cohen resembled a Mossad man. It is this appearance of normality that makes catching 'terrorists' so difficult, since they spend most of the time not wearing masks.

Unlike its counterparts in other countries, the aims of Germany's Red Army Faction are less immediately apparent. People know that the IRA is fighting to drive the British out of Northern Ireland and reunify the country; that the Palestinians are fighting to regain what they see as their land; that ETA is fighting for an independent Basque homeland. What these groups have in common are clearly defined historical roots and clearly defined political goals, however undesirable and unobtainable they may appear to the states and societies they attack. All are nationalist 'terrorist' organizations. But the RAF is driven by revolutionary ideology not the desire to recover lost land. It wishes to destroy imperialism, overthrow capitalism – which was epitomised by West Germany – and establish a Marxist socialist state. Although there are strong elements of Marxist philosophy in the IRA, PLO and ETA, the ideology is not the end in itself. With the RAF, it is. But the Red Army Faction was also something more and had to be so to attract its nucleus of young, middle-class, well-educated revolutionaries. The story of Silke Maier-Witt gives an insight into why at least one member of the group did what she did. The Red Army Faction is also a product of German history.

In 1940 Silke's father, Hans-Joachim Maier-Witt, sought permission to marry an attractive, clear-eyed, blonde woman called Sieglinde Sievert, who worked as a customs officer in Hamburg. But getting permission was much more than the formal courtesy of asking Herr Sievert for the hand of his daughter in marriage: it entailed putting the request in writing to a higher authority. The archives reveal that Hans-Joachim was a dedicated Nazi. In 1933 he joined the SA, the Sturm-Abteilung, the 'Stormtroopers' who, from their origins as a disguised army reserve in the 1920s, became Hitler's bloody instrument on his road to political power. A year later, after Hitler had overthrown the Weimar Republic, Hans-Joachim joined Himmler's rival militia, the SS, the Schutz-Staffeln, whose firing squads executed the SA's leaders.[6] In 1937 he formally joined the Nazi Party and was given his party card and number: 5 299 253. The letter Hans-Joachim wrote seeking permission to marry Sieglinde was addressed to his SS superiors. They wanted not just the assurance that both spouse and bride were pure Aryan, uncontaminated by alien blood, but the genetic proof. Only in this way could the purity of Hitler's vanguard be ensured. Both had to complete the *Erbgesundheitsbogen*, the 'Inherited Health Form', and submit it with birth certificates and complete family trees. Remarkably, my colleague Tilman Remme dug deep into history and found all the original documents. Spread out before us and producer Stephen Walker were nearly four centuries of Germany history. Silke Maier-Witt was its child. The Maier-Witt family tree stretched back to the early eighteenth century, to 8 June 1726, when Michael Mayer was born. On 5 May 1763 he married Anna Maria Naschold in Altensteig and the Maier-Witt line began, with the 'Witt' added later. Both lines were pure, and Hans-Joachim and Sieglinde were given permission to marry. They had no wish to do so in church – which also pleased the SS, to whom National Socialism was the only true religion. On 23 April 1941 Hans-Joachim and Sieglinde wrote again to the SS applying for a marriage loan. The letter ended 'Heil Hitler'.

On 21 January 1950, Silke Maier-Witt was born in Nagold in the Black Forest area to where her father had moved to run a sawmill. Six years later, Sieglinde died of breast cancer. Silke's grandparents commuted from the big family house in Hamburg to look after her. Hans-Joachim remarried but the marriage was of short duration. He then married for a third time, providing Silke with her second stepmother, Ilse, whom Hans-Joachim had got to know while the family was living in the Black Forest. The Maier-Witts then moved back to Hamburg, where Hans-Joachim took over another sawmill in the grime of the city's harbour area. Ilse was all that Hans-Joachim could have looked for in a wife. She was gentle, kind, and devoted to her husband and family, clearly always subordinating her own needs to theirs. By this time Ilse had two boys and two girls to look after. She would rise early every morning and prepare a cooked breakfast for her husband and children. When Hans-Joachim came home from the sawmill at lunchtime there would always be a hot meal waiting on the table. In the evening, dinner was a family ritual, the table neatly set with sparkling glasses and shining silver. No doubt Hans-Joachim would sit at its head, presiding over the family and household of which he was master.

Silke was his favourite daughter, for whom he wanted the best. 'I was good at school and I didn't cause too many problems,' she reflects. 'My father always wanted me to be something special, you know, to study and do all the things he never did. And he was proud of me too.' To further his ambitions for his daughter, Hans-Joachim sent Silke to one of the most exclusive girls' schools in Hamburg, the Heilwig Gymnasium, although it meant travelling three hours each day on public transport. The rich girls arrived in their own cars. The contrast between home and school was dramatic, and Silke, never one to make compromises, wanted the best the school could offer, but the best was not always something that the family could afford. 'Silke always wanted what the privileged girls had,' remembers Ilse, 'but with four children to look after we couldn't provide it. All had to be treated the same. Tennis lessons, for example, were out of the question. When she went out to buy a coat, Silke was given a limit, which she resented. She always felt she was having the coat forced upon her. But she worked very hard, always did her homework and always came top of the class. If a friend beat her, she would work even harder to win back her place, and then say she never worked hard.'[7] We met one of Silke's classmates, Sabine Seliger, who remembered her as a quiet, self-effacing girl who never pushed herself to the front. In photographs Silke was always the one in the background. Popular and always ready to help, Silke was known to her classmates as 'die gute Mawi' – 'the good M-W'. There was, however, another side to her which was only occasionally glimpsed. In a biology lesson one day, the class was dissecting an ox-head. Silke took hold of the eye, held it up before her friends and gradually squeezed it until it burst. Sabine told us the story, sitting in the school laboratory where it happened, wincing as she recalled the gruesome scene. 'It was horrible,' she shuddered. 'We were all amazed that the good M-W should do such a thing. It was then I realised that there was a different side to her, a sadistic, violent streak.'[8]

Life at home for Silke was never easy. As she grew into her teens, she found the routine more and more claustrophobic and her father's authoritarian nature unbearably oppressive. She felt she was never able to be her own person, caught between numbing domesticity and an inflexible patriarch. Never one to suffer in silence, Silke kicked against it, upsetting her stepmother, Ilse, and enraging her father, who was not used to having his authority challenged. 'At first they got on well,' Ilse recalls. 'The problems only started when she got older – sixteen, seventeen, that difficult age. Maybe I didn't notice them much, I was always so busy – with the family, with the housework. She often came to me but I always sent her to her father because I thought he could talk to her more, but that didn't help much. Silke always wanted to get what she wanted. She had her own head and you always had to agree with her. If you didn't, then that wasn't quite right. And he got angry and he cried as well. It was difficult to get talking. Silke would have liked to, but somehow it just didn't work the way she would have liked.' The biggest source of friction between father and daughter was the Second World War. The more Silke read about it at school, the more she wanted to know. Her father had been a Nazi. What did he do? What did he know? Why did he go along with fascism? These were the questions with which she confronted him. There were frequent explosions of anger which Ilse would hear from the kitchen. She stayed out of sight, not wishing to get involved. The rows were monumental. After one celebrated exchange, father did not speak to daughter for fourteen days.

'When I read about how many Jews were killed, I thought I could never be accepting my father's generation.' Silke explained. 'He never answered my questions. I couldn't believe they never knew anything about it. He got mad at me for asking. He kept saying that somebody else had told me all this and asking who put it into my head. He got mad not because of the question, but because I was asking it.' Silke told me it was important to appreciate how she felt at that time in order to understand what she subsequently did. Ironically, the anger that lay behind these arguments with her father was the force that drove her into terrorism. 'I felt fascism was coming up again and I had to do something,' she said. It was not an excuse. To Silke it was fact. Contemporary history, too, played its part. She went to America on an exchange for a year, an experience she did not enjoy. The campuses were ablaze, as students demonstrated against America's involvement in Vietnam. The response was brutal. At Kent State University, Ohio, one of America's quieter seats of learning, National Guardsmen shot four unarmed students dead. Silke returned to Germany, went to university and started to study psychology, but it was Vietnam that obsessed her. Images of America's suppression of a small nation in the name of democracy left an indelible impression on her mind. 'To see the pictures on television at that time of Americans killing these Vietnamese people, and these people struggling for freedom, was really something. I remember pictures of napalm bombs and a naked child running out of the jungle, in flames. For the first time I knew what "imperialism" meant.' 'Die gute Mawi' had become a radical student activist.

By this time she had left home and moved into squats and communes around Hamburg. From time to time, Ilse would, at Silke's invitation, go and inspect them. She saw the conditions but never the people. She was horrified, and felt that Silke was deliberately inviting her to visit to rub in the contrast between the chaos in which she now lived and the order in which she had been brought up at home. Ilse refused to rise to the bait, yet became increasingly apprehensive. Every time there was an anti-Vietnam War demonstration, she feared Silke might have been one of those arrested. And it was not just Vietnam. By 1972 terrorism had exploded on the German scene, and the names and faces of the Baader–Meinhof gang became internationally famous, sworn enemies of the state and heroes of the politicized young. Ilse and Hans-Joachim used to say how dreadful the new phenomenon was and wondered what it must have been like for the poor parents of the young men and women involved.

In June 1972 the leaders of the gang were arrested for a series of terrorist attacks including those on the Springer Press building in Berlin, a police station in Augsburg and the American army base in Heidelberg in which four US soldiers were killed. In their violent campaign of bombings, kidnapping and bank robberies, the like of which post-war Germany had never seen, five people were killed and 54 injured.[9] Andreas Baader (founder of the RAF), Ulrike Meinhof, Holger Meins, Jan-Karl Raspe, Gudrun Ensslin and Brigitte Mohnhaupt were given long sentences and sent to Stuttgart's Stammheim prison which, complete with bullet and bomb-proof courtroom, had been specially constructed to take terrorist prisoners. The prisoners went on two collective hunger strikes soon after their arrest, in protest against their conditions and the way they alleged they were being treated. They claimed they were being 'tortured', not physically in the sense of being ill treated, but psychologically, because they were kept in permanent isolation that led, they maintained, to sensory deprivation. The hunger strikes and the claims of torture had a powerful impact on Silke Maier-Witt and thousands of young people like her. The effect was even greater when one of the hunger strikers, Holger Meins, died of starvation in November 1974. It was his death that propelled Silke Maier-Witt into terrorism. She contrasted what she saw as his strength with her own weakness, a contradiction that was to haunt her throughout her terrorist career. 'It really affected me because I though he died fighting and he fought without compromise whereas I always did compromise.'

Silke decided to become actively involved, not in the RAF, but in the groups that were formed around the country to support the prisoners. They were known as the 'Committees Against Torture'. It was there that she met Susanne Albrecht, another middle-class girl from Hamburg whose family, unlike Silke's, really did have the money to support the lifestyle of a rich young student. Susanne, like Silke, had rejected her comfortable middle-class background. The two became friends and moved into a flat together with another young activist called Karl-Heinz Dellwo. Five months after Holger Meins died on hunger strike, the RAF hit back, announcing themselves as the 'Holger Meins Commando'. At midday on 24 April 1975, six members of the group seized the German embassy in Stockholm and took twelve hostages, including the West German ambassador and military attaché. The attaché was fatally wounded in the attack. They held the embassy for twelve hours, demanding the release of twenty-six of their imprisoned comrades, together with $520 000 and an aircraft to fly them to an undisclosed destination. When the Bonn government refused to capitulate, they blew up the top floor of the building, killing the economics attaché. One of the terrorists was killed in the process. The five RAF survivors surrendered. One of them was Karl-Heinz Dellwo, Silke's flat-mate. She was astonished when she found out, having no idea that he was actively involved in the RAF. She thought he was just a fellow traveller like Susanne and herself. The reality was brought home when the police came and searched the flat and took Silke away for questioning. 'I knew him, and he was not so very different from me. A bit more courageous, perhaps. And then I thought: It can't be so hard after all because, if he was able to do it, I could be next. At the time I didn't feel I could do it. I was shocked too, because of the brutality of what they did.' I pressed her on 'brutality'.

But they killed two innocent people in Stockholm. Did you think that you could do that – kill anybody?
At that time I thought I could not, but I thought I would have to force myself to do things like that, because of what we were aiming at. I thought it was justified in a way.
But how did killing those two people in Stockholm achieve, or help achieve, what you were aiming at?
Well, I didn't think about that at that time. They were trying to get out the prisoners and somehow I tried to justify it. If they had released them, nobody would have been killed. I suppose I put the blame on those who didn't release the prisoners.

Stockholm was a watershed in Silke's life. She had been hovering on the brink for some time, but now she decided to take the fatal step and enter the world of the Red Army Faction. Twice, memory of family and friends might have dissuaded her. Ilse and Hans-Joachim bumped into her by chance when doing their Christmas shopping in Hamburg. They were appalled at what they saw. Silke was unkempt, dirty and drawn, reeking of cigarette smoke from substances legal and otherwise. Ilse begged her to come home. 'You're always welcome,' she said. 'Why don't you come back? Forget about politics. Don't discuss it. It always causes trouble.' For a time, Silke obliged, but only came back at breakfast time and then went away as suddenly as she had come. Her old school friend, Sabine, also saw Silke before she disappeared from view. They met in the university library where Silke was working before she abandoned her studies. 'She looked dreadful and obviously in need of help,' remembers Sabine. 'I felt guilty because I knew I should have listened, but I had my own life to lead and I didn't bother. I only wish I had made the effort and then perhaps things would have been different.'

After Stockholm, Silke left university and asked her parents to forward all her papers. She destroyed every one and went underground – becoming one of the 'illegals'. That was in the spring of 1977. The leaders of what became known as the 'first generation' of the RAF – Andreas Baader, Gudrun Ensslin and Jan-Karl Raspe – had just been sentenced to life imprisonment, Ulrike Meinhof having committed suicide in her Stammheim cell on 9 May 1976. At first, Silke started stealing passports to provide false identities for what she came to know as 'the group'. Gradually, she became more deeply involved and soon reached the point of no return:

getting her gun. It was part of the ritual. Silke had never seen a real, live gun before, let alone handled one. She remembers the date vividly: 7 April 1977, the day the RAF shot dead West Germany's Federal Prosecutor, Siegfried Buback, on the way to his office in Karlsruhe. The attack marked the beginning of an unpredictable onslaught that year in which the RAF struck a succession of lethal blows at the heart of West Germany's political and economic establishment. Buback was the co-ordinator of the country's anti-terrorist operations and the man responsible for the successful prosecution of the Baader–Meinhof gang. The group threatened more attacks to 'prevent the murder of our fighters in prison'.[10]

At the time of the killing, Silke was in Amsterdam, where the group had a safe house. 'I met some of the "illegals" about midday and they told me what had happened. They asked me if I wanted to stay with them now. I thought about it and said "yes". Everything was fixed and I got my weapon that night. It was a Colt Combat Commander, the one the American police use. It was big. It was the first time I had ever had a weapon in my hand. They showed me how to use it and how to take it apart and put it back again. Nobody really talked about what it meant. It meant a lot, you know, because now I had a weapon I was supposed to use it somehow.' I pointed out that it meant killing people. 'Yes. But I didn't really think about it very much, you know. It was just a necessity, because everybody had one. So I just took it and always hoped I didn't have to use it. It was just that way in the group.' The group member who showed her how to use her Combat Commander was Peter-Jürgen Boock, currently in gaol in Hamburg serving the thirteenth year of a life sentence. Boock, too, has renounced the RAF but has always refused to betray his colleagues. Boock is uncomplimentary about Silke Maier-Witt's credentials as a terrorist. He and other members of the group's inner circle, to which Silke never belonged although she yearned to be admitted, used to refer to her and Susanne Albrecht as 'the Hamburg aunts'. He described her reaction to the weapon:

I tried my best to give her the feeling that this gun is not only an instrument of killing but part of the ritual of going 'underground'. It means you burn your legal passport and you get a falsified passport. You wear a gun from that moment. I got the impression she wore the gun like a fashion accessory. Taking it is like crossing a line. There's no going back. Everybody who's coming into the group has a chance to say no at that moment and nobody would do anything. But after you take the gun, after you get your falsified passport and after you come into the circle of the group, you can't leave it any more. You can't go and say, 'Well, that's it. It was a mistake. I'm going home.' It's impossible.[11]

Silke's family had no idea what had happened to her and grew increasingly anxious. Then they heard her name on the news. Silke Maier-Witt was wanted by the police in connection with the murder of Jürgen Ponto, the chairman of the Dresdner Bank, West Germany's second largest financial institution. Ponto had been shot dead during a bungled kidnap attempt by a man and four women at his home near Frankfurt on 30 July 1977. The RAF had never intended to kill him but planned to hold him against the release of the newly sentenced prisoners. A dead hostage was no bargaining card. Jürgen Ponto was the godfather of Susanne Albrecht's sister and a close family friend. Albrecht was said to have gone to the front door with a bunch of flowers to gain admittance for the potential kidnappers. Once they were inside the house, Ponto resisted abduction and was shot dead by the man. Susanne Albrecht is now in prison near Bremen. We paid her a brief visit but she did not wish to talk. She married while in hiding in East Germany and had a small son who knew nothing about his mother's past. She is still clearly devastated by what happened sixteen years ago.

Soon, Silke Maier-Witt's photograph appeared on 'wanted' posters, alongside Susanne Albrecht's. Ilse and the family were utterly devastated. 'We talked all night long. Why did it happen? For what reason? Of course I blamed myself a lot. I felt guilty. I am the second mother. Maybe I did something wrong, I don't know. You think about it more afterwards. When the family is so big, you've got lots to do. We could have looked after Silke more. We should have talked to her more. But you're so busy with day-to-day things that you don't really think about it. Those kind of thoughts turn up later. All parents make some mistakes but that's no reason for dropping out or getting into terrorism. It was terrible. I really was ill, because I thought all of it was my fault.' Ilse could not hold back her tears.

Subsequently, the police obtained their first direct evidence of Silke Maier-Witt's direct involvement in terrorism. On 25 August 1977 the RAF launched a rocket attack on the Federal Prosecutor's office in Karlsruhe in an attempt to kill Siegfried Buback's successor. The attack failed, and the RAF abandoned their home-made rocket. Silke's fingerprints were found on the box in which it had been packed prior to delivery to the target. 'It made me wanted even more,' she said. 'I was marked.' But the RAF remained obsessed with the release of the prisoners – the cause that had superseded any ideological goal. One precedent suggested that if they kidnapped the right person the state would probably give in. On 27 February 1975, a group calling itself the 2 June Movement (named after the date on which a student was killed during a demonstration in 1967) had kidnapped Peter Lorenz, a senior West Berlin politician, on the eve of the mayoral election in which he was a candidate. The state had capitulated, released five prisoners, and put them on a plane to Aden. It had also paid the ransom demand of $50 000.[12] Peter Lorenz had been released, urging the state to show its determination to 'fight terrorism and radicalization'. The federal Ministers of Interior and Justice had justified the action on humanitarian grounds and denied it set a precedent by giving in to terrorists. They were wrong.

For their final, desperate attempt to free their prisoners, the RAF could hardly have selected a more appropriate target, from the political and ideological point of view. At sixty-two, Hanns-Martin Schleyer was one of West Germany's most prominent industrialists at the pinnacle of its economic establishment, president of the German Employers' Association and president of the Federation of West German Industries. As his son, Hanns-Eberhard, told me, 'He was a symbol of capitalism, a symbol of the ruling class in Germany.'[13] But, to the RAF, their target was another equally potent symbol: of West Germany's Nazi past. Documents reveal that Hanns-Martin Schleyer had been a member of the Hitler Youth from 1931 to 1935 and had subsequently joined the Nazi Party and the SS. During the war, he served as a junior SS officer in Czechoslovakia. His Nazi Party number is filed as 5 065 517 and his SS number as 227 014. To Silke Maier-Witt and her comrades, Schleyer was evidence that old Nazis lived on and flourished in the highest echelons of the state.

I asked Hanns-Eberhard about his father's Nazi past. Initially he said, 'The facts are not correct' until I pointed out that we had seen his file. He was dismissive. 'This might be true that this was an argument the terrorists used. I would think it enabled them to even strengthen their position, particularly with regard to foreign reaction. But I think, as far as Germany is concerned, what was more important was to hit him as a target who represented capitalism and German industry. That was the primary target.' Hanns-Eberhard had known his father was top of the RAF's hit list and had discussed with him what attitude the family should take in the event of his abduction. He said they should act in accordance with the government's decision if it were based on a powerful argument.

On 5 September 1977 the discussion ceased to be hypothetical. Hanns-Martin Schleyer was kidnapped in Cologne and his driver and three body-guards were shot dead, sprayed with machine-gun bullets. Silke Maier-Witt was one of those who had reconnoitred the route. 'At that time I felt the brutality of that action,' she told me. 'All right, I had questions in my mind about whether it had been necessary to kill four people just to get one. But I didn't put these thoughts into words. It was a kind of excitement too because something had happened. The real thing started now.' The RAF issued its ransom demands: the release of eleven prisoners, including the surviving leadership, Baader, Ensslin and Raspe, and Karl-Heinz Dellwo, who had been involved in blowing up the West German embassy in Stockholm; a payment of DM 100 000 a head for each of the eleven; and a plane to fly them to the country of their choice. At the very beginning, a committee was set up under Chancellor Helmut Schmidt to co-ordinate the state's response. Its first decision, made in secret, was not to give in to the kidnappers. Hanns-Eberhard Schleyer, who knew nothing of the decision at the time, gave the impression he felt betrayed by his father's friends. 'I lived under false hope, and, of course, I liked to live under false hope. I didn't like to hear that the state was not going to give in to the terrorists.'

His father was held prisoner for six weeks, much of the time in a flat south of Cologne. Forensic photographs show the apartment was sparsely furnished. There was a floral-patterned mattress on the floor, which served as the prisoner's bed. A cupboard had been lined with sheets of foam, into which he would be bundled and silenced if rescue was at hand. Chains to which he could be manacled had been fixed to the woodwork. Four drawing-pin holes were left where once hung the RAF banner in front of which Hanns-Martin Schleyer had been video-recorded making desperate appeals for his freedom.[14] The image was dreadful: a gaunt, haunted man looking far more than his sixty-two years, begging for his life. It remains, like the famous photograph of the hooded figure of the Black September gunman at Munich, one of terrorism's most harrowing images. Peter-Jürgen Boock was one of Schleyer's guards and produced the videos. 'He was not the kind of guy I thought he might be. He was very eloquent. He tried his best to manipulate us, and we, of course, wanted to manipulate him. But he was prepared for a situation like this. I always thought he was very, very clever. If he took a step, he had thought about it for a long time and knew exactly where he wanted to go. He definitely did not think that he was going to die. He thought until the last moment, I guess, that his friends in government and in economic circles would help him and do their best to make the deal.' Silke Maier-Witt's role was, as Boock pointed out, never central to the operation. Her job was to deliver the letters and demands, including one to Schleyer's son. She would take the train to some distant location and post the letters from there so their origin could not be traced. The envelopes survive in her handwriting.

As the weeks went by and the government showed no sign of giving in, the RAF took one further dramatic step in conjunction with its ideological allies, the Popular Front for the Liberation of Palestine (PFLP), whose training camps it had used in Yemen. On 13 October 1977 four gunmen hijacked a Lufthansa 737 jet, flight LH 181, as it left Majorca for Frankfurt with eighty-six passengers on board. They issued the following 'ultimatum' to Chancellor Schmidt.

This is to inform you that the passengers and the crew . . . are under our complete control and responsibility. The lives of the passengers and the crew of the plane as well as the life of Mr Hanns-Martin Schleyer depend on your fulfilling the following:

1. Release of the following comrades of the RAF from prisons in West Germany – Andreas Baader, Gudrun Ensslin, Jan-Karl Raspe, Verena Becker, Werner Hoppe, Karl-Heinz Dellwo, Hanna Krabbe, Bernard Roessner, Ingrid Schubert, Irmgard Moeller, Guenter Sonnenberg – and with each the amount of DM 100 000.
2. Release of the following Palestinian comrades of the PFLP from prison in Istanbul – Mahdi and Hussein.
3. The payment of the sum of 15 million US dollars according to the accompanying instructions.
4. Arrange with any one of the following countries to accept to receive all the comrades released from prison:

   1. The Democratic Republic of Vietnam.
   2. Republic of Somalia.
   3. People's Democratic Republic of Yemen.

5. If all the prisoners are not released and do not reach their destination, and the money is not delivered according to instructions, within the specified time, then Mr Hanns-Martin Schleyer, and all the passengers and the crew . . . will be killed immediately.
6. If you comply with our instructions, all of them will be released.
7. We shall not contact you again. This is our last contact with you. You are completely to blame for any error and faults in the release of the above-mentioned comrades in prison or in the delivery of the specified ransom according to the specified instructions.
8. Any try on your part to delay or deceive us will mean immediate ending of the ultimatum and execution of Mr Hanns-Martin Schleyer and all the passengers and crew of the plane.[15]

For nearly five days negotiations continued, as flight 181 criss-crossed Europe, the Middle East and Africa. On 16 October, during a refuelling stop in Yemen, the hijackers shot dead the captain, Jürgen Schumann, in full view of the passengers.[16] The following day, the aircraft took off from Aden and landed in what was to be its final destination, Mogadishu in Somalia. There was to be no repetition of Munich. Learning from its tragically inept handling of the Olympic hostage crisis, West Germany had set up and trained an elite commando unit, known as Grenzschutzgruppe-9 or GSG-9, along the lines of, and with the help of, Britain's SAS, the

Special Air Service. This was the first time GSG-9 had gone into action in a terrorist emergency and the first German military operation outside its borders since the Second World War.[17] The commandos stormed the plane and, within seven minutes, all the hostages were freed. Three of the four hijackers died in bursts of concentrated gunfire. The commandos returned home from Mogadishu to a heroes' welcome, a triumphant symbol of the state's decision not to give in to terrorism. Within hours of the rescue came the almost equally dramatic news that the three remaining founders of the Red Army Faction had committed suicide in their top-security cells in Stammheim prison. Andreas Baader and Jan-Karl Raspe had both shot themselves through the head with pistols believed to have been smuggled in by their lawyers. Gudrun Ensslin had hanged herself from a window-frame with an electric cord.[18] There was the inevitable outcry of 'state murder', believed by many of the RAF's supporters outside the walls until the myth was destroyed by the 'Ausstieger' following their arrests in 1990.

Mogadishu and the suicides of the RAF's founding leadership sealed Hanns-Martin Schleyer's fate. Hanns-Eberhard had made two last attempts to save his father's life. The letters he received via the courier, Silke Maier-Witt, showed a man at the end of his tether. 'He finally appealed for his life. He asked the government to give in – but, more than that, to take a decision. This was very important. He was not able any longer to stand the situation.' Hanns-Martin Schleyer wanted to know whether he would live or die. First, his son tried to deliver a ransom of DM 32 million which he had picked up from the Bundesbank in Frankfurt and loaded into two suitcases. He had been instructed to make his first contact with the RAF at a hotel in the city. He notified the government of his intention. When he arrived, he found the lobby swarming with journalists. Hanns-Eberhard has always suspected that the government had tipped off the press in order to torpedo any final rescue attempt. The only recourse left was an appeal to the Constitutional Court on the grounds that the federal constitution makes it incumbent on the state to protect the life of every citizen. The appeal was heard in an extraordinary atmosphere as the government was trying to resolve the hijack crisis. But the ruling went against him: the court upheld the government's case that its obligation to any single individual was overruled by its wider obligation to the citizen body as a whole. Hanns-Eberhard finally went on television and made his last plea. It was already too late. His father was being taken across the border from Belgium, which was his last place of captivity, to be 'executed' and dumped in the French town of Mulhouse.

I asked Peter-Jürgen Boock how Hanns-Martin Schleyer died. He said he was not there at the time, but those who were had told him what happened. 'After they passed the border, there was a kind of wood, a small wood, where they parked the car. They had told Mr Schleyer that he would just be brought to another place and that he should not be disturbed about being moved. He didn't know what was coming to him, so he had no chance to react. They took him out of the back and fired two shots into his head.' A phone call was made to the French police indicating where the body could be found. Silke Maier-Witt, as an accessory, was found guilty of his murder. Looking at her face, I found it almost inconceivable that she could have been involved in such a brutal act. How could she have done it?

It was such a bloody and such a terrible thing but at that time it was as if I had switched off these kinds of feelings. I feel awful about it, but it was like that. I don't think I'm a brutal type of person and I don't think all the other ones were too. It was not that they were eager to do it. It was just that we felt compelled to do it because of what we wanted. *Not brutal? This helpless man, pleading for his life, who was shot and dumped in the back of a car. Not brutal?* Of course, yes, it's brutal, but at that time I did not let these thoughts affect me. It's what I think is the worst part of my part in that story, you know, because I wondered how long I could stand it. It's what people can do just because they think it's justified. *But you could have got out . . . you could have said . . .* No. *. . . this is enough, four people dead . . . Hanns-Martin Schleyer murdered . . . I've had enough . . . I'm going . . ,* Yeah, but there would not have been a chance to go. Where should I have gone? I was 'wanted' and I knew what would happen if I got caught. There was no chance to get out.

What Peter-Jürgen Boock had said about Silke's initiation with the Colt Commander was true. There was no way out.

The murder of Hanns-Martin Schleyer was the turning-point in the West German state's response to the RAF. To put it bluntly, he was sacrificed in order to send a clear message to terrorists. The group was in disorder. Their gaoled leaders were dead. Any residual sympathy among the radical young had largely evaporated. They had achieved nothing. According to Silke, the group's main preoccupation in the aftermath of Schleyer's 'execution' was the search for drugs to supply an ill Peter-Jürgen Boock, who had become addicted to morphine. It was, as Silke admitted, a sick and disgusting end. She was lost, disillusioned and trapped. Directionless and leaderless, the group left for the PFLP's training camp in Aden. The change had a remarkable effect on Silke. She was no longer hunted. For the first time she felt free. Her heart was never in the training sessions on how to make bombs and hit targets with RPG-7s, and her comrades noticed and criticized her attitude. Any sign of deviation was a threat to the group. She also absented herself from the interminable ideological discussions that stretched late into the night. She sat in on one when her comrades considered a suicide mission to blow up a débutantes' ball in Germany where local burghers introduced their daughters to newly arrived young American officers. Two women members of the group had infiltrated the ball the year before with remarkable ease. Silke was appalled at the idea and said so, confirming the view the hard core of the group already had of her – that she was weak and unreliable. Silke sought solace in baking bread. 'I did it good. It was not a very important thing for the group but I enjoyed it. I had a glimpse of living when we were down there in Aden and I wanted to stay there. I even got ill, I suppose, so I wouldn't have to leave.' Silke also grew very fond of 'Mahdi', one of her young Palestinian hosts. (To our knowledge, he was not the person whose release was sought in the hijackers' communiqué during the kidnapping of Hanns-Martin Schleyer.) 'Mahdi' and his PFLP comrades also made her think about her own commitment and the cause she had embraced. It seemed empty alongside that of the Palestinians. 'I saw that they had a different attitude towards their fight. They did the same thing, but they fought for their people and put their heart into it. I only put my head into it. Never my heart. In Aden, I had the definite feeling that whatever we did it was no use, but there was, at the same time, the feeling of no way out. If it would have been possible, I would have stayed there and lived a remote life, you know, but I couldn't, there was no chance. The Palestinians could not take us, so it was just a kind of fatalism to go back to Europe and stay with the group.'

Despite Silke's attitude, Aden and contact with the Palestinians reinvigorated what was left of the RAF as they planned operations for their return, the main purpose of which, it appeared, was to show the world that the Red Army Faction was still in business. General Alexander Haig, the Supreme Commander of NATO forces in Europe, was to be their next target. Time was short, since the general was due to retire and return to America at the end of June 1979. He had also declared his intention to run for US President. Alexander Haig was as obvious a military target as Hanns-Martin Schleyer had been an economic one. Like Schleyer, Haig took precautions, but they too were of no avail. The only difference was that Haig survived – by a split second. Schleyer had been a Nazi and, to the group, Haig was the next best thing: a Vietnam veteran, decorated with the Distinguished Service Cross for leading his troops into battle near An Loc.[19] The PFLP provided the plastic explosives, 12 kilograms put together by Peter Jürgen Boock at the camp in Aden, and then sent via Yemeni diplomatic bag to Rome. From there, they were taken via Paris to Brussels and then 50 kilometres south to Mons, where General Haig had his office just outside the city at Casteau, the site of SHAPE (Supreme Headquarters, Allied Powers, Europe). As with all the RAF's attacks, the preparations were painstaking. The target was invariably hit. Silke Maier-Witt spent several weeks checking out Haig's route to his office from the château that was his official residence about 11 kilometres outside the city. It was what she did best, because no one ever suspected her. She sat in cafés, rode on buses and took nonchalant strolls pushing a bicycle past key points along the route, to establish, most importantly, in which vehicle the general was travelling. He had two routes to his office, one that went directly through Mons, and the other, the 'back' route, which passed more picturesquely through the Belgian countryside. Each morning, for security reasons, the three-vehicle convoy randomly varied the route, making the decision immediately prior to driving through the front gate of the château, known to the security people as 'the choke point'. Left meant Mons. Right meant the scenic route.

Silke worked closely with another member of the group, Werner Lotze, who planned the operation. Lotze is another *Aussteiger* now in gaol in Berlin serving his sentence. The two spent hours in the woods with a motorized camera photographing the general's convoy as it thundered by at high speed through the countryside. From the intervals between the photographs, Lotze calculated its speed. Haig's driver was a fast-talking, even faster-driving, US soldier called Hans Hooker, who had little respect for Belgian speed limits at the wheel of his armour-plated Mercedes 600. His nickname was 'Leadfoot'. 'He was endowed with a foot that was as heavy as his physical frame – and that was substantial. In other words he had a proclivity to drive at very high speeds,' recalls a grateful Alexander Haig.[20] Lotze and Silke got together the equipment necessary for the attack: a Honda 550 motor bike purchased for cash in the Netherlands, walkie-talkies bought in Antwerp and batteries to assemble the bomb. Lotze decided that the best place to plant the explosives was by a canal bridge near a cement factory in the countryside outside Mons where the person pressing the button, the detonator, would have a clear view of the road. Both Silke and Lotze told us the name of the man who triggered the bomb, and Silke said she was prepared to give evidence against him, but since, at the time of writing, he has not been tried before a court, I have not mentioned his name. I refer to him simply as 'the detonator'. Over four or five nights, other members of the group dug a tunnel a metre under the road, planted the bomb and left it there for about two weeks.

At 8.20 on the morning of 25 June 1979, General Haig left home for his last week at the office a few minutes behind schedule as he had lingered over breakfast talking to house guests from Palm Beach, Florida. Hans

Hooker therefore had to make up for lost time, which he was capable of doing with relish. He told producer Stephen Walker it was 'a bright, balmy, beautiful June Monday morning. Sunshine. No clouds'.[21] At the gate, Hooker turned right. As the Mercedes 600 came to the canal bridge, Hooker, as was his wont, seeing there was no traffic, 'really accelerated' towards the canal bridge. It was Hooker's speed that probably saved the general. At 8.30 a.m. there was a tremendous explosion, detonated via a command wire from 500 feet away. Haig, thinking he had come under rocket attack and fearing an ambush might lie ahead, yelled at Hooker to stop. Hooker slammed on the brakes, locked the steering wheel and thrust the tank-like Mercedes into a vertiginous spin. The moment Haig leaped out of the car, he knew it was a bomb, 'because asphalt was still raining from the sky'. The Mercedes miraculously survived the force of the blast. 'The trunk was blown up like a rubber balloon from the force of the explosion. It came within a split second of doing the job.' Two of Haig's escort were slightly injured. The explosion left a crater in the road 12 feet wide. 'Because the bomb was under human control, that's probably why we were saved,' reflects Haig. Hooker was phlegmatically proud. 'Timely transportation at all times. That is what we did. We accomplished our mission and the general was able to return to his family and to his country.' The moment 'the detonator' jumped on to the back of Lotze's Honda, he knew he had failed to kill Haig. 'I don't think I managed it,' he yelled at Lotze. 'I've just seen the car jump off the road – one metre, one metre fifty. I don't think we've succeeded.'[22] Alexander Haig, the scourge of international terrorism, survived. Asked at a subsequent press conference whether he thought the attempt on his life was linked with his intention to run for President, he replied ebulliently, 'That intention of mine has not so far been received with enough enthusiasm to justify so drastic a reaction.' He added that he had advised his wife to arm herself with a rolling pin.[23] It was, he noted, not quite what he had in mind when he said he wanted to go out with a bang.

Silke was involved in one more operation later that year before she finally made the decision to quit. The outcome sickened her. On 19 November 1979 the group planned to rob a bank in Zurich. In the shoot-out, an elderly woman, a passer-by, was killed. It was too much for Silke. 'It was the moment when I felt that I couldn't justify it any longer. We were just trying to get money to keep on going without really knowing what to do or what we were doing. And somebody got killed just for the money. This was just the point where, well, it was over. I couldn't do it any more and everybody knew it too.' I pointed out that the elderly lady was Jewish, knowing the agonies of conscience Silke had gone through in her discussions about Nazism and the death camps with her father. 'Yes, I know,' she replied sadly, her face expressing what words could not. 'It was too much.' Zurich marked the end of the group. Eight decided to leave. There was no attempt to stop them. The question was where to go. 'We had plans of going to Angola or Mozambique or a country like that, an African country. But nobody really had an idea where we could stay.' Then suddenly they were told they could go to Prague and then on to East Germany. The fraternal socialist countries were prepared to assist. The Stasi gave Silke a new identity and even carried out minor cosmetic surgery on her face. She became Sylvia Gersbach, a Soviet comrade born in Moscow on 18 October 1948.

> I tried to push my past away and I started to try to live in the GDR as a different person. I had then a complete GDR identity, living there all my life. It was difficult because I couldn't really identify with that woman I was supposed to be. I was a widow who had a very sad life, you know. No parents any more. Her husband dead. Living with her mother-in-law and helping her die. All kinds of stuff like that. It was really a history I could not identify with. I had to learn the dates and tell stories about it but I never talked much about where I came from. The only chance I had to talk about my real identity was with Stasi people.

East Germany was not the socialist paradise of which Silke had dreamed. She found it drab and claustrophobic, and its people hardly fired with revolutionary zeal.

> They didn't want to talk about politics. I thought they were dedicated to socialism, in a way, but they were not. I mean they were just people doing their work. They were, in a way, even more petty bourgeois than they had been in the West. I found it amazing that even young people were content to live a life I would never have been content with when I was nineteen years old. I was not finished. I wanted to get to know life and what I'm living for. They were trying to get married early, trying to get an apartment of their own and a car and a little piece of land. It looked as if they didn't want anything else. In a way, I was almost attracted to a quiet life like this. I remember riding my bicycle to my workplace and thinking: Oh, God – this is what you do until you are sixty years old and that's it. And I felt as if I had lived my life and it could end then, because there was nothing more to come.

When the Berlin Wall came down, Silke was almost relieved; she almost felt liberated. She knew it meant arrest and imprisonment but it was also a release from the numbing tedium and oppressiveness of a state and society she had come to despise, although it had harboured her for a decade. It was as if Sylvia Gersbach and the old Silke Maier-Witt were buried in the rubble of the Wall. It offered a new start, ironically in the state whose values and institutions Silke Maier-Witt, the terrorist, had fought to destroy. But the prerequisite of this new beginning was clearing the slate. 'I had to find my way back to my own history,' she explained. 'I had to talk about it.' That is why she was prepared to betray her former comrades, by giving evidence at new trials arising out of her testimony, although many of the newly accused were already in gaol serving sentences for other crimes. The other *Aussteiger* did the same. But turning state supergrass did not come easily. Silke agonized when I asked her how she could betray those with whom she had lived, fought and struggled. 'I didn't want to betray them. All of them were arrested already and I didn't realize that it would be used for new trials in the end. But, of course, I felt that if I didn't talk I would get a life sentence. In the beginning I didn't do it because of that. I just talked to get things said and to take my part of the responsibility. You cannot keep on killing people, not in the times like we have now. You cannot do it any more. You cannot stick to those politics. You have to stop it, and my way out of it was that I talked about it.' In a way, her interview with us was the public part of that process.

Silke's family could not believe it when they discovered she was alive. They had heard nothing from her and knew nothing of her since she had gone underground in the spring of 1977. For all they knew, she was dead. 'It was unbelievable, it was really wonderful when she reappeared. I can't describe it now,' Ilse said, overcome with emotion. The irony was that Silke felt she had been abandoned by the family and that they no longer wished to know her; and the family felt that Silke would never want to see them again. Silke wrote her stepmother a letter in which one word said everything: she called Ilse 'Mutti' – mother. Silke wrote another letter too. It was far more private and personal. It was addressed to her father, Hans-Joachim, and it was written in her gaol cell on 2 February 1991. The letter was never sent because Hans-Joachim had died of a heart attack in January 1978, a few months after the murder of Hanns-Martin Schleyer. Silke had last seen him in hospital around the time she went underground. After his funeral, a German tabloid newspaper splashed a headline accusing Silke of killing her father. It was, in the whole of my many conversations with her, the most sensitive and painful issue of all. Was the only person whom Silke Maier-Witt ever killed her father? At the time, Silke confesses she blocked out such feelings and it is only now that she realizes the unbearable suffering she caused. She does believe that she was partly responsible for his death. 'I think it was grief that killed him. It must have been awful for him. Now I realize how much he must have suffered because I was his favourite daughter. He always wanted to get closer. I remember one time he said he just wanted to take part in my life a bit. But I couldn't at that time. I was just in confrontation with him. There was no chance to really talk it over. And now it's too late. He's dead.'

In her letter to her father, Silke wrote the things she had never been able to say when Hans-Joachim was alive because she had never understood him and why he took the position he did on the past. Ironically, East Germany brought understanding. Her letter is a form of catharsis.

Dear Father,

What I want to tell you doesn't come easily. Where shall I begin? Do you remember our argument – the one about concentration camps? In school, I had heard about a book called 'Documents of National Socialism' that gave the numbers: millions of people had been murdered in the gas chambers and met their deaths in the concentration camps. About you, I knew fragments, only fragments – and not even from you yourself. You were in the SS. You were 'denazified'. You were in the war and you talked about your *Kamaraden*.

And then came my question – or was it more an accusation? 'You should have known all this. You should have prevented all this.' You blocked the question. 'Who put that idea into your head?' you said. The fact that you would not take me seriously was what angered me. You said, 'But I didn't know.' And then there was a furious row and silence for two weeks. At the end, I was certain of one thing – that under those circumstances I would have resisted. I will never let anything like that happen again – that we Germans should do something like that. But I never thought it through. From then on, the whole subject was taboo. I was 17 or 18 at the time. Today, more than 20 years later, I remember it very clearly and I am ashamed of it. In my own way, I became guilty. Today, I too have to say, 'I didn't know.'

Later then, when you were in hospital seriously ill, I came to see you. At that time, you didn't know anything about my life. But I saw you weak, helpless and no longer a strong father – and I understood. You could not acknowledge that you had made mistakes: that you had wasted the best years of your life for something that turned out to be so dreadful, so wrong. And then there was a glimpse of understanding. In a moment, it was all over when your strength returned and you were back home. It was a chance we both missed. How difficult it is to put all this in words. How often I thought about it at night. We cannot talk about it any more. I can only write it down, what happened to me.

The first time it hit me was just before I was arrested in the autumn of 1989. There was one report after another – revealing the true face of socialism. I had been a member of the party – and wanted to be a member – to have the opportunity to change things, not to leave it to everybody else, but to do it myself. I had defended the East German regime against its niggling detractors and against those who thought that capitalism was God. Whatever I heard about the GDR before, I thought was an exaggeration: the environment wilfully destroyed; the party bosses living a life of luxury; the inhumanity, lies and deceit; and even the arms trade. Above all there was the almighty power of the Stasi, who were everywhere and saw everything. And me? I was caught up in it all. At first I didn't want to look at it properly and see what was really going on. I presumed I could judge when I could not. A seamless change from the RAF to the Stasi? Wasn't it all about self-denial? Isn't that what I learned from you – self-denial?

After the collapse of East Germany, I sensed that I had reached a dead end. So this is what Nazi Germany was like – to collaborate without wanting to see. But why? And where do I go from here?

Silke Maier-Witt is likely to spend another couple of years in prison and then she will be free to start her life again. I asked Dirk Buechner of the BKA, to whom she had poured out her terrorist odyssey over thirty-two meetings, whether she would be in any danger from the RAF upon her release. The same, I assumed, applied to the other *Aussteigers*, most of whom had also turned supergrass. I imagined the IRA, for example, would have had no hesitation in 'executing' her for her betrayal had she been one of *its* members. He said he thought there was no threat as she had only given evidence against the other *Aussteiger* and those already in gaol. 'To the RAF, she's a non-person.' If the RAF were minded to take action, it could probably do so, for as we will see in the final chapter 'Today and Tomorrow', the 'third generation' of the RAF (Baader–Meinhof being the 'first' and Silke Maier-Witt being part of the 'second') continued as a lethal terrorist force throughout the 1980s. It still exists today, although probably with fewer than twenty members.

Silke will return home to the big family house where the table is still neatly laid and fresh flowers adorn every corner. Photographs of her father stand beside them.

6 · THE VILLAGE

Forty kilometers inland from San Sebastian and northern Spain's Atlantic coast stands the village of Ordizia. Ordizia used to be a beautiful place. The heart of it still is. Its centrepiece is the Plaza Mayor, a covered square whose vaulted ceiling is held aloft by twelve giant Corinthian columns through which children dart and hide in games of Basque 'tag'. The roof affords protection from the burning sun of high summer and the driving rain and snow of deep winter. Ordizia is a place of extremes in more ways than one. Nestling in the fold of a valley with snow still dusting the peaks beyond, Ordizia is where Spain's own 'terrible beauty' was born.[1] The village is a cradle of ETA, Euskadi ta Askatasuna, 'Basque Homeland and Freedom', the organization whose violent campaign for Basque independence has claimed over 700 lives in the past twenty years and which the Spanish state is now close to defeating. Madrid stands on the brink of this remarkable success as a result of measures that include those which many of the British public would no doubt like to see its state use against the IRA and its Loyalist counterparts: covert assassination and deportation.

A stone plaque on the fringe of the Plaza Mayor reminds visitors that the pillared cover has graced Ordizia since 1875 thanks to the munificence of Don Carlos, the pretender to the Spanish throne, who pledged to 'guard and fulfil the rights of Guipuzcoa', the province which, along with Alava, Vizcaya and Navarra in Spain and Labourd, Basse Navarre and Soule on the French side of the border, constitutes the ancient Basque region of Euskadi. Opposite the square stands a squat but pleasing old town hall faced with stone emblems of cannon, drum, castle and crown reminding Ordizia's 10 000 citizens of their rebellious past. Today, militant and more moderate rebels dominate the council chamber inside: three belong to Herri Batasuna (HB), 'Popular Unity', which is the political wing of ETA;[2] three to the Partido Nacionalista Vasco (PNV), the century-old Basque nationalist constitutional party not unlike Northern Ireland's moderate nationalist Social Democratic and Labour Party (SDLP);[3] and five other political parties whose roots also lie in resistance to Spanish rule.[4]

Although it may be surprising at first to find the politics of urban socialism and the language of revolution in a setting where more conservative ideologies might be expected to flourish, ETA is, above all, a nationalist organization with predominantly rural roots. The Basque countryside is the paradigm of Basque 'ethnicity'. Beyond the columns of the Plaza Mayor and the picture-postcard streets, stand high-rise blocks of workers' flats and the factories where they spend their days. Ordizia is now a village only at its heart. Balconies are strewn with washing even in the pouring rain as if their owners were grateful for the free rinse. The river Orio, which once gushed clear from the mountains, now flows muddy brown and sluggish, long polluted by the factories that line its banks for almost the length of the valley as far as San Sebastian and the Bay of Biscay. The sunrise industries have not risen over the mountains; ETA's twenty years of bombing and killing have seen to that. Despite the rural setting, Ordizia is home to an urban proletariat that for years has regarded Karl Marx as its mentor. Economics and class struggle have fashioned the village's politics as they have those of scores of others dotted around the Basque countryside.

On a gently rising hill behind the village square is the old school that gave Ordizia's young 'Etarras' their first taste of formal education. They were the children of the 1950s and 1960s who grew up in a climate that was not only moulded by the social and political changes affecting the rest of the youth of Europe but also conditioned by the authoritarian Spanish state. Hitler and Mussolini had gone, but Franco survived until the Generalissimo and his ideology were finally buried on 23 November 1975. Francoism and the evolution of ETA are inseparable. Franco had crushed the Basque country in the civil war of the thirties with the aid of his ally, Hitler, when the Luftwaffe had laid waste the city of Guernica, an action immortalized by Pablo Picasso's painting of that name. Like Guernica, the degree of autonomy which the Basques had traditionally enjoyed from Madrid was destroyed. All resistance was brutally crushed. The Basque language and culture were outlawed. To speak the native tongue was to commit an act of subversion inviting reprisals. In schools throughout the region, the day began with the singing of the fascist anthem, 'Face the Sun'. The mutinous and sluggish were ritually punished. Boys were forced to stand with their fingers clustered upright while teachers smashed them with a rod. Girls were forced to stand or squat with arms outstretched and their hands loaded with books. Resistance was sullen and silent. In Ordizia, as throughout the Basque country and much of Spain, young people came together in groups known as *cuadrillas*, gatherings of around twenty friends which, in many cases, became the units from which ETA grew. *Cuadrilla* is virtually untranslatable. It is not exactly a gang because that word has the wrong connotations, and it is more than just a group of friends because the relationships are so lasting and deep. A *cuadrilla* is usually formed at school by boys and girls when they are between ten and fourteen years old. They do everything together. There is no formal structure, no official membership, no initiation ceremony. They are as informal and loose as fraternities and sororities in American colleges are exclusive and tight. A *cuadrilla* lasts for ever, the bonds becoming stronger with age and experience. In the Basque country of Franco's Spain, the notion of the *cuadrilla* became even more important since it expressed a shared identity in the face of external hostility and repression by the state.

Remarkably, one particular *cuadrilla* in Ordizia provided ETA with some of its most famous recruits, who became not only its gunmen and bombers but its politicians, martyrs and leaders. Their story is a microcosm of the rise and fall of ETA and the Spanish state's response. As *cuadrillas* are egalitarian, not hierarchical, the group had no particular leader. Rigidity and structure were for the Francoist world outside. Talking to its surviving members today, it is difficult to believe they were once 'terrorists': they could not be more different from the stereotype. Some became fugitives in France, others spent time in gaol. Some were wounded, others met violent deaths at the hands of both the Spanish security forces and their own kind. One was deported to an island in the Atlantic where he died in exile. One of their colleagues from a suburb of Ordizia was assassinated by mercenaries financed by the Spanish state. Another was, until recently, ETA's top military commander. Some rejected violence once democracy replaced Franco. These were the men and women who twenty years ago fought for two goals: the defeat of Francoism and Basque independence.

Today the members of the *cuadrilla* are middle-aged. I refer to them by the first names and the nicknames by which they are still known. All of them reminisce with remarkable frankness. 'Koldo' looks the least like a former 'terrorist'. His appearance is as neat and precise as his words. He produced some yellowed newspaper cuttings that told of his exploits in the 1970s alongside a picture taken at the time which bore little resemblance to the intense and bespectacled features of the older man opposite. Looking at the old photograph, I could see the young Koldo in the role of ETA 'terrorist'. Today I could not. The newspapers told of how he had narrowly escaped death when he fell four storeys from a rooftop having been shot through the ankle by the police as he was trying to escape. The washing lines saved him and broke his fall. He points them out today with gratitude and relief. While he was explaining what happened, some of the more elderly residents of the flats came out on to their balconies and began discussing whether the man down below was the ETA person who had ruined their washing all those years ago. Koldo, diplomatically, shook his head. He showed us with enormous pride his Gastronomic Society, the dining clubs that are such a rich feature of Basque life, pointing to the photographs on the wall of its founder members in 1931 and proudly declaring that he was member no. 110.

I asked him why he had become involved in ETA. 'Because of the oppression of the Spanish state,' he said. It was not difficult to see why. His mother and father, however, being of a generation that had lived through the horrors of the civil war, had no wish to see their children involved in illegal organizations that seemed to have no chance against the weight of the Spanish state. 'Our parents didn't want us to join. They knew we ran a high risk and that we'd probably end up in gaol, in exile or dead. I didn't tell them I'd joined. They found out by drawing their own conclusions. I already had a cousin in exile after he'd been involved in a shoot-out in Bilbao. They told me not to do it but it was too late. I had already taken the decision.' Koldo told me that all members of the *cuadrilla*, including the girls, who formed the original ETA 'commando',[5] had started off as Boy Scouts, complete with woggles, neckerchiefs and traditional Boy Scout hats. 'Powell was the boss,' he explained, as if the organization Baden-Powell founded had, like ETA, spawned factions with military and political wings. The Scout group, run under the auspices of the Catholic church, failed to satisfy the deeper hunger of the *cuadrilla*. In the end, they were expelled because of 'ideological differences': 'We wanted to give it a more political and cultural angle.' Gradually, Koldo and the others were drawn towards ETA in the wake of the enormous publicity the organization had received after the Burgos trial in December 1970 in which fifteen ETA leaders were sentenced to long periods in gaol for banditry, military rebellion and what the Francoist state called 'terrorism'. To young Basques before Burgos, ETA had been just a name. After Burgos, the initials became a symbol of heroic resistance to fascism. Franco's gamble of making the trial public backfired. The result in the Basque country was not condemnation of 'terrorism', as the authorities had hoped, but waves of sympathy and lines of recruits.

Yet the arrests and trial of ETA's leadership had 'de-articulated' the organization. Those still at liberty had to start again from scratch. Potential recruits were identified and approached. Initially, the contact would be oblique. First, would they like to come to a meeting? Then, would they care to put up some posters? Paint Basque flags on the corner of the street? Perhaps they might 'liberate' a *multicopista* (the hand-cranked printer that predated the photocopier)? Each stage was a test. Koldo passed them all. Then a radical lawyer asked Koldo if he would like to go to a clandestine meeting on a promenade of San Sebastian. He was to carry a paper under his arm for identification. He went along with another member of the *cuadrilla* known as 'Pakito'. It was October, the time when Atlantic breakers crash against the sea walls of Gros Beach and promenaders watch lone surfers riding the waves. Koldo and Pakito were not the only ones there. It was a bizarre ETA recruiting convention attended by young people from all over the area, all presumably carrying papers under their arms. One by one, each pair was approached by the ETA co-ordinator. The promenade must have been alive with furtive whispers as the recruiter, acting on behalf of ETA's Executive Committee, stalked his likely candidates. Perhaps the surf drowned out the whispers. He emphasized the importance of security and gave each couple printed instructions on how to make a bomb. He also provided the name of a contact with whom they were to liaise from that point on.

Koldo and Pakito returned to Ordizia, and the *cuadrilla*'s newly formed commando went to work. Koldo described how their first, crude bombs worked. They were known as 'biro bombs'. The top of the 'biro' was snapped off, releasing acid to flow down the tube. The acid 'ate' the detonator and the plastic explosive 'goma-2' went off. (The bombs were also known as *goma-dos*.) The group's first target was the bust of Zerama, the statue erected in honour of the man who had written the music to 'Face the Sun'. The explosion decapitated the stone-faced Zerama. The second was a small bomb attack on the Sala de Fiestas in Ordizia, the Basque equivalent of the local dance hall. I could understand why the *cuadrilla* attacked a Francoist symbol, but why a dance hall? 'We felt that these good-time activities were distracting people from the real cause,' said Koldo in earnest reply. (Franco had invested heavily in football, bullfighting and other recreational pursuits to distract citizens from politics.) Above all, Koldo is earnest. The third target was more political – the memorial tablet in Ordizia's church erected in honour of Franco's supporters who died in the civil war. The group set up the attack but the bombing itself was carried out by a unit from outside. The tablet was shattered.

Pakito was an enigma to the rest of the *cuadrilla*. Today, they speak of him in hushed tones and with some reluctance. Few wished to have their names attached to quoted comments for fear of unpleasantness in the village or worse. No one at the time ever dreamed that Pakito would rise within the organization as he did. 'He didn't look like a leader and didn't have the character of a leader,' said one. 'He was quiet, introvert and sullen at times. Like a dead mosquito,' ventured another. Some members of the *cuadrilla* remembered him going round the village collecting swill for the pigs on his family's farm in the hills above Ordizia. 'We used to stand under the trees in the square chatting and he used to pass us by, head down, clearly embarrassed, carrying buckets on his way back up to the farm. The image is burned in my brain. It must have been humiliating for him.' All remarked that he was very reserved but restless. 'It seemed as if he had never broken a plate in his life. He was a bit of a fox, and academically he was nothing.' One described how Pakito used to go to ETA Executive Committee meetings and ostentatiously place his gun on the table as a clear indication of how he saw the means to the end. 'A butcher,' was one description. 'He was very bad. If he threatened to kill you, he would no doubt carry it out.' Pakito was like no other member of the *cuadrilla*. Only a minority spoke warmly of him.

'Tanke' could not be more different. He is a giant of a man, more like a beefy rugby forward than a terrorist who once went to Uruguay to teach and learn from the Tupamaros.[6] The Tupamaros had been enormously impressed by ETA's military prowess after it had assassinated Franco's Prime Minister, Admiral Luis Carrero Blanco, on 20 December 1973 with a massive bomb placed under the road. So they invited some of their Basque revolutionary comrades over to swap notes. The ETA commando had dug a tunnel from the cellar of a building on the route that the Prime Minister regularly took from mass to his home. In the huge remote control explosion, the car was blown over the 65-foot wall at the back of the church and landed on a balcony above the courtyard inside.[7] Carrero Blanco never stood a chance. It was Tanke who was ordered to collect the explosives and drive them to Madrid. 'We took the car. We knew it had explosives inside but we did not know what they were to be used for. We had no idea what was going to happen. We'd call it "a messenger job". When we found out what they were used for, there was tremendous joy, because Carrero Blanco was the hardliner of fascism. For us it was a liberation. It was like a party.'

While we talked, Tanke lit cigarette upon cigarette, most of them resting between the fingers of his huge hands, seldom making the journey to his lips. When Tanke was five years old, he knew no Spanish and learned it the hard way from a Francoist teacher who meted out punishments similar to those visited on children who failed to sing 'Face the Sun' with the expected enthusiasm and conviction. He talked of the torture that used to be commonplace at the hands of Spain's paramilitary Civil Guard, whose old barracks still stand by the river in Ordizia. A standard trick was for the Guards to confiscate you identity card if they saw you on a demonstration. They would then tell you to come to the barracks to get it back. There was no choice. You had to do so. Beatings and electric shocks were routine practice, and Tanke even described how some detainees were laid on a bench and edged closer and closer to a whirling sawmill blade in order to get them to talk. Other members of the *cuadrilla* confirmed the stories, but there was no other mention of the sawmill. Although its more extreme

forms have disappeared, the culture of using ill treatment to extract information appears to have continued, even in a democratic Spain headed by a
socialist government publicly committed to human rights. Throughout the
eighties, Amnesty International reported on cases of brutality against
prisoners. While we were filming in the Basque country in 1993, the United
Nations published its latest report on the incidence of torture and abuse of
human rights around the world. It concluded that Spain's record was still
'not satisfactory'. The President of Spain's Human Rights Association,
Jose Antonio Gimbernato, declared: 'Spain occupies the last place among
most developed countries of the West in fulfilling fundamental rights.'[8]

Gradually Tanke became more and more involved in Basque culture,
organizing Basque events and bringing Basque singers to the festival. At
the weekends, Tanke and the *cuadrilla* would take to the hills, marching
through fields and woods speaking Basque and singing Basque songs. In
Ordizia, Basque nationalism and politics were closely intertwined. Tanke
became involved with the workers and began to organize strikes in the
railway works in Beasain, which is situated right next door to Ordizia,
effectively making the two communities economically one, although they
remain great rivals. The only trade unions in Spain at the time were
vertically integrated and run by the fascists as part of the Francoist state.
Soon Tanke drew attention to himself as an active militant, being noticed
not only by the Civil Guard but by the ETA leadership in the area. After
Burgos, ETA was decimated and desperate to grow. Tanke and other
members of the *cuadrilla* were ideal material. 'I was pinpointed,' he said.
'Someone approached me – I can't remember who it was – and said, "How
about doing something for us?"' Tanke agreed. I asked him if there was any
initiation ceremony as with the Red Army Faction's gun or the IRA's oath
of allegiance. He smiled and said no: sliding into ETA was like sliding into
bed. Tanke was one of the *cuadrilla* who was lucky to be alive. In August
1974, while part of a unit on its way to kidnap the King of Spain's brother-
in-law, he was stopped at a checkpoint outside San Sebastian. There had
been a robbery that morning and the Civil Guard was everywhere. Tanke
managed to escape after a shoot-out but was pursued. There was another
gun battle. 'There were eight Civil Guard Land-Rovers all shooting at
once. You are already mentally prepared for that sort of thing. You already
know that he who walks must one day fall down. It's a nasty feeling. You
are hemmed in.' Tanke was shot six times and spent the next three years in
gaol. He was released in July 1977 under the general amnesty that followed
the death of Franco. 'I didn't ask for it,' he said. 'I had no choice. There was
great joy that Franco had gone and gratitude towards those who had
brought him down.'

'Loli' agreed with Tanke that getting involved with ETA was the most natural thing in the world in the Ordizia of the early seventies. Loli is one of the three women members of the *cuadrilla* who became involved with ETA. With a smiling face and sparkling eyes, Loli is lovely. When my colleague, Nigel Townson, took me to meet her, she invited us in out of the torrential rain and immediately put slippers on our feet. On a scale of stereotypical 'terrorists' Loli would be nowhere in sight. 'The transition to ETA is very simple,' she said. 'You learn the language, become part of the culture, go to the mountains, and then someone will ask you to do something, like handing out leaflets. It starts like that and then each time you do something more dangerous. You don't stop to think. You get involved because of the situation. You had to do something. You either end up in prison, in France or dead.' The sentiments were, by now, familiar. Loli knew what joining ETA meant. Her brother-in-law once escaped through a window in Guernica, but was pursued to the mountains and shot dead.

One of Loli's best friends in the *cuadrilla*, Jon García, also joined ETA, although she never knew it at the time. Jon García is a well-groomed, good-looking man with fine features and an even finer moustache. 'The *cuadrilla* was a good means of camouflage for those in ETA,' he said. 'You could hide as part of a larger group without drawing attention to yourself.' I asked why he joined. 'Because they asked us to. I had no great burning desire to do so. ETA at that time was very much a political organization. Someone from that front got in touch and asked if I was interested in entering the military side. He said they needed the strength as there was important work to be done. So I joined. An ETA veteran came to give us training in the use of weapons and explosives.' Some of the training was done at Tanke's family farm in the hills above Ordizia, while other instruction took place in the Sierra de Aralar, the mountains that rise from the valley to the east. But Jon García only lasted a year. He decided that ETA lacked a coherent Marxist outlook, with its increasing concentration on the military campaign: to him, political organization required greater emphasis.

Jon García originally joined ETA with another friend from the *cuadrilla*, 'Txinto'. Txinto was, by all accounts, the best and brightest of the group. Both abandoned their university studies to devote themselves full-time to ETA. Although there were political differences between Txinto and other members of the *cuadrilla*, he never let them interfere with friendships and would go out of his way to avoid political debate if he felt it would jeopardize the relationships by which he set such store. After a year, Txinto too withdrew from ETA but, even more disillusioned with the left outside, rejoined in 1976. He never admitted to his friend that he had done so. Jon García kept in touch with Txinto, who, he said, became 'very pessimistic'.

'Txinto originally believed that one last push would deliver the revolution but in time he became resolved to gradual evolution. At one stage he told me that, if it didn't work in a couple of years, he'd retire to the hills and buy a farm.' Txinto never did. He was killed on 11 January 1978 after a shoot-out in Pamplona where he was sharing a flat with another ETA member. According to Jon García, the two were warned that the police were after them and decided to cross the mountains to the safety of France. Just after leaving the house, Txinto's colleague realized he had left his mountain boots behind. He returned to pick them up and was ambushed. Txinto heard the shooting and ran to help his friend. He returned fire, killed a policeman and was badly wounded in the process. Another policeman is said to have finished him off with the *tiro de gracia*. A simple plaque is now mounted above the family gift shop in Ordizia just off the Plaza Mayor; it bears the simple inscription: 'Txinto. Born 19.8.53. Died 11.1.1978.' Jon García and Txinto's family were devastated by his death.

'Yoyes' was the most hard-line and uncompromising of the three women in the *cuadrilla*. She was also the most militarily active. Talking and reading about her reminded me of the IRA's Mairead Farrell, who was shot dead by the SAS on 6 March 1988 while planning an operation in Gibraltar.[9] Yoyes's coolness on operations was legendary. I met one of her former comrades (now living a couple of miles outside Ordizia) who had carried out his first mission alongside a far more composed and experienced Yoyes. His ETA codename was 'Esmith'. It had originally been 'Smith', one of several English names used by ETA as *noms de guerre*. His comrades admired his English punctuality so they called him 'Smith'. 'Smith' became 'Esmith' for ease of pronunciation. The couple's target was the Francoist trade-union headquarters in Renteria, an industrial suburb of San Sebastian. Esmith was from a border village nearby and was working in Renteria, so he was familiar with the area. He remembered that the date was May Day in 1972 or 1973. Three operations had been planned simultaneously, each to be carried out by different ETA commandos. Yoyes was one of the *liberados*[10] who came in to carry out the attack. Esmith had never met her before. They were to pose as a young couple out for a stroll. Esmith was given a gun, detonator and '*goma*-2' explosives. It was the first time he had carried a weapon. The explosives were concealed in the front pocket of his 'kangaroo' anorak. He was even more nervous because there were police around. Perhaps they had received a tip-off. He dug his teeth into the cap of the 'biro', ripped it off and rammed it into the package of explosives. He had fifteen to twenty minutes to plant the bomb and get away. He took Yoyes's arm and walked up to the window of the trade-union building. Yoyes and Esmith embraced. 'My gun was tucked in the back of my trousers. I had my arm round Yoyes and she had her hand in her pocket on the pistol. She was very calm. I really admired her. She was a professional. I was a complete amateur.' Esmith planted the bomb and the couple adjourned to a bar to wait for the explosion. The bomb went off. No one was hurt. 'I was still incredibly nervous. It was Yoyes who calmed me down.'

Yoyes was interviewed for a BBC *Panorama* programme on ETA reported by Richard Lindley. When I watched that interview again, her words and demeanour confirmed the impression I had already received of her from talking to other members of the *cuadrilla*. She said violence was the only way.

> Nothing else gives even the possibility of winning independence. All the rest is promises – promises that independence can be won by peaceful means. It's all a lie. We just can't win that way. The only possibility we have of gaining our liberty is through violence. They don't give us any choice.
> *Is what you believe enough to die for?*
> That's not really how we look at it. Either we fight or we die anyway. If we die fighting, well, that's the way it goes. But, if we don't fight, the Basques will certainly perish as a people and even in this so-called 'democracy'. We kill so that we can live so the Basque people can survive.[11]

Esmith got to know Yoyes even better when the two were on the run in France but lost touch with her in the mid-seventies after ETA split into two wings: ETA Politico-Militar (PM) and ETA Militar (M). The split, like the split between the Provisional and the Official IRA, was bitter and murderous. The approaching death of Franco was the catalyst. With the dictator gone and a fragile democracy born, there were acrimonious debates between those in ETA (PM) who believed that *lucha armada*, 'armed struggle', was no longer appropriate and those in ETA (M) who believed that the transition made no difference and that the *guerra revolucionara*, the 'revolutionary war', should continue until victory was achieved. On 23 July 1976 the architect of ETA (PM)'s political strategy, 'Pertur', was kidnapped and assassinated, allegedly by his rivals, who were opposed to any political settlement. His body was never found. Pakito, at the time a member of ETA (PM), was one of those who opposed Pertur's political strategy and subsequently defected to ETA (M). During Spain's first post-Franco democratic elections in 1977, ETA (PM) declared a ceasefire on condition that several of its key people were released from gaol. The new democratic state obliged. As the split widened, the members of the *cuadrilla* spilt accordingly. Loli, who by now was in France, stayed with ETA (PM) and astonished the French priest by marrying someone from

ETA (M). Koldo, too, backed ETA (PM). Txinto went with ETA (M) until his death in Pamplona in 1978. Tanke and Yoyes both went the same way and joined Pakito in ETA (M).

Another member of the *cuadrilla* known as 'Juanra' joined ETA (M) too. Juanra, like Txinto and Jon García, was one of the more intellectual members of the group and was studying for a degree at Vitoria University. It was Juanra who later recruited Yoyes into ETA. Around the same time he had also recruited another woman called 'Bixen' whom he had known since their days in primary school. She was later to become Juanra's wife after both went on to study at the same university in Vitoria. Bixen, an active member of HB who today lives in Ordizia with her son, is far more like Yoyes than Loli. While talking to us in the HB headquarters in Ordizia with a column of intense HB activists streaming in for a meeting, she rolled and squeezed a silver cigarette paper with ferocious intensity as if releasing the tension and anger through her fingers. Whereas Loli is gentle, warm and smiling, Bixen is tough and suspicious that her cause will be misrepresented by a media she deeply mistrusts. With some reluctance, she told us about her husband, Juanra. She was not used to being asked seemingly banal questions such as 'What was he like?' 'It's difficult to answer,' she said, squeezing the silver paper still tighter. 'He knew how to listen to people and how to help them. He had a lot of friends. He read a lot and knew a lot about international politics. I learned through him. He was very close to his son. But he dedicated his life to the cause above and beyond his family.' In his second year at university, police uncovered an ETA commando cell and one of its members put the finger on Juanra. Further study was out of the question. Juanra had to flee to France to join Koldo, Pakito, Tanke, Loli and Yoyes, who were now living across the border as ETA refugees beyond the arm of the Spanish authorities. Bixen stayed behind to finish her studies before taking a job as a teacher in San Sebastian.

Through the 1970s and early 1980s, to the anger and frustration of Madrid, France became a haven for ETA fugitives as the Irish Republic once used to be for the IRA. But France was more than just a bolt-hole where ETA members initially enjoyed the status of political refugees; it was also a training, logistical and operational base from which its commandos could launch attacks across the border with virtual impunity. Despite constant representations by the Spanish state, the French were prepared to do very little to help solve Spain's problem. Between 1977 and 1981 there were twenty-nine requests from Madrid to Paris for the extradition of ETA suspects. Paris granted not one.[12] To the increasingly beleaguered Spanish government, the notion of international co-operation against terrorism was a joke. At the time, Paris had two main reasons for its less than helpful attitude: with 200 000 Basques of her own in the three Basque provinces on her side of the border, she was not inclined to do anything that would stir up trouble; and her government, not convinced that democracy had taken firm root, still regarded ETA as the organization that had been the revolutionary cutting edge of the struggle against Franco. France's reservations about the strength of the new democracy were overcome in February 1981 when King Juan Carlos bravely saw off an almost pantomime coup by army and Civil Guard plotters. They took over the Cortes, the Spanish parliament, by firing shots in the air in front of the television cameras; but the military stayed loyal to the King.

Yet France still showed no signs of moving against ETA with any conviction. Even when François Mitterrand and the French socialists came to power, some ETA refugees were still given legal papers. Juanra was one of the fortunate beneficiaries; this enabled Bixen to join him in Bayonne. But things were about to change. Bixen first became aware of it on 6 October 1983 during a police interrogation. She had been arrested at 3 a.m. while staying with her sister in Ordizia. Bixen had only recently married Juanra in France. The two sisters were taken to San Sebastian, held for two days and submitted, she says, to psychological but not physical torture. Her interrogators wanted to know who had been guests at their wedding. 'It was already very cold,' she told me, 'and they turned on the air-conditioning to make it even colder. They brought my sister to the cell and she had nothing to do with ETA. They tried to devalue her by calling her names. One of them was a policewoman. It's very hard being insulted by another woman.' Bixen told them she wanted to talk politically, about HB's policies and the future of the Basque country. Not surprisingly, her interrogators were not interested; instead they tried to 'turn' their subject and entice her to collaborate. They said her husband was going to be killed and that she was destined to become a widow. 'Why carry on if you know he's going to die? Why not come and help us?' Bixen saw it as a warning of what was to come, the so-called *guerra sucia*, the 'dirty war'.

The instrument of the *guerra sucia* was a secret right-wing 'hit squad' known as GAL, the Grupos Antiterrorists de Liberación, somewhat freely translated as 'the Getting Rid of Terrorists Group', for that is precisely what its members did, using terrorists methods themselves. GAL's killers were mercenaries mainly recruited from France and Portugal who were paid for each 'hit'. The financing of some of GAL's activities was traced back to secret state funds in the Ministry of the Interior in Madrid. Although it has never been conclusively proved, there is impressive circumstantial evidence that the Spanish state adopted the option Israel rejected and set up a killer squad sufficiently removed from the state to ensure 'plausible deniability'. But GAL's plausibility as an independent agent became less and less, engulfing the Spanish government in a scandal of

Watergate dimensions. Between 1983 and 1986 some twenty-seven Basques, including French civilians and Basque 'innocents', were assassinated by GAL's mercenaries, most of them on French soil.[13] When I asked a senior French intelligence officer in Paris who had been intimately involved in the fight against ETA whether GAL might have had an origin independent of the Spanish state, he burst out laughing. The same question met the same response from a well-informed observer in Madrid. I suggested that perhaps Basque businessmen, fed up with paying ETA's so-called 'Revolutionary Tax' (extortion money), might have provided the funds for GAL. He said I must be joking. Both the socialist government and parliamentary party blocked any investigation.

GAL, it appears, was brought into being out of Madrid's frustration: the purpose of the organization was not just to liquidate those the French were unwilling to touch but to galvanize the French government into action – although, remarkably, it appears that there was a degree of complicity with GAL at certain levels of the French security services. On both counts GAL succeeded. GAL's nineteenth victim, Juan Maria Otegui, came from a suburb of Ordizia. He was not a member of the *cuadrilla* because he was slightly older, having been born in 1942, but he knew its members as comrades-in-arms from the same village. Otegui was assassinated in France on 2 August 1985 on the road from Bayonne to Saint-Jean Pied de Port as he was returning home from his work at the Denek co-operative. Two unidentified men on a motor-cycle pulled out of a side road and shot him from behind. Otegui died within minutes. He left behind a widow, Karmele Martínez Aguirre, and a young daughter, Nagore. I met Karmele in a coffee shop in Bilbao where she nervously sipped mineral water. She had moved back to the city to start a new life. Her husband's death had come as no surprise. 'We knew it was probable,' she said. 'His name was on wanted posters in Madrid. There was a reward of 7 million pesetas [probably around £50 000 at the time].' I asked if there had been any warning, since GAL had already been terrorizing ETA fugitives in France for nearly two years. She said they had been forewarned two or so months before her husband's death. 'There was a general climate of fear. A captain from the gendarmerie came to our house and told my husband to take care as there was a GAL unit operating in the area and he was on a hit list. What precautions he took were a matter for himself. We were offered no protection. We were surprised as we'd never had anything to do with the police and they'd never visited us before. My husband was a very confident person who didn't get frightened easily. I asked him to stop work for his own safety but he refused. He said he'd rather be killed by GAL than end up in gaol. I always knew he would die violently.' Not satisfied with assassinating Otegui, GAL returned several months later and almost killed his wife. The trail from that attack opened the window on how GAL was recruited and financed.

The state officials who were the front men – and eventually the fall guys – for the operation were a senior police officer from Bilbao, Detective Superintendent Jose Amedo, and a middle-ranking colleague, Detective Inspector Michel Dominguez. For the purposes of setting up and running the GAL operation, they used the pseudonyms 'Ricardo' (Amedo) and 'Eduardo' (Dominguez). The following reveals the link between them and the attempted murder of Otegui's wife. On 31 January 1986 the two police officers went to Lisbon to meet a Portuguese intermediary who would do the recruiting for them. Following Portugal's disengagement from Angola in the seventies, there were plenty of tough, hardened veterans around not averse to earning a few million pesetas. Amedo and Dominguez met the recruiter in a hotel and then took him to dinner at a restaurant called 'O Pescador' in Cascais by the sea just outside the city. Their guest, Mario Correiro da Cunha, was a former paratrooper and veteran of the wars in Angola and Rhodesia. We met him in Lisbon. He certainly looked the part right down to the Ray-Ban 'Aviator' sunglasses. He still leaps out of aeroplanes for fun. Karate is his other favourite pastime. Physically he seems well equipped to do both. The meeting was one of our more sensitive encounters. Mario da Cunha was reluctant to talk. He said 'Ricardo' and his colleague had asked him to help recruit men to carry out *cobros dificiles* – 'difficult repayments'. We spent ages trying to work out precisely what *cobros dificiles* were. The phrase means using unorthodox methods to get money back from those who are reluctant to pay. Da Cunha said the men were 'bodyguards'; I suggested they were 'heavies'.

He said he was introduced to 'Ricardo' by a former Angola comrade, Antoniò da Macedo, whom he had not seen for years but who had been working in an area in Portugal notorious for smuggling and drug-running. Da Cunha claims he was suspicious at first: 'A light went on in my head.' The two men they met were not introduced as Spanish police officers but da Cunha said his suspicions were aroused when he saw 'Ricardo' take out his Visa card to pay the bill (12 940 escudos – around £50 at current 1993 exchange rate). He noticed 'Ricardo's' ID card with another name under a photograph of a man in military-style uniform. 'Then the light in my head turned on a little bit stronger. I thought he must have been army or police.' The name on the Visa card was Amedo; the number 4.940.000011865.4719; the account at the Banco de Bilbao. Despite his suspicions, da Cunha did as he was asked, recruited three mercenaries to carry out the allegedly unspecified *cobros dificiles* and received a postal order for 50 000 escudos (around £200 at 1993 exchange rate) for his troubles. The recruits were Paulo Fontes and Rogerio da Silva, who worked in security at the US ambassador's residence in Lisbon, and da Cunha's old Angolan friend, Antonio de Macedo. Da Cunha is also said to have told his superiors in the Portuguese intelligence services (for whom he was also allegedly working) about his meeting and his mission. If this was so, it is inconceivable that they would have not passed on the information to their colleagues in the Spanish intelligence services with whom they worked closely countering the Iberian pennisula's drugs and other criminal networks. When da Cunha was subsequently arraigned for involvement in recruiting mercenaries for GAL, he told the Lisbon court that he felt 'obliged to investigate what was happening ... they were only interested in recruiting people for surveillance services, the security of businesses and eventual difficult payments, *cobros dificiles*. ... I want to emphasize again that these gentlemen never referred to GAL, ETA or any other organization.'[14]

This statement, although not strictly speaking inaccurate, does not tell the whole story. When Paulo Fontes was subsequently arrested in France, he 'sang' and filled in the complete picture. He said that Rogerio da Silva made the first approach when they were working together at the American embassy in Lisbon. After the initial meetings with Amedo and Dominguez, events moved with alarming rapidity. This is Fontes's statement.

On 5 February 1986, he [Rogerio da Silva] offered me a job, backed by the Spanish and French police, which involved kidnapping Spaniards who lived in France. Fifteen million escudos [around £60 000 at 1993 exchange rate] would be paid for the operation. Since this appeared to be something quasi-official, I didn't regard it as at all risky. I met Mario [da Cunha] and he confirmed that we would kidnap a person in France and bring them to Spain, that we would be backed by the Spanish and French authorities, and that we would have to meet two Spanish policemen for the details. The policemen confirmed the kidnapping. We met the policemen the same day as Mario [5 February]. They didn't say who they were but in Bilbao said they were 'Eduardo' and 'Ricardo'.

The two Spaniards [Amedo and Dominguez] took us to Bilbao by car and put us up in a hotel on 6 February. The next day they explained that we were not to kidnap someone but to kill them. The person was a refugee in France who had carried out assassinations in Spain. We accepted this new contract. A man called Jean Louis [allegedly a French gendarme] would show us all the targets over the next few days. He said there was not one target but several because 'one was dealing with the same thing, given that these people were wrongdoers of the same order sought by the Spaniards'.

We [Fontes, Rogerio and Macedo] went to the Bar des Pyrénées but didn't carry out the action because of the number of people around the three targets. The two Spaniards said 'we were wrong not to have also killed the women given that these were just as dangerous as the men and given that one was dealing with people who belonged to ETA'. This was the first time that the two Spaniards had cited the purpose of the action, namely, ETA.[15]

On 8 February 1986, only three days after the meetings in Lisbon, the three mercenaries mounted their second operation in France. Their French contact, Jean Louis, told them that 'all the men with beards in the bars of the district and the people with them were people from ETA and there was no need to distinguish between them'.[16] Guns at the ready, the mercenaries walked into the Bar Batxoki in the port of Saint-Jean de Luz. It was known as a refugees' drinking place. The brother of an ETA leader was inside at the time. Also there was Karmele Martinez Aguirre, the widow of Juan Maria Otegui, who had been assassinated by other GAL killers only five months before. Karmele was in the bar with her three-year-old daughter, Nagore, talking with friends. Suddenly someone screamed, 'To the floor!' Karmele was standing with her back to the door. 'It was a strange moment. I realized that people were coming in with guns. I was aware of the noise but not the bullets. I grabbed my little girl and dived to the floor. It was only afterwards that I realized that the little girl was not my daughter. I didn't even register being hit.' Karmele was wounded in the leg and spent twenty-seven days in hospital. Nagore was hit in the buttock and detained in hospital for five. Karmele has no doubt who was behind the killing of her husband and the attempted murders in the Bar Batxoki: 'The Spanish government, of course. The Socialists [PSOE]. It's crystal clear it was funded and organized by them. It all smacks of a state operation.' Fontes carried out one more abortive 'hit' on 13 February 1986 against the Bar Consolation, also in Saint-Jean de Luz, in which an ETA member, Juan Ramon Basanez Jauregui, was seriously wounded. No one was killed. Fontes was arrested at the railway station trying to make his getaway. Two days after his arrest, he wrote to his sister, telling all. 'Policemen sent me to kill members of ETA,' he said. 'The money promised at the beginning of the operation was sufficient to buy a house, set up a business, buy a car and even travel through Europe and North Africa. I risked myself. I lost.' Gradually the other mercenaries who had been recruited elsewhere were arrested. Some, like Fontes, confessed. Another member who chose to talk was Christian Hitier, a former right-wing OAS terrorist,[17] who had also been recruited by Amedo. After his arrest, Hitier made the following admission.

Amedo recruited me, together with Dominguez, to work for the Spanish government, making it clear that we were dealing with official missions. I collaborated with him in the hope that this would solve the problems over my papers and nationality, although I also hoped to receive an economic reward. First he asked me for some information. After he asked for a greater degree of commitment, such as recruiting activists and planning specific missions, that is to say to wipe out Etarras and refugees, which was his objective. He never referred to his superiors in concrete terms. He always referred to 'the government' and to missions of an 'official' character.[18]

Amedo and Dominguez were finally arrested by the Spanish authorities on 13 July 1988 and put on trial in January the following year. They were found guilty of attempted murder and given sentences of life imprisonment. Both appear to have grown increasingly reckless in their activities, believing that they enjoyed a state immunity as if Franco had still been in power. Amedo was shown to have squandered millions of pesetas, presumably money intended for GAL, in the casinos of San Sebastian and elsewhere. In the end, realizing that they were being left to twist in the wind, on 24 July 1987 they murdered Juan Carlos García Goena, a man who had nothing to do with ETA, apparently in order to put pressure on their superiors to stand by them. The killing had the opposite effect. Enough was enough. Amedo and Dominguez were reined in. The man who broke them, putting the legal seal on the prodigious endeavours of the young journalists Melchor Miralles and Ricardo Arques, who had pursued the story with great courage and tenacity, was a young Spanish investigating magistrate from Madrid, Judge Baltasar Garzón. Garzón became a popular hero, the 'Mr Clean' who exposed the 'dirty war'. Garzón took endless statements from GAL operatives, the families of their victims, survivors of GAL attacks, and the Spanish police and security forces themselves. Crucially, he was able to obtain an admission from the Director-General of the Spanish police, José María Rodríguez Colorado, that Amedo's trip to Portugal to recruit Fontes, da Silva and Macedo was paid for out of secret state funds, *fondos reservados*, held by the Ministry of the Interior.[19] Judge Garzón wanted to know more. How much money was used in all? What was it used for? And on whose authorization? But every door was closed. The matter went to the Cabinet and the Cabinet refused all access and any further detail. Such matters, the government declared, were a state secret, '*secreto de Estado*', the exposure of which would endanger state security, '*la seguridad interior del Estado*'. GAL had had the desired effect. Garzón got as far as he could.[20] Those who laboured with him had no doubt the smoking GAL gun lay behind the closed doors of the Ministry of the Interior. Amedo and Dominguez stayed silent throughout.

The impact of GAL on French policy was dramatic. After GAL's first bloody year in which it claimed around a dozen victims, extradition, which Paris had hitherto been reluctant to carry out, was placed on the French agenda. In 1984 five ETA suspects were sent back to Spain and twenty-three deported from France without due legal process and right of appeal.[21] The countries which received the first and subsequent batches included Togo, Gabon, Sao Tome, Capo Verde, Cuba, Panama, Venezuela, Ecuador and the Dominican Republic. France was simply dumping Spain's problem overseas. The carrot she generally offered host nations was French aid. France's biggest catch was the ETA leader, Eugenio Etxebeste, 'Antxon', who was arrested in France on 31 July 1984 and deported to the Dominican Republic ten days later. There he remains today, a crucial figure, with telephone access to key people in the Ministry of the Interior in Madrid should the Spanish government, as seems possible at the time of writing, decide to reopen negotiations with ETA.

Included in the list of deportees was a member of the *cuadrilla*, Juanra, who had been living in Bayonne with his wife, Bixen. By this time Juanra had legal papers. Once GAL started to operate in the autumn of that year, Juanra, as an obvious target, went underground. He did not make the same mistake as Otegui. France argued, with some reason given GAL's murderous record, that the presence of Basque refugees in her midst was leading to instability. Refugee round-ups began but Juanra escaped the net, at least until October 1985 when he was detained carrying a firearm in a bar in Biarritz. Bixen returned home to find her husband in handcuffs in a police car and officers searching the house. He was detained for three months in police custody. Then, suddenly, in February 1986, Juanra disappeared. Bixen traced him to Bardeluc on the French-German border. She drove to see him and discovered within a week that her husband was to be deported. One morning he was put on a train to Paris, then on a plane to Senegal, then on a light aircraft to the Cape Verde Islands off the coast of West Africa which, at the time, were ruled by a Marxist-Leninist government. According to Bixen, Juanra was escorted all the way by the same police officers who had arrested him in the bar in Biarritz. Two months later, Bixen and her son followed him to the rocks of Cape Verde. 'It was the deconstruction of a militant,' Bixen said bitterly. 'It was illegal. There were no papers and no appeal. Deportation is not better than gaol. It's just different. It's a repressive system that has the same ends as prison, and exile is open-ended.'

Juanra was not alone on the Atlantic island. He subsequently had the company of fourteen other ETA members who were treated as revolutionary heroes by the Marxist government. But their country was now even further away than their cause. Juanra became editor of the foreign section of *Noticias*, a local newspaper whose circulation and impact were somewhat limited. In 1989 Juanra met an unfitting end for a revolutionary. He went for a swim and drowned. Foul play was not suspected. Bixen blames those responsible for his deportation and collusion between France and Spain. 'If he hadn't been deported, he would not have drowned.' Juanra's body was given a revolutionary send-off as it left Cape Verde on a plane bound for the Basque country. Bixen returned to Ordizia. At home, Juanra was buried as a hero. Another member of the *cuadrilla* was gone.

The Spanish state not only hammered ETA militarily but used an array of carrots too. Without going into complex political detail, over the years Madrid gave the Basques much of what they wanted in a skilful attempt to weaken ETA's support and HB's political appeal. The Basque country was recognized as an 'Autonomous Community' as part of the post-Franco constitution and approved by local referendum in October 1979. The first Basque parliament was elected in March 1980. In 1982 the region was allowed to recruit and organize its own police force, the Ertzainza, whom ETA found it tactically difficult to target as they would be killing their own people. The original intent was that the Basque Police should eventually replace the Spanish National Police and the hated Civil Guard. This will happen in 1994. These concessions differed considerably but not entirely from what ETA demanded. On 1 February 1978 ETA (M) set out its position. It said it would discuss a ceasefire if the state would concede the following five points as a basic minimum for negotiations to get under way.

1 Total amnesty for all prisoners, exiles and deportees.

2 Legalization of all political parties, including those whose programme includes the creation of an independent Basque state.

3 Expulsion from Euskadi of the Civil Guard and National Police.

4 Improvement in the living and working conditions for the popular classes and especially the working class.

5 An autonomy statute that, as a minimum, recognizes the national sovereignty of Euskadi, authorizes Euskera [Basque] as the principal official language of the country and provides for Basque government control over all law enforcement authorities and military units garrisoned in the Basque country, and endows the Basque people with adequate power to adopt whatever political, economic or social structures they deem appropriate for their own purposes and welfare.[22]

Those points still reflect ETA's position today.

Amnesty or pardon was another weapon that bit deep into ETA's support. It was offered and taken at several strategic points in the twenty-year campaign. The move was not impeded by morality but dictated by *raison d'état*. Most of the *cuadrilla* took it during or within a few years of the establishment of democracy. After Tanke accepted amnesty in 1978, Loli and Koldo followed suit. 'I originally thought that we could engineer a Bolshevik-type coup, and the people would rise up and bring ETA to power,' Koldo reflected. 'I changed my mind on violence whilst I was in prison when I realized that ETA could not match the military might of the state. At first I thought that the military campaign should only be conducted in *support* of the political struggle, but then I realized that it was a brake on it. I reached that stage of thinking in 1980.' But the most controversial acceptance of a pardon was made by none other than Yoyes, a pillar of ETA (M). In 1981 she surprisingly severed her connections with the organization and went into voluntary exile in Mexico. In 1984 she returned to France and went through the legal procedures to accept amnesty or 'social reinsertion', as it was more grandiloquently and bureaucratically called. She returned to her home in Ordizia amid great publicity. Her defection was a triumph for government policy, not just because Yoyes was Yoyes, but because she was the first ETA (M) leader to accept amnesty. Apparently she had been given an assurance by the then leader of the organization, Txomin Iturbe, that she would come to no harm. The assurance held good for a year until Txomin was arrested and deported, thus compromising his control over the organization.[23] On 10 September 1986 Yoyes was in one of Ordizia's more modern squares with her three-year-old son when she was approached and shot dead. Her assassin, an ETA member called José Antonio López Ruiz, 'Kubati', was subsequently arrested and gave the following chilling account to the police.

I went up to Yoyes and said, 'Are you Yoyes?' She asked me who I was. I said, 'I am from ETA and I have come to execute you.' Immediately, I fired two shots from my pistol into her breast. She fell to the ground and I finished her off with another shot to the head.[24]

Esmith, whom Yoyes had initiated on his first operation, had bumped into her at the village's Basque festival a week or so before her killing. They had planned to meet up and talk about old times. 'I had a tremendous sense of impotence when I heard what happened,' he said. 'I was ready to cry. We had both been exiles – she to Mexico and I to Venezuela. We had both decided that violence was no longer justifiable. Her return was delicate. Yes, I cried.' One of ETA (PM)'s former leaders, who had been a father-figure to the *cuadrilla*, was in Ordizia at the time of shooting, watching a pelota match, the Basque national game, in the indoor courts near the square. He remembers someone shouting, 'They've killed Yoyes!' He ran to the square and saw her covered body. 'I found it difficult to control myself,' he told me. 'I was overcome with blind madness. I never thought it would have happened. If she had been with us, with ETA (PM), it never would. The repercussions were profound. Even those around HB at the time initially didn't believe it.' Koldo, too, broke down when I raised the subject of her death.

The killing of Yoyes effectively sealed the fate of the government's amnesty programme which, to date, had seen the release or return of over 300 former Etarras.[25] That was, no doubt, why Yoyes's killing was ordered. It may have had the desired effect, but it rebounded badly on those who had ordered her assassination. Ordizia, Spain and the whole Basque country were horrified. ETA paid the price in support. Her death was ETA's self-inflicted wound and a turning-point in the fortunes of the organization. It was a victory for the state, not its enemies.

By the close of the eighties, only one active member of the *cuadrilla*'s original ETA cell remained: Pakito. The intellectuals and the thinkers had all gone. Following her husband's death on Cape Verde, Bixen had returned to Ordizia and devoted her energies to HB. To outside observers, only the 'headbangers' were left, driving the group further and further down the cul-de-sac of the military campaign. A bomb placed in the underground car park of the Hypercor supermarket in Madrid on 23 March 1987 killed twenty-one people and wounded thirty-nine. A warning was given, but the time allowed was not enough to evacuate the premises. By the nineties, Pakito had become ETA's senior military commander. The Olympic Games in Barcelona came and went without incident despite ETA's threats: another triumph for the state. As ETA's support dwindled still more, the security of its military leadership grew even more precarious. On 29 March 1992, ETA's military command was decapitated. A French SWAT (Special Weapons and Tactics) team stormed a house near Bidart, a French town a few miles over the border, and arrested Pakito and his two fellow commanders, 'Fitti', ETA's explosives expert, and 'Txelis', its chief ideologue. Txelis had been spotted some time before, placed under surveillance and video-recorded by the French police whom he eventually led to the house where the three regularly held their meetings. They were thought to be in the process of planning an operation to release some of their comrades from a Spanish gaol. Apparently, his captors found Pakito on the top floor of the house, tearing up documents and flushing them down the toilet. No resistance was offered. Pakito was taken to Paris and charged with 'association de malfaiteurs' – 'association with wrongdoers', the French equivalent of a conspiracy charge. On 18 June 1993 he was sentenced to ten years.

In 1992 the state dealt a critical blow to ETA's financial infrastructure. With its fund-raising mechanism destroyed, there was no regular source of income to oil the organization's wheels. Kidnapping, which had in the past raised millions of pesetas for ETA, had already ceased to be a viable option because there was insufficient support or manpower to carry out such operations without serious risk to those involved. A more lucrative, regular and less hazardous alternative was extortion, or what ETA euphemistically called the 'Revolutionary Tax'. Any businessman in the Basque country was fair game, regardless of the size of the business. Some enterprises were actually very small, employing only a handful of workers. The 'collection' of the 'tax' followed a regular pattern. One of ETA's victims in the early 1990s was a small businessman from Beasain, Ordizia's industrial suburb. First, he received a standard computer-printed letter from ETA. Each one was personalized to reflect the requirements demanded of the particular individual. The letter he received read as follows.

The revolutionary socialist Basque organization of national liberation, ETA, is notifying you of your obligation, given your financial resources, to play your contractual part in the process of the national and social liberation of the Basque country. To that end, we inform you of our decision to demand from you an obligatory economic contribution to fulfil the numerous needs that the aforementioned process calls for.

Taking into account the information in our possession of the resources you have, the amount demanded is 5 million pesetas [around £25 000]. This quantity shall be paid in cash and in pesetas or if not in French francs and, of course, in used notes.

For the formalization of the payment, you will have to establish contact with the habitual radical nationalist channels within two weeks from the date of receipt of this notification. It goes without saying that you should not notify the Spanish police or the Basque police of this demand, otherwise you would have to contend with the painful consequences of what your behaviour would bring.

Nor should it be necessary to say that the demand we address to you, far from any motive of any personal, collective gain, has no other objective than that of guaranteeing the development of a free, just, united Basque society, without doubt demonstrated by the incalculable commitment and generosity of each one of the militants of our Organization, who, as you well know, pay for their efforts with many years of struggle and gaol and even with their own lives.

We await your contact.

Yours most sincerely,

ETA

When two weeks had passed and the businessman had failed to make contact with the 'habitual, radical nationalist channels', a second letter was sent. This was normal practice, since few recipients of ETA's demands were inclined to respond to the first communication. A second customized standard letter was then sent. Menace replaced formality.

As you have not initiated in the time foreseen the payment of the Revolutionary Tax that our Organization, ETA, notified you of beforehand, and as we have not received any news from you, we finally demand that you make effective payment of the sum we have asked of you.

We remind you that you should initiate payment of the afore-mentioned quantity from the 15th day of receipt of the present and last warning. The payment will be made effective in pesetas or in French francs, and in used notes. Use for this the usual Basque means and with the greatest discretion.

If you persist in refusing to pay, or you contact the police, you will automatically become the target of repressive measures against your property and person that the Organization judges opportune. There will not be another warning.

The businessman heeded the warning and went across the border to Biarritz to use 'the usual Basque channels' to make contact with ETA. The warnings he and scores of other Basque businessmen received were not given or taken idly. One in Guernica received a letter bomb that blew off his hand and blinded him in one eye. In Biarritz, the businessman agreed to pay up. On 14 November 1991 he went to the Café Zelaya in San Sebastian as instructed by his contacts with a packet of Winston cigarettes in his hand and a copy of the magazine *Interviu* under his arm. He also carried a million pesetas (around £5000). He was nervous because he had not brought with him sufficient money to meet ETA's full demand. His contacts demanded the other 4 million pesetas they had asked for and threatened him again. He said he had not got the money. He was, however, persuaded to find it. A month later, on 18 December 1991, the businessman again went to a rendezvous in San Sebastian, this time the Café Guretxea, where he handed over a further 2 million pesetas. He was still 2 million pesetas short. His contacts said they would 'stop by the office to pick up the rest'. But on 29 January 1992, before they collected the balance or threatened the businessman further, they were arrested by plain-clothes detectives from the Ertzainza, the Basque police. The arrests were the culmination of a year-long operation involving 100 officers to break the 'Revolutionary Tax' network. It was named 'Operation Easo' after the location in San Sebastian where much of the money was handed over. The handovers were secretly video-recorded without the knowledge of either party. Four men were charged: one was a member of HB, ETA's political party; one worked for *Egin*, HB/ETA's newspaper; one was from LAB, the Patriotic Workers' Council, part of ETA's trade union; and one was from HASI, the Basque Popular Socialist Party, part of the élite political group that directs the revolutionary nationalist coalition. Ten businessmen gave evidence in open court, including the person from Ordizia's industrial suburb and one of his neighbours. The sums of money demanded totalled 400 million pesetas (around £2 million), although it is estimated that ETA probably received less than half that amount. On 27 April 1993 the four men were found guilty. ETA's fund-raising network was substantially undermined, and with it much of the climate of fear in the Basque country's villages, towns and cities that had made the extortion of the 'Revolutionary Tax' possible in the first place. Significantly, it was not the central security organizations of the state, the Civil Guard and Spanish National Police, that had carried out 'Operation Easo' but the Basque country's own police force. For the Ertzainza, it was a political triumph as well as an unprecedented security success.

With its funds dried up, its military structure largely destroyed and its political base eroded even further after HB's setbacks in the general election of June 1993, ETA now seems on its last legs. The members of Ordizia's *cuadrilla* who either left the organization or took amnesty are sanguine about ETA's condition. Only Tanke says he would probably join ETA today if he were still a young man. He refuses to accept it is finished. 'While there still is a political motive and while there are still no liberties and sovereignty for the Basque people, ETA will never be defeated. It may be severely beaten up but not entirely defeated.' Few of the others agree.

Fresh slogans have recently been painted on the walls of Ordizia around the old Plaza Mayor: 'Gose Greban-Pakito', 'Pakito Hunger Strike'. Did anyone care apart from supporters of HB? People shook their heads. It is likely that, in the wake of Felipe González's unexpected victory in the general election, there will be moves by the new government in Madrid to enter negotiations with ETA once again. I asked one of Madrid's senior anti-terrorist chiefs, who had been involved in the abortive negotiations with ETA in Algeria in 1989, what he would say to ETA members should he meet them again. He smiled and said: 'Surrender.'

But reports of ETA's death were premature. On 21 June 1993, a car bomb exploded in central Madrid during the rush hour. The target was an unmarked military vehicle. All seven occupants were killed: four colonels, a sergeant, a naval captain and a civilian driver. More than a dozen civilians were injured, some of them seriously, including two girls aged eight and fifteen who were waiting for the school bus: one lost her eye and doctors thought they might have to amputate the leg of the other. The newly re-elected Spanish President, Felipe González, described the attack as 'a terrible crime' and said it was ETA's response to its political wing's poor showing in the recent general election. The killings may also have been ETA's retaliation for the ten-year gaol sentence passed on Pakito by a French court three days earlier. The message to the new government was clear: ETA was still in business.[26]

7 · THE SEEDS OF CONFLICT

At 9.07 a.m. on 7 February 1940, a small door opened in the gates of Winson Green prison, Birmingham. It was Ash Wednesday, the day of repentance. A prison officer emerged and posted up two black-edged notices.[1] A few minutes earlier, as a distant clock struck nine, the hundreds waiting outside the gaol had bared their heads. In the street opposite, a milkman carried on with his delivery. Police and plain-clothes detectives far outnumbered the bystanders. Those who had kept vigil through the night were allowed in groups of a dozen at a time to approach and read the brief statement. Signed by the prison governor, the under-sheriff and the prison chaplain, it declared, 'Judgement of death was this day executed on Peter Barnes and James Richards in our presence.' James Richards was an orphan. His friends knew him as McCormack, the name by which he subsequently became best known. Barnes and McCormack secured their place in history as the last members of the Irish Republic Army, the IRA, to be executed in England.

Two hours later, the coroner declared that they had been executed simultaneously on a double scaffold: the cause of death was dislocation of the neck and death was instaneous. The jury returned verdicts of judicial hanging. Barnes and McCormack had been found guilty of the murder of twenty-one-year-old Elsie Ansell, one of five civilians who died when an IRA bomb planted in the panier of a delivery bicycle exploded in Coventry the previous summer. The victims ranged from an eighty-one-year-old pensioner, James Clay, to a fifteen-year-old schoolboy, John Corbett Arnott. The two other victims were recorded as Gwilym Rowland, a fifty-year-old local council worker, and Rex Gentle, a thirty-year-old clerk. Elsie Ansell was only a fortnight from her wedding day. Their bodies were cut to ribbons by the shrapnel. Some were only identifiable by the rings on their fingers.[2] It was the most bloody incident in the IRA's wartime bombing campaign in England, launched on the long-held Republican premise that England's difficulty was Ireland's opportunity. Over half a century later, on 20 March 1993, IRA bombs exploded in a Warrington shopping centre, killing two young boys, Johnathan Ball, aged three, and Tim Parry, aged twelve. Public opinion in Britain and Ireland was outraged. Nothing seemed to have changed. The following weekend, under the title 'The Patriot Shame', the *Independent on Sunday* ran an editorial drawing the parallel between Warrington and Coventry. It concluded:

> We have been here before and often. The killing of children has dramatically heightened resolve to find a solution to a very old problem. The trick will be to keep that resolve in focus, so that Johnathan Ball and Tim Parry become neither martyrs in the blood-for-blood tradition of Ulster, nor as obscure as Ansell, Rowland, Clay, Arnott and Gentle, who 54 years ago went into that good night.[3]

At their trial, Barnes protested his innocence, while McCormack declared, 'as a soldier of the Irish Republican Army, I am not afraid to die, as I am dying in a just cause.'[4] The IRA has continued to haunt successive British governments for most of this century.

Barnes and McCormack were buried in England and their names and deed forgotten, except for their entry in yellowing newspapers and the IRA Martyrs' Roll of Honour. Forgotten, that is, until July 1969, when, as a gesture of goodwill to Dublin, the Home Office gave permission for the disinternment of their remains for reburial in Irish soil. An estimated 5000 attended the ceremony at a small country cemetery at Mullingar in County Westmeath.[5] It was conducted with all the trappings of an IRA funeral: guard of honour, last post, shots over the coffin and funeral oration. But it was the delivery of the Republican eulogy at the graveside that gave Barnes and McCormack a far more contemporary place in history. For here, on a summer's day in 1969, the public at large first became aware of the growing split within the IRA that was to give birth to the Provisionals before the year was out.

The oration was given by Jimmy Steele, an IRA veteran from Belfast. What he said stunned the crowds gathered around the coffins and the prominent Republicans on the platform. They belonged to a very different IRA that bore no relation in ideology, strategy and tactics to the Provisionals of today. In 1962 the IRA had rejected violence, forsworn the 'armed struggle' and embraced the idea of unifying the Catholics and Protestant working class to forge a socialist revolution and establish a workers' republic. Such Marxist dogma was anathema to traditional IRA supporters who saw it as a betrayal of all the IRA stood for: the use of armed force to remove the British presence from the North. To them, an IRA without guns was an IRA without purpose. Audaciously, Jimmy

Steele attacked the current leadership and the policies it had pursued: they were policies, he said, that had left the Catholics in Belfast unprotected from Loyalist attack and brought discredit on the Republican Movement, the composite name for the IRA and its political wing, Sinn Fein. His audience did not need the situation spelling out halfway through a year of increasing violence as Protestant extremists clashed with Catholic civil rights demonstrators across Northern Ireland. Prophetically, Steele warned of the consequences of the IRA's unreadiness.

The IRA veteran, Joe Cahill, was present to hear the words of his longtime friend. Cahill had been gaoled by the British during the Second World War and interned from 1957 to 1961 during the IRA's border campaign. He had then resigned from the IRA because of ideological differences. Jimmy Steele said what Cahill and many other Northern Republicans had long wanted to hear. 'There was dissatisfaction throughout the country at the road the Republican Movement was going,' Cahill told me, 'and the feeling was that this particular ceremony was a good opportunity to talk to a gathering of Republicans from all over Ireland. Jimmy Steele told them the Republican Movement would have to get back on the right course, on the true road to freedom: they'd have to prepare for the day when there'd have to be a fight, an armed struggle. That was the only way to free Ireland. I personally was delighted. I came out of the graveyard with Jimmy and it took him fully half an hour to get out, with people congratulating him for saying what needed to be said, thank God.'[6] Steele was subsequently dismissed from the IRA for giving voice publicly to what many had been whispering within the Republican Movement since the civil rights movement had exploded into violence in 1968–9. With Barnes and McCormack laid to rest once again, it was only a matter of time before the fundamental difference of opinion within the IRA became a formal split.

The differences had been growing since the failure of 'Operation Harvest', the IRA's border campaign fought from 1956 to 1962. From the military point of view, the campaign was a fiasco. Attacks were launched on border crossings, police barracks, military installations and the occasional BBC transmitter, but the loss in terms of property and human life was negligible compared with today. Eighteen men died, six of them members of the IRA, twelve of them members of the security forces. In the IRA's present campaign, since 1969 over 3000 people have died and the damage to property runs into billions of pounds. The damage alone caused by the bombing of the Baltic Exchange in the City of London in 1992 cost nearly £400 million and the devastation of Bishopsgate a year later over £300 million.[7] The border campaign failed chiefly because the authorities in both Dublin and Belfast interned IRA suspects on both sides of the border and because the IRA was never able to generate the degree of popular support necessary for a successful campaign. Attacks were restricted to the country-side. Urban areas remained unscathed.

In 1962, when the border campaign was called off and the internees released, the IRA painfully reassessed its position. Its predecessors had made an indelible mark on history during the Easter Rising in 1916 when a handful of 'Volunteers' seized the GPO in Dublin and impertinently de-clared the establishment of the Irish Republic before being arrested, exe-cuted and martyred by the British. The IRA then fought a bitter guerrilla war against the British army and the Black and Tans which led to the signing of the treaty in 1921 that created the Irish Free State and dominion status for twenty-six of Ireland's thirty-two counties. Britain retained political control of the six counties that became known as Northern Ireland because the million Protestants who lived there, and whose ancestors had been there since the Plantation of Ulster at the beginning of the seventeenth century,[8] wanted to have nothing to do with their Roman Catholic neigh-bours in the South. In the newly formed Irish Free State a civil war followed partition after those members of the IRA who opposed the treaty de-nounced their former comrades for betraying the Irish Republican cause and accepting the partition of Ireland. Throughout the 1930s and 1940s the IRA had waged desultory campaigns in the North, culminating in the failure of the border campaign in 1962.

The man who took on the unenviable task of reviewing the IRA's strategy and tactics was Cathal Goulding, a Dubliner who had spent most of the 1950s in Pentonville prison after a raid in 1953 on the armoury of Felsted School in Essex. His accomplice on the raid was a young Englishman with Irish Republican aspirations, John Stephenson, who later grew to fame or notoriety as Sean MacStiofain, the Provisional IRA's first Chief of Staff. Goulding was elected IRA Chief of Staff in 1962. 'I was the shakings of the bag,' he said, 'but I was really interested in the job. I wanted to do something.'[9] He recognized that in the forty years since partition, the IRA had achieved precisely nothing. 'The IRA in 1962 numbered only a few hundred, whereas those who fought on the Republican [IRA] side in the civil war were counted in thousands. Every decade we became smaller. Every campaign we entered into, we came out losers. We lost our material and we lost good men. In fact, we lost everything.'

Goulding's first action was to initiate a series of debates, IRA 'encounter groups', in which Republicans deliberated on the past and future of the organization. The discussions went on for eighteen months. The new Chief of Staff made his purpose clear. 'I wanted to try and emphasize the fact that we were really pissing against the wind unless we became politically active, unless we could offer ordinary people something, even in the interim. I wanted the IRA to adopt a socialist policy with a socialist objective, to become involved in politics, which the IRA had always refused to do.' Goulding was bitterly critical of the IRA's long-held policy of 'abstentionism'. 'They wouldn't recognize the government here [in Dublin] and they wouldn't recognize the government in the North and they wouldn't go into government themselves unless the election were held on an all-Ireland, thirty-two-county, basis. And yet they still paid their income tax, they still held driving licences and they conformed in every way except they refused to enter into politics. I wanted to try and get a cohesive policy, a policy that would say, we are a socialist organization and our objective is a workers' republic, or whatever it might be.' In particular, Goulding was anxious to form links with the Protestant working class in the tradition of the eighteenth-century father of Irish Republicanism, Wolfe Tone, whose aim was to unite Catholic, Protestant and Dissenter to rid Ireland of the English Crown. Goulding's IRA was wedded to the principle of non-sectarianism: British imperialism was the enemy, not the Protestant working class. 'They've been in Ireland for three or four hundred years. As far as I'm concerned, they're Irish. It's just that they have a different attitude as a result of their religion. Sectarianism was a big weapon in the Six Counties. I thought we'd break down that terrible hatred between Catholics and Protestants in the North. And that was the main objective that we had.' However starry-eyed he may have been about the prospect of Catholic and Protestant unity, Goulding got his way on the new direction the Republican movement should take. The military campaign which had always been the basis of the IRA's existence – or 'armed struggle', as it later became known in revolutionary parlance – was relegated to the cupboard of Republican history although never thrown in the dustbin lest at some future date it be needed again. But, from the practical point of view, 'armed struggle' was out. Goulding was nothing if not a realist after the embarrassing failure of the border campaign.

> The notion that the IRA was going to rise up some day and free Ireland and get rid of the British was a ridiculous pipe-dream, for the simple reason that we never had the support of the people, North and South, to do it. We couldn't match the Free State [Irish Republic[10]] army and we certainly couldn't match the British army. We could carry out a campaign possibly in the Six Counties for a while but not in the Twenty-Six Counties, because people didn't like to see the Gardai [the Irish police] or Irish soldiers being shot. The IRA in the North can exist but only within the Catholic ghetto areas, because when they shoot a policeman, they shoot a Protestant. And when they shoot a British soldier they antagonize the Protestants because they look upon him as being part of their country.

With the military option thus discarded, the IRA threw its energies into social and political agitation. Some of its campaigns seemed a trifle incongruous. 'Fish-ins' were organized on private property to assert the right of the people of Ireland to the fruit of its rivers. Power now flowed from the end of a rod, not from the barrel of a gun. But violence was never completely excluded, although it was violence against property rather than persons. There were attacks on foreign companies and investors, the architects of 'economic imperialism' in Ireland: buses ferrying strike-breakers in an industrial dispute with an American company were destroyed; farms owned by foreigners were attacked; and a foreign-owned oyster boat was blown out of the water.[11] The IRA change of direction was received with little enthusiasm by the Fianna Fail[12] government in Dublin. A politically active IRA, marching and demonstrating about social and economic conditions in the Irish Republic, was not welcome, despite the fact that its activities hardly shook the foundations of the state.

Not surprisingly, the dramatic change of direction which Goulding and his colleagues forced on the Republican movement was bitterly opposed by the traditionalists like Joe Cahill. Cahill and those like him were regarded by the Goulding leadership as right-wingers: they were fundamentally opposed not only to the relegation of the military campaign but to the number of communists and Marxists who now swelled the IRA's ranks. The IRA remained at heart a conservative, Catholic organization, many of whose volunteers attended mass, and still do, despite the inevitable charges of hypocrisy. Marxism was the ideology of the ungodly. Joe Cahill resigned from the IRA in disgust. He felt the organization was being hijacked. 'I had a feeling that ultra-left politics were taking over. As far as I was concerned, the main purpose of the IRA and Sinn Fein was to break the connection with England and get rid of the Brits from Ireland. They'd gone completely political, and the military side of things was being run down. The Republican movement was being led off the true path of Republicanism. Sooner or later there'd have to be a showdown. A split was inevitable.'[13] Cahill resigned in 1964 but it was to be another five years before the historic split finally came. It happened because the ideological differences that had driven Cahill and others out of the Republican movement were exacerbated by the situation that evolved in Northern Ireland, forcing the two factions within the IRA even further apart.

There is no doubt that ultimate responsibility for the evolution of that situation rested with Britain. After partition, Northern Ireland had been given its own parliament complete with its own Cabinet and Prime Minister. The parliament buildings were located at Stormont, a leafy suburb just outside Belfast. It was originally intended that, within a short period of time, Stormont and the parliament of the new Irish Free State, Dail

Eireann, should elect a Council of Ireland, a structure designed to be the political springboard for ultimate Irish unity. In 1925 the British Prime Minister, David Lloyd George, optimistically heralded the compromise as a solution to the problem that had dogged Britain for centuries. As he told the House of Commons:

> The freedom of Ireland increases the strength of the Empire by ending the conflict which has been carried on for centuries. . . . Incidents of that struggle have done more to impair the honour of this country than any aspect of its world dominion through the ages.[14]

But Lloyd George's optimism was never fulfilled. Stormont became a permanent fixture in the Northern political landscape of a now divided Ireland. It was, on the face of it, a mini-Westminster with many of the rituals and procedures of the Mother of Parliaments grafted on to it. But there was one fundamental difference: Stormont was inherently undemocratic. The border of the new province had been deliberately drawn to guarantee an inbuilt Protestant/Unionist majority within the state, with the result that Protestants outnumbered Catholics by two to one. Majority rule therefore meant Protestant rule until the day beyond the imagined boundaries of time when Catholics outnumbered Protestants. Stormont became known as 'a Protestant Parliament for a Protestant People' with its own police force, the Royal Ulster Constabulary (RUC), which was 99 per cent Protestant, and its exclusively Protestant paramilitary adjunct, the Special Constabulary or B Specials,[15] as they became notoriously known to Nationalists throughout the province. Northern Ireland was, in the words of Michael Stewart, Labour's Foreign Secretary in the 1960s, 'a police state'[16] backed up by a draconian Special Powers Act, instituted in 1922, empowering the forces of law and order 'to take all steps and issue such orders as may be necessary for preserving the peace and maintaining order'.[17] This legislation, applicable nowhere else in the United Kingdom, was targeted at the Nationalist community in general and the IRA in particular.

Once Stormont was established, the policy of successive British governments was to let it get on with the business of running the province: history had taught generations of British politicians that North Ireland was a tar baby and none wished to intervene and run the risk of getting stuck. But the Nationalists who represented the Roman Catholic community did not help matters by opting out of conventional political life on the basis that they did not recognize the state or its institutions. To many Unionists, Nationalists were the enemy within, Dublin's Trojan Horse bent on the destruction of the Northern Ireland state. As evidence, they pointed to articles 2 and 3 of the Irish constitution of 1937 which laid claim to the six counties.

Article 2. The national territory consists of the whole island of Ireland [Eire], its islands and territorial seas.

Article 3. Pending the re-integration of the national territory, and without prejudice to the right of the Parliament and Government established by the Constitution to exercise jurisdiction over the whole of that territory, the laws enacted by that Parliament shall have the like area and extent of application as the Saorstat Eireann [the Irish Free State] and the like extra-territorial effect.

Given the inbuilt sectarian contradictions in the North, discrimination by the Protestant majority against the Catholic minority became institutionalized. The gerrymander, the rigging of political boundaries, was the most blatant example of the principle in practice. Londonderry, or Derry as Nationalists called the city,[18] had the inverse of the province's population ratio. Here Catholics outnumbered Protestants by two to one. The Unionist answer, to maintain political supremacy in the city that was the symbol of Protestant resistance,[19] was to draw the boundaries so as to produce a majority of their own kind on Londonderry City Council. The result was that in the sixties, in a city where there were roughly 14 000 Catholic voters and 9000 Protestant voters, the local gerrymander produced a council with twelve Protestant councillors and eight Catholics. In Dungannon, County Tyrone, the pattern was much the same: 53 per cent of the voting population was Catholic, yet its council consisted of fourteen Protestants and seven Catholics. The franchise itself was distorted by a property qualification for local council elections throughout the province whereby, in order to vote, a citizen had to be a ratepayer, that is the owner or tenant of a property. This discriminated against Catholics who, in addition to being the minority population, were also the most socially and economically disadvantaged. The slogan of the subsequent civil rights movement, 'One man, one vote', was based on this anomaly. There was also undoubted discrimination in the allocation of local authority housing: the Unionist-controlled Fermanagh County Council, whose electorate was roughly equally divided between Protestants and Catholics, built over 1500 houses between the end of the war and 1969 and over two-thirds of them went to Protestants. But the principle of looking after one's own extended to Nationalist-controlled local authorities too: in Newry in the early sixties, there were 765 council houses of which only twenty-two were inhabited by Protestants.[20] On the same basis, there was widespread discrimination in employment, the most glaring example of which was the shipyard of Harland and Wolff, whose giant cranes rise above Protestant East Belfast: in a workforce of 10 000 only 400 were Catholics. In 1969, the Labour Government's famous report, chaired by Lord Cameron, into the cause of the civil conflict in Northern Ireland, concluded:

> The weight and the extent of the evidence which was presented to us concerned with social or economic grievances or abuses of political power was such that we are compelled to conclude that they had substantial foundation in fact and were in a very real sense an immediate and operative cause of the demonstrations and consequent disorders. . . .[21].

Such extensive discrimination, of which Nationalists too were in some cases guilty, was the inevitable consequence of the way in which the state had been created. The seeds of internal strife were sown at birth.

Under Harold Wilson's administration in the sixties, the problem of Northern Ireland continued to lie dormant, despite the efforts made by a group of 102 Labour backbenchers known as the Campaign for Democracy in Ulster to alert the government to the situation that they were convinced was about to explode on Britain's doorstep. One of its leaders, Paul Rose, was parliamentary private secretary to the Cabinet Minister, Barbara Castle. 'I remember her patting me on the head and saying, "Why is a young man like you concerned about Northern Ireland? What about Vietnam? What about Rhodesia?" I just looked at her with incomprehension and said, "You'll see when they start shooting one another." And she was totally oblivious to this. I think their priorities were focused on other things to the extent that they were totally blinded as to what was going on in their own backyard.'[22] Even the walls of Westminster were deaf. Since 1922 and the ruling of the then Speaker of the House, Mr J. H. Whitely, there had been a convention that questions relating to Northern Ireland could not be raised in the House of Commons. The province's matters were matters for the province's parliament. The result was that, before the outbreak of serious rioting in Derry in October 1968, the time spent on Northern Ireland matters at Westminster averaged less than two hours a year.

In 1967 Paul Rose and two other leading members of the Campaign for Democracy in Ulster, Dr Maurice Miller and Stanley Orme (who in 1974 became a Labour Northern Ireland Minister after the introduction of direct rule in 1972), visited Northern Ireland to investigate discrimination, electoral practice and unemployment. Their subsequent report described Unionist reaction to their visit as 'hostile and provocative': they were regarded as 'anti-Ulster' and 'interfering and unwelcome'. They submitted their damning report with its recommendations for a Royal Commission to the Home Secretary, Roy Jenkins. The recommendation was rejected.

Jenkins, who probably knew more about Ireland than anyone else in the Cabinet, told the House of Commons why he and his government were against intervention.

> Successive governments here have refused to take steps which would inevitably cut away not only the authority of the Northern Ireland government but also the constitution of the province ... there is a great deal to be said for not trying to settle the affairs of Northern Ireland too directly from London. Before this government was formed, I spent a good deal of my time studying and trying to write about 19th century and early 20th century history. No one can undertake detailed studies of that period of British history ... without being left with the conviction that, despite the many attributes of the English, a peculiar talent for solving the problems of Ireland is not among them. ... Fewer issues in the past have shown a greater capacity to divert and dissipate the reforming energy of left wing British governments than deep embroilment in Irish affairs.[23]

But there was apparent good reason for Labour's political lassitude. In 1963, Captain Terence O'Neill became the new Prime Minister of Northern Ireland: he was a patrician, laid-back liberal, at least compared with most of his predecessors. The Labour government, elected the following year, was relieved that the province seemed to be in good hands and, given time and gentle encouragement, reform would inevitably follow. The view from the Irish Republic was much the same. Dublin and Westminster both kept their fingers crossed that their hopes for a new dawn would materialize.

From the outset, Captain O'Neill was anathema to ultra-Loyalists epitomized by the young cleric, Dr Ian Paisley. Paisley and his supporters saw any word or hint of reform as a sign of treachery to be resisted at all costs. When O'Neill invited the Irish Prime Minister, Sean Lemass, to Belfast, Paisley took to the streets: inviting the enemy to sup at Ulster's table was committing the cardinal sin. The words 'O'Neill must go!' were emblazoned on Loyalist banners. And go O'Neill did. He resigned on 30 April 1969, pushed out by Unionist hardliners who believed he was soft on the enemy. The Protestant backlash was not a cliché. It was alive and marching and self-evidently capable of grinding the hopes of O'Neill and Downing Street to dust. To posterity, O'Neill's main achievement was to provide a glimpse of what might have been. The Labour Cabinet uttered a sigh of disappointment and hoped for the best once again.

Today Roy Jenkins, now Lord Jenkins, makes no apology (although he admits that with hindsight he might have acted slightly differently). 'I don't believe that anyone had a solution, any more than anyone's had since. I don't feel very guilty. Maybe one ought to have moved in, but I very much doubt if it would have done any good. The point is – and has been since 1886 onwards – that you cannot move in certain directions without incurring the intransigence of the majority, even if the narrow majority. I have a great lack of faith in the ability of any Englishman, or, in my case, Welshman, to impose solutions upon Ireland.'[24] Lord Callaghan, another Welshman who succeeded Roy Jenkins as Home Secretary in 1967, has much the same view. 'I never do believe, frankly, that anybody from this side of the water understands Ireland and I've never flattered myself that I understand the situation fully. I think very few people do. Certainly we didn't have enough understanding of it at that time.'[25] The political ignorance at the time was not surprising, given the status of Northern Ireland in the Home Secretary's dispatch box. 'When I asked for a list of the matters to deal with in the first week I became Home Secretary, Northern Ireland wasn't included in them. London taxi cabs were but not Northern Ireland.'[26]

The result of this inactivity on the part of the Labour Cabinet was the emergence of the civil rights movement, determined to force the reforms that the British government knew were necessary but was loath to compel Stormont to introduce. The point of no return was the march in Derry on 5 October 1968 when demonstrators were wantonly batoned by the police, undeterred by the fact that their charge was being recorded by television cameras in scenes that were soon to be paraded before a horrified world. One of the casualties was the then Westminster Republican Labour MP, Gerry Fitt, who made dramatic political capital out of the blood that ran from his head. Suddenly Westminster was finally forced to take notice of the demand for civil rights. The Cameron Report did not shrink from criticizing the police.

> The use of batons was probably unnecessary and in any event prema-
> ture, as the major part of the demonstrators were obeying their
> leaders' advice to disperse quietly. The baton charge was lacking in
> control and degenerated into a series of individual scuffles . . . some
> very damaging pictures of police violence were seen throughout the
> United Kingdom and abroad.[27]

In the following months, tension and violence increased even more as march followed march and law and order gradually broke down. Loyalists were determined that civil rights demonstrators should not gain control of the streets. In Derry, where the clashes were fiercest, barricades were erected in the Nationalist area beneath the ancient city walls known as the Bogside. 'Free Derry' was born. Here, the Queen's writ was deemed not to run and Citizens' Defence Committees took over the protection of the nationalist population within its perimeters. The Catholic community become increasingly alienated from the police and the stage was set for the emergence of the Provisional IRA.

Loyalists have always maintained that the civil rights movement was merely a front for the IRA, who infiltrated its ranks and manipulated its activities to undermine and destroy the state. But the reality is not as straightforward. There is no doubt that the IRA was deeply involved in civil rights, as Cathal Goulding readily admits: 'The Army Council of the IRA together with the Communist Party set up NICRA [the Northern Ireland Civil Rights Association].'[28] But this was part of the IRA's new strategy of creating a broad, popular front of workers, trade-unionists, Republicans, Nationalists[29] and activists of all political persuasions to challenge the Stormont regime and ultimately the Dublin government. The action was, however, to be purely political, since the tactic of 'armed struggle' had been firmly rejected. Loyalists remain unconvinced even by Lord Cameron's perceptive analysis of the IRA's involvement in civil rights.

> We have investigated this matter with particular care in view of the extent to which it is surmised that the IRA had become a prominent or even dominant factor in shaping or directing policy of the Civil Rights Association. There is ample evidence that in most of the larger demonstrations promoted by the Civil Rights Association identified members of the IRA have taken part as marchers or stewards. In point of fact, it has been noticeable that as stewards they were efficient and exercised a high degree of discipline on marchers or demonstrators. There is no evidence – and had there been we have no doubt that the vigilance of the RUC would have observed and prevented it – that such members themselves either incited to riot or took part themselves in acts of violence. Here no doubt they were acting in accordance with the well known current policy of the IRA itself . . . there is no sign that they [the IRA] are in any sense dominant or in a position to control or direct policy of the Civil Rights Association.[30]

There is no doubt, even with the benefits of hindsight, that the civil rights movement and all that flowed from it was the direct result of the Labour government's failure to heed the warnings and intervene in a way that would have rectified the legitimate grievances of the Catholic minority. Had it done so – and it would have required considerable political courage to stand the convention of nearly half a century on its head – events would almost certainly have taken a different course, provided, of course, that Westminster had been prepared to face up to violent Loyalist resistance to reform. Even as late as 1967, a poll showed that two-thirds of Northern

Ireland's Catholic minority approved of the existing constitutional status of the province as part of the United Kingdom.[31] Civil rights, not the border, was the issue.

If blame is to be apportioned for the 'state of terror' that has now existed in Northern Ireland for nearly a quarter of a century, it must be shared between Westminster, Stormont and Dublin. Westminster contributed to the strife through its inaction and indifference; Stormont through its blindness and bigotry; and Dublin through its interference in the internecine politics of the IRA. Throughout the turbulent months of 1969, each community in Northern Ireland lived with its own anxiety. Unionists feared that the growing militancy of the civil rights movement, which they saw as simply a cloak for the IRA, threatened the constitutional position of Northern Ireland within the United Kingdom. Nationalists feared that they would become victims of a Loyalist pogrom, left undefended by a police force which experience told them was both Protestant and partial. Memories of the onslaught against Catholics in Belfast during the birth pangs of the Northern Ireland state were still a powerful part of oral tradition: between 1920 and 1922, 23 000 Catholics were driven out of their homes and over 500 Catholic-owned shops and businesses were set alight and destroyed.[32] Nationalists were convinced that history was about to repeat itself.

Traditionally, the role of the IRA in Belfast had been to defend Nationalist enclaves from such Protestant attack; but the takeover of the organization by Marxists and communists in the early sixties meant that such a role was no longer politically correct. To the new leadership, the ideal of Republicanism was the alliance of Catholic, Protestant and Dissenter in the face of the enemy: that enemy was England, not Protestant fellow Irishmen. For Cathal Goulding and his comrades, defending Catholics from Protestant attack was a sectarian act that was a denial of the true meaning of Irish Republicanism. During the IRA's border campaign of 1956–62, orders had been given to remove arms from Belfast to avoid the danger of sectarian conflict.[33] According to Goulding's utopian analysis, Protestants would have the scales stripped from their eyes, see the error of their ways and be recruited as allies in the class struggle. That was the theory that drove the IRA through the sixties. The main reason why the IRA failed to defend Catholics in Belfast in August 1969 was not only because it *could* not but because such an action would have been contrary to principle. The crucial fact is generally overlooked.

That was the view from IRA headquarters in Dublin. The men on the ground in Belfast, however, saw it differently. As the threat of Loyalist attack became ever more imminent as the summer of 1969 drew on, anxious voices within the Belfast IRA warned the leadership in Dublin of the need to prepare for defensive action. They were not crying wolf. At the beginning of August, Lord Scarman, whose equally impressive report on the disturbances took over where Lord Cameron's left off, recorded serious rioting and the threat of 'invasion' by Protestants at the bottom of the Shankill Road where Loyalist 'territory' meets the Catholic Unity Flats. Lord Scarman's observations also give the lie to the general perceptions that all RUC men were sectarian bigots.

> In the course of these riots, the Protestant mobs made a determined attempt to invade Unity Flats and also appeared in force on the Crumlin Road. They were successfully resisted by the sustained efforts of the police, who incurred the anger of some sections of Protestant opinion by their baton charges up the Shankill Road.[34]

This was but one of many such recorded incidents at the time. As the temperature rose, Goulding came under increasing pressure from some of his men in Belfast. 'We had a dump under what we called General Head-quarters[35] control amounting to a couple of hand-guns, about fifteen sub-machine-guns and some rifles, mainly .303s, plus a few American carbines. That was the entire armament that we had. Now the Belfast lads were saying to me, "You want to give us more guns. There's going to be trouble." And I said, "There's not going to be that kind of trouble".' Nevertheless, Goulding had to pacify his increasingly restless troops on the ground. 'People said, "Send up arms." I said, "I've only got one cache." So I sent a circular to units around the country and asked them to make whatever arms they had available for defence in Belfast. Cork, for example, listed three rifles, about six revolvers and a couple of Sten guns. But I really didn't want guns up there. I wanted people doing the right thing.'[36] However strong Goulding's faith in his men's ability to do 'the right thing' and remove the sectarian scales from Loyalist eyes, the time for dreaming was over. Weapons were what Belfast wanted, not political lectures. But few weapons arrived, with the result that when the North exploded in August 1969 the IRA was left naked without arms and credibility.

Events moved at alarming speed, triggered by the determination of Protestants to carry on with their traditional summer marches to show they were not intimidated. To Catholics, these parades, which had always been an assertion of Protestant supremacy, were a gauntlet across the face. Pressure grew to ban the Apprentice Boys' annual parade in Derry, due to be held on 12 August, since it was bound to provoke the Catholic majority in the city and in particular those who lived in the Bogside. Harold Wilson was minded to heed the warnings and intervene over Stormont's head, but, as he remarked in his memoirs, 'unwiser counsels' prevailed.[37] Those counsels are thought to have been those of the Home Secretary, James

Callaghan, who later made no apology. 'I don't like banning marches. I allowed the great march on Vietnam to go ahead. I'm a libertarian in these matters. I don't remember whether the Apprentice Boys' march was intended to go through areas that would have provoked the Catholics, but, if so, I think I would have taken – I certainly ought to have taken – a different view. I think at the beginning we were living from day to day. That is to say we responded in an emergency with an emergency action, namely to put the troops in. I said publicly at the time that I hoped they would be out as soon as order was restored but I'm on record as having said that I'd thought it would take at least ten years. I said that literally within days or weeks of them going in. I said ten years. It's been twenty.'[38]

The Apprentice Boys' march did not pass through Catholic areas but came perilously close to them. Youths from the Bogside threw stones, and the predicted confrontation erupted. The legendary 'Battle of the Bogside', in which stones and petrol bombs from the Catholics were met with CS gas from the police, was a turning-point in Irish history. The police, exhausted and depleted, could not hold out and British troops were moved in on 14 August 1969. It was a fateful political decision whose consequences were never envisaged at the time. The ramifications of direct military intervention had been discussed at Cabinet level with the Stormont government over the preceding weeks, and Britain had warned that such a step would have serious constitutional implications. But, in the event, Britain did not carry out her veiled threat to introduce direct rule, or at least some delimitation of Stormont's powers, and the army was deployed unconditionally. Not that the labour Cabinet displayed any great enthusiasm for the move. 'I don't think anybody wanted to send the troops in. That was the last thing we wanted to do,' reflects Lord Callaghan. 'We held off until the last possible moment until we were being begged by the Catholics in Northern Ireland to do so. What an irony of history that it was they who begged us to send the troops in. And I can understand why. Their lives were in danger and we had to respond to that, especially as the police seemed to be exhausted and quite incapable of controlling the situation.'[39]

Direct rule from Westminster stayed on the back burner for another two years. Many of those involved in civil rights believed at the time that Westminster's refusal to grasp the nettle and take over the running of the province when troops were deployed was a fatal mistake. Hindsight makes them even more convinced that they were right. 'The British government made its major mistake at that time,' argues the veteran civil rights leader, Austin Currie.

When the British government was forced to send in the troops, that was the time that Stormont should have been suspended. It was clear to me and was clear to anybody who had any political savvy that the British government couldn't commit the British army without committing itself politically as well. There was no way that the British government could commit British soldiers and leave the political control entirely in Northern Ireland, and it should have taken that extra step and said, 'Law and order has broken down. That's the reason we've had to commit British troops in the first instance. Let's recognize that reality and suspend Stormont as well.' Had that happened in 1969, then I believe that a lot of the trouble and a lot of the deaths that occurred after that would have been avoided because you had the initial stage where the pretence was kept that Stormont was still in control.[40]

But Labour Cabinet ministers of the time still stand by their decision to leave Stormont untouched. Lord Callaghan maintains: 'You have to do things as they become politically possible. Not only would it have been impossible at that time to have abandoned Stormont because public opinion wouldn't have been ready for it, but we would not have been in a position to handle the situation.'[41]

Within twenty-four hours, troops were also on the streets of Belfast after savage rioting was provoked by Catholics in order to take some of the pressure off people in the Bogside. There were a few shots from the Catholic side, presumably from the small number of guns the IRA had been able to muster. Lord Scarman described the RUC's response:

The police, who believed by now that they were facing an armed uprising, used guns, including Browning machine guns mounted on Shorland armoured vehicles. Four Catholics were shot dead by police fire: one Protestant was killed by a shot fired by a rioter in Divis Street. Catholic houses were burnt by Protestants.[42]

Belfast, or at least the western part of the city, was ablaze.

At the height of the rioting the Irish Prime Minister, Jack Lynch, went on television and made a provocative speech.

The Stormont Government is evidently no longer in control of the situation. . . . The Government of Ireland can no longer stand by. . . . The Government of Ireland has requested the British Government to apply to the United nations for urgent dispatch of a peace-keeping force to the Six Counties. . . . Many injured do not want to be treated in Six County hospitals, so Irish Army authorities have been instructed to establish field hospitals in Donegal and other points on the border.[43]

Tradition has long had it that Jack Lynch used the phrase 'the Irish Government can no longer stand *idly* by', but history records that he did not use the word, 'idly', however regrettable the loss.[44] His words were greeted with a mixture of consternation, rejoicing and amusement. To Loyalists, it was confirmation of what they had always feared: that, given the slightest opportunity, Dublin would try to get its hands on the North. To Nationalists, it was a trumpet call indicating that the Irish Fifth Cavalry was at hand. To the British government, it was a sign that Jack Lynch had gone over the top. 'Everybody was in a very jumpy state,' Lord Callaghan explained.

> I was on holiday and the Home Office rang me up late one night after he'd made this speech and said, 'We think you ought to come back. We don't know what Prime Minister Lynch is going to do.' Well, I knew Jack Lynch as a very sensible Minister of Finance when I'd been Chancellor of the Exchequer before, and it seemed to me to be out of character with that rather reserved and self-controlled personality that I knew. But the situation was such in Northern Ireland – we hadn't experienced anything like it for years – that I thought I'd better go back to the Home Office. I went up that night and we said, 'What on earth is Jack Lynch thinking about? He can't really mean he's going to invade Northern Ireland. He couldn't be so stupid.' And of course he wasn't. He backed off. I think he made that speech in order to quieten public opinion in the South initially and perhaps to alert us to the strong feelings there about what was happening in the North, which was of course directed at us as to why we weren't protecting the Catholic population.[45]

Lynch was under great pressure at home, not least from the more staunchly Republican members of his Cabinet – the most prominent of these being the Minister for Finance, Charles Haughey; the Minister for Local Government, Kevin Boland; and the Minister for Agriculture, Neil Blaney. These men were to play a key role in subsequent events. To them, the crisis in the North presented the opportunity to complete the unfinished business of 1921. I asked Neil Blaney to explain his thinking at the time.

> It was my convinced view that really this was the final break-up of the entity that is Northern Ireland and therefore would have brought about the situation wherein we could have ended the division of the country and I think that we missed opportunities.
> *What did you want the Irish army to do?*

To go into the Bogside. To go into Derry. To go straight off into the west bank of the Foyle where the thing had really caught fire on the night of 12–13 August.

An invasion?

No. Protective.

But it's a foreign army entering British soil, isn't it?

I'd have looked on it as the home army entering home territory. I remember arguing at a meeting that we had the same right to protect any citizen of the Six Counties as we would have had if it had happened in Cork. I mentioned Cork deliberately because Jack Lynch came from Cork.[46]

On the face of it, such sentiments were not only a Republican dagger pointed at the Loyalist heart but a direct challenge to the IRA, which had wiped Irish unity, and the use of force to achieve it, off its agenda. More traditional Republicans in Belfast like Joe Cahill and the veteran Jimmy Steele, who had dared express his disquiet at the reburial of Barnes and McCormack the previous month, saw the ground being cut from under them. They felt that the IRA, not ministers in Jack Lynch's Cabinet, should be raising the national question and offering military assistance to the beleaguered Catholics in the North. Cahill and Steele knew that the IRA had been humiliated and felt the consequences each day on the streets. 'Walking down the road with Jimmy,' Cahill recalls, 'we were met by a group of people who actually spat on us. And they used what was to become a very familiar term at the time – and it was very, very insulting. They said, "IRA – I Ran Away." That was the reaction of the people to the IRA at the time. When I reported back to the IRA in August '69, one of the first tasks I was given was to organize a defence group in Ballymurphy. When I went into Ballymurphy, I was told to get out. I wasn't wanted. I was a member of the IRA. The IRA had deserted them. They didn't want us. "Get out!" they said.'[47] Sean MacStiofain, who was to become the Provisional IRA's first Chief of Staff, had a similar experience. Unlike Cahill, he had remained loyal to his old comrade, Cathal Goulding. 'I went up to Belfast shortly after the pogroms in August and I was told that I was the only one from "down there" who was acceptable "up here". I tried to reason with them and I suppose I tried to make excuses for them. I was hoping against hope that the events of '69 would restore some sanity in the Republican movement and perhaps persuade Goulding and others that their policies were wrong and that we could remain united and face the future together. But things didn't work out that way.'[48]

Meanwhile, the Dublin government was in the process of taking more active steps. The extent to which the whole of Jack Lynch's Cabinet were aware of what was afoot remains unclear, since Mr Lynch himself has never been prepared to elucidate. I did write to him to discover whether he was prepared to discuss his recollections of the period, but the answer was no. Charles Haughey also declined a similar request. It would be astonishing if the Cabinet did not at least know the broad thrust of what was being done, although ministers who sat around the table may have been spared a few of the more controversial details. What drove the Fianna Fail government to act and make contingency plans was fear of the so-called 'Doomsday' situation in which law and order in the North would completely break down and Nationalists would be left undefended and exposed. In the charged atmosphere of those months between the summer of 1969 and the spring of 1970, such concerns were firmly rooted in reality, not Republican fantasy, as Kevin Boland, the Minister for Local Government, was well aware.

> We had to be prepared to give whatever assistance we could, whether it be effective or not, in the event of an all-out onslaught on the ghetto areas and isolated rural pockets taking place. Everybody believed it was only a matter of time until it happened. Eventually the Minister of Defence was instructed to consult with the army authorities and report back on what could be done. When he did, he said that the army had neither the military nor the financial capacity to give any worthwhile assistance. I think Mr Lynch thought: Well, that's that finished; we can't do anything to help. But a few of us kept up the pressure that we must do it, whether it was effective or not. Eventually, the decision was taken at a full Cabinet meeting that authority would be delegated to the Minister for Finance, Charles Haughey, and the Minister for Defence, Jim Gibbons, to provide whatever assistance could be provided in these expected circumstances.[49]

Whether Mr Blaney and others acted as they did with the knowledge of Mr Lynch is a question that only he and history can answer when key Cabinet papers are made available. But there is little doubt that ministers did know about one of the first actions the government took in response to the immediate crisis in the North: the organization of military training for volunteers from Derry at Fort Dunree, a historical military monument across the border in Donegal. It was undertaken by the Irish army, obviously in the greatest secrecy. 'It was decided to give basic training to groups of individuals in what they call "military street fighting",' recalls Kevin Boland. 'Whether that was discussed at Cabinet level, I don't know. I think it probably wasn't. But it was done with the knowledge, I would say, of the whole government.'[50]

Clandestine training in urban guerrilla warfare – for that is what it amounted to – had to be planned with great care, and the person chosen to organize it had to be selected with equal precision. The man deemed to combine all the required skills of discretion, enterprise and cunning was one Captain James J. Kelly of Irish military intelligence. Four years earlier, Captain Kelly had served with distinction in the United Nations Truce Supervision Organization in Palestine. His Chief of Staff wrote of him:

> Captain Kelly performed his duties in an excellent manner. He is a sincere, warm and friendly officer, well-liked and respected by his associates. He possesses a sharp wit and astute intelligence. He is a clear, logical thinker, cool and unruffled in emergencies. He plans ahead, weighs the consequences and implications of events and actions, arrives at sound conclusions, and takes timely, decisive and appropriate action.[51]

With such a curriculum vitae, Captain Kelly seemed to have the perfect credentials. He also came with the added advantage of having some first-hand knowledge of the North, an attribute notably lacking in most of those who sat around the Cabinet table. Captain Kelly became Dublin's 'Mr Fixit' and the key figure in the bizarre and controversial events that followed. Initially ten volunteers made the journey from Derry to Fort Dunree to learn how to handle guns under the instruction of the Irish army. I pointed out to Captain Kelly that he would not have had many cadres with ten people. He responded to the observation wide-eyed, as I had clearly misunderstood the scale of the operation. 'The point is that the plan was to carry on for weeks. You could have ended up, for example, with say ten multiplied by twenty and then you would have had two hundred people who could have trained other people. You could have had twenty from Derry, thirty from Belfast, ten from Lurgan and so on.' I then observed that, once the recruits in 'military street fighting' returned to the North, they would have had nothing to fight with. He looked at me again, eager that light should dawn. 'Well, the guns were supposed to be there in this "Doomsday" situation – the Irish government was going to supply the guns.'[52] However incredible it may seem, that is what the plan was. The training, however, was brought to an abrupt end when the press got wind of the first ten recruits. There was political panic and the training was hastily scuttled. But, crucially, the plans to supply weapons went ahead.

The original request for guns had been made to the Dublin government by Republican Stormont MPs who journeyed south in the wake of the Loyalist onslaught on the night of 15 August 1969 on the Nationalist areas of West Belfast. The sight of whole streets on fire, torched by rampaging Protestant mobs, and of Catholic families loading their cherished possessions on to anything on wheels, convinced both victims and horrified

spectators that the long-awaited Loyalist 'pogrom' had begun. Lord Scarman observed, 'these eruptions . . . may with some justice be described as
"invasions" – given the ghetto pattern of much of Belfast.'[53] The fact that
the RUC was unable or unwilling to stop the devastation seemed further
evidence that Nationalists would have to defend themselves.

Paddy Kennedy was one of the Stormont MPs who went knocking on the
most important doors of Dublin. 'I met with Mr Lynch, Mr Blaney and Mr
Boland. Mr Lynch, I think, was reluctant to accede to this request for guns.
It's all very well looking at these events from hindsight but he could
appreciate the request. I think he also saw the dangers of providing guns
just to ordinary citizens. He felt that once he had parted with guns he didn't
know where they would finish up or how they would finish up. Mr Blaney
was greatly concerned at what was happening and he was anxious to
provide whatever help he could. He felt that perhaps guns would be
necessary to come into Belfast.' Kennedy said that he had seen Mr
Haughey much later and told him, too, that Nationalists wanted guns.
'There was no secret about what we were asking. We were in fact looking
for firearms to defend the Catholic areas.'[54]

IRA men also made the journey to Dublin and passed through some of
the same ministerial doors. Jim Sullivan, adjutant of the IRA's Belfast
Brigade, explained that arms were being sought for limited use. 'I pointed
out that at no time would any weapons be used for an attack on any group of
people in the North. They'd only be used in their defence.'[55] Those whom
Sullivan met in Dublin had no doubt who Sullivan was. When I interviewed
him in the autumn of 1992 off the Falls Road in Belfast, he was clearly
ailing. The following day he died. His recollections therefore must be
assessed with that in mind. He told me that on one visit to Dublin he was
offered several hundred rifles which had once belonged to the Irish Territorial Army. Certainly this fits with the facts. When the Territorials were
re-equipped with more modern weapons, the old rifles were offered for sale
on the open market. They appear to have been withdrawn, however, when
it came to light that one client was a cover for Loyalist paramilitaries. The
government stockpiled the guns lest they ever be needed to meet such an
emergency in the North. Besides being the IRA adjutant in Belfast, Sullivan was also chairman of the Citizens' Defence Committees (CDCs) in the
North, local organizations which had been established to do precisely what
their name indicated. These were to be the units through which Dublin was
to channel arms and money to the North. It was axiomatic that the Defence
Committees were dominated by the IRA. 'They were, by and large, the
same organization,' explained John Kelly, who was to become a leading
figure in the early Provisional IRA. 'Remember that the only people who
had any knowledge of arms were the IRA. There were no other people in

Belfast on the Nationalist side who had a knowledge of guns and how to use them. So, naturally, they were the people who were looked to at this period for defence purposes.'[56] The IRA's close involvement with the Citizens' Defence Committees was confirmed by Lord Scarman, who stated, 'undoubtedly there was an IRA influence at work in the Derry Citizens Defence Association in Londonderry, in the Ardoyne and Falls Road areas of Belfast, and in Newry.'[57]

There were, indeed, anxieties at Irish government level, as Paddy Kennedy indicated, about the hands into which any arms would fall and the use to which they would be put if consignments were sent to the North. Although the Goulding IRA was little more than a Marxist thorn in the Dublin government's side and was certainly no military threat, there was a disinclination on the part of ministers to provide weapons to an organization that was politically hostile to the supplier. From the beginning, such a fact was blindingly obvious to Captain Kelly, who recognized there was a problem:

> Certainly we discussed the possibility of people in the North support-ing any Dublin government effort. If, for example, the Dublin government decided to cross the border – and there were some elements in Cabinet from as early as August '69 talking about that – they would be interested to know if there were people in the North who would support them in their efforts. The IRA had a curious attitude at that stage. They wanted to overthrow both right-wing governments – North and South. I remember discussing it with some people at the end of 1969 and they were talking about a 'pre-revol-utionary situation' where you'd have numbers of people killed which would provide the opportunity for a proper revolution so they could overthrow and eliminate both governments. So, if you have people talking in that way, it was very difficult to see them getting money handed over to them from a Government they were going to overthrow.[58]

It does not follow, however, as those who subsequently became the 'Official' IRA argued at the time and have argued since, that the tactics of the Dublin government were premeditated: to split the IRA and establish a non-Marxist armed wing, the 'Provisionals', who would be ideologically more sympathetic to Fianna Fail and with whom the ancestors of the 'Soldiers of Destiny' could do business. The fact that this happened does not mean that the Machiavellian fingers of Fianna Fail were pulling the Provisionals' strings. There were powerful ideological differences behind the now imminent split.

Dublin first had to check out the likely recipients of its munificence to make sure not only that they were willing but that they were the right people. Towards the end of August 1969 Neil Blaney made the first contact via a Northern intermediary with a man who was, at that time, a Northern IRA commander. His name was Francie Donnelly.[59] The meeting took place along the shores of Malin Head in County Donegal. Blaney was in a rowing boat at the time enjoying the warmth and sunshine of a late summer's day. He came ashore and sat down on the beach to talk with Donnelly. Much of what he said appears to have been in code, but neither party had any doubt about what was potentially on offer. They chatted for half an hour or more, discussing the Northern situation in general and finally getting round to the point of the meeting. Given the passage of time, recollections of the conversation were somewhat imprecise when I interviewed both Neil Blaney and Francie Donnelly about their encounter. This is what Donnelly recalled:

> Blaney was making enquiries about whether people would be prepared for the defence of the population if weapons were available for them. He wanted to know what amount of weapons would be needed, and that sort of thing, without possibly seriously committing himself to saying that they *were* available, you know.
> *Did he indicate that weapons would be available?*
> Aye, I think he made some indication of that, you know, that weapons would be available under certain given situations. But he didn't quantify that or say what the situation might be. Obviously he was thinking that if there was any serious increase in violence from the Protestant or the Unionist population that would be a time where there'd have to be some intervention.

I then put Donnelly's account to Neil Blaney, who sat relaxed in his native Donegal, sucking on his pipe. He is adept at distracting his interlocutor, brushing away the awkward question with the strike of a match or a cloud of smoke. Compared with some of Mr Blaney's initial utterances, the Delphic Oracle was a model of clarity.

> Well, I wouldn't quite agree with that. But the thrust of it, yes, I would, without being able to remember the detail of any conversation I had with anybody. It was my view that, since we, as a government through our army, were not prepared to provide protection for the people up there, then anything, including the procurement of arms for people to defend themselves, was on as far as I was concerned.
> *You were prepared to assist with that as far as you could?*
> Absolutely. Quite. And what I might add, as well, there was a great

deal more people then who had the very same view. In fact I know very few who didn't have that view, who would now deny that they ever even thought of it.

Did you offer guns and money?

Money rather than guns because we didn't have them.[60]

At the time, this was true. Blaney's first approach to Donnelly was merely an exploratory exercise. Towards the end of September, a follow-up call was made, this time by Captain Kelly, whom Donnelly had never met before. He was working on his farm and was surprised to find an officer from Irish military intelligence turning up on his doorstep. Again, recollections of this conversation are not as precise as history would like and I reproduce what the two men told me. This meeting is important because, for the first time, it appears that there was talk of the Northern members of the IRA splitting from the Goulding leadership in Dublin and setting up a separate Northern Command. In the light of what subsequently happened when the IRA split, this meeting is obviously highly controversial. Critics would argue that Donnelly's recollection is self-serving because his wing of the IRA, the 'Officials', lost out when the split came. It is easy to blame your enemies for history. This is Donnelly's recollection of the encounter.

There was a long, again general, discussion on the Northern situation – what could happen or might happen. There were a few interesting questions about how Fianna Fail would be accepted if the party were to set up branches in the North. Captain Kelly was very adamant – very inquisitive – about what the position was with regard to weapons. He wanted to know whether we had arms or not – and if any were likely to be forthcoming. He then went on to ask about a Northern Command structure – I'm not exactly sure if those were his words but that's what it amounted to.

What did he mean by 'a Northern Command structure'?

I think he was implying there was too much control from headquarters in Dublin and that it would be better if people in the North who knew the situation better would be willing to procure the necessary equipment for defence.

Breaking from Dublin? Separate from Dublin?

Well, I think that's what it implied, you know. That's what he was more or less saying.

Captain Kelly was asking you to do a lot for him. What was he offering you in return?

Well, again, Kelly wasn't being very definite about what he was

offering. There were promises that, should the situation arise and should there be a Northern Command, supplies would probably go direct to the North.
Supplies of . . .?
Of weapons, possibly, and money. It would come directly rather than go through the then headquarters, the GHQ staff at that time. It was that sort of generalization, you know, but it'd be hard to pin down any particular thing.
Did Captain Kelly say, 'If you do this we will provide you with guns'?
Not directly, no. But the implication was there, as usual, that that's what they would be doing. That would be the trend if we had a Northern Command.
Is your analysis the analysis of hindsight?
No. No. I wouldn't be giving it if it was.

When I put Donnelly's recollections to Captain Kelly, he was as meticulously circumspect as Neil Blaney had been about his original meeting with Donnelly on the seashore at Malin Head.

I more or less tested out his feelings on Fianna Fail, although I wasn't interested in Fianna Fail, strangely enough. I was an army officer working for the government, and the government happened to be Fianna Fail.
Did you say to him if you want support from the Irish government then you would have to detach yourself from your leadership in Dublin?
Well, if this leadership, as I defined it, was seeking to overthrow the Dublin government he would, *ipso facto*, have to state that he didn't support that policy. Let's put it that way.
If he was going to get support?
Well, the point is I could not in conscience go back and say to my superiors, 'You must support Francie Donnelly in Derry because this fella is a member of an organization that wants to overthrow you'! It's an unreal situation.
Were you testing out how flexible Francie Donnelly might be?
I suppose you could put it that way.
Did you mention to Francie Donnelly the possibility of breaking with the Dublin leadership and possibly setting up a separate Northern Command?
Well, I don't think I would ask Francie Donnelly himself about a Northern Command – it's not terminology I would use – but there were people in the North talking about it at that stage and I'm sure it came into the conversation possibly. It would be logical.[61]

By coincidence, on the day that Captain Kelly paid his unexpected visit to Francie Donnelly, 22 September 1969, IRA dissidents in Belfast, whose disaffection had been growing ever since the humiliation of August, attempted a coup against the existing Goulding IRA leadership in Belfast. They had planned the move a month earlier on 24 August at a secret meeting held in the social club in Andersontown's Casement Park.[62] Among those reported to have been present were those who became the nucleus of the Provisional IRA leadership. They included Jimmy Steele, whose claim to fame was not only his speech at the reburial of Barnes and McCormack but the fact that he had spent longer in prison than any other IRA man in Belfast; Seamus Twoomey, who rejoined the IRA in 1969 and went on to become commander of the Provisionals' Belfast Brigade and subsequently Chief of Staff; Leo Martin, who became the Provisionals' first Officer Commanding (OC) the Six Counties; the young Gerry Adams, who, after gaol in the early to mid-seventies, became Sinn Fein's first Westminster MP; John Kelly, who was at that time one of the vital links between Dublin Cabinet ministers and the IRA; Billy McKee, who became the Provisionals' first Belfast Commander and front-line figure in the Provisional IRA's initial engagement in Belfast;[63] Jimmy Drumm, who became a prominent member of the Sinn Fein Executive (Ard Chomhairle) and whose wife, Maire, was assassinated in hospital in 1976 by Loyalist gunmen dressed as doctors; and, from Dublin, David O'Connell (Daithi O'Conaill), who had been an IRA hero in the 1956–62 border campaign and who is thought, perhaps erroneously, to have succeeded Sean MacStiofain as the Provisionals' Chief of Staff. Also present was Joe Cahill, who for so long had been a vociferous critic of the Goulding leadership in Dublin and who was the Provisional's Belfast Commander when internment without trial was introduced in August 1971.

The meeting decided that an ultimatum would be issued to Billy McMillen, the IRA's OC in Belfast, and his adjutant, Jim Sullivan: unless Cathal Goulding and three of his named senior colleagues on the IRA's General Headquarters Staff resigned, the dissidents would take over and Belfast would go it alone. Fourteen of the IRA's seventeen areas in the city voted to support the proposal. As Joe Cahill reflected, McMillen and Sullivan 'didn't have a lot of choice because the vast majority of IRA volunteers in Belfast were prepared to break with Dublin'.[64]

On 22 September 1969 Joe Cahill and seven others presented the ultimatum to McMillen and Sullivan, who were holding a meeting in Cyprus Street. Cahill remembers that Sullivan went off at the deep end. 'Jim was fairly hot about it and wanted to know what the hell was going on. It was stronger language than that actually. He shook people's shoulders and demanded to know who was behind what he called "a mutiny". I suppose

voking a shoot-out, stung by a
ded was a group of 'pansies'.
llivan remembered the scene
whether we're a 'pansy' group
t McMillen intervened and told
groups sit down and talk. He was
A violent exchange was avoided
ations were demanded, McMillen
dissidents were to be drafted on to
rved on the Dublin leadership that
rned out to be fewer than sixty. In

he Dublin government had not been
pounds were being channelled to the
North, a good   n the hands of the IRA, although this
may not have been the inten   he Taoiseach and every member of his
Cabinet. Some would argue that, once the money reached the North, the
government had no control over its use and its application to 'the Relief of
Distress', the purpose for which it was sent. Government money was also
used by Captain Kelly to buy guns on the Continent. These controversial
and complex financial transfers were authorized at ministerial level. The
process started at a Cabinet meeting on 16 August 1969, the day after the
Loyalist 'pogrom' in Belfast. The Dail Public Accounts Committee, which
investigated these transactions and whose remarkable report is vital in
unravelling this tangled financial web, notes it was decided that 'a sum of
money – the amount and the channel of the disbursement of which would be
decided by the Minister of Finance [Charles Haughey] – should be made
available from the Exchequer to provide aid for the victims of the current
unrest in the Six Counties.'[66] Overall, between 20 August 1969 and 24
March 1970, the sum of £100 000 was paid out of public money as Grant in
Aid for the Relief of Distress in the North. These payments grew from
relatively small beginnings, each one, as the Public Accounts Committee
subsequently reported, 'individually authorized either in writing or orally
both as to the amount and payee by the then Minister for Finance, Deputy
Charles J. Haughey, personally'.[67]

The government made no secret of the fact that these funds were to be
administered by the Irish Red Cross Society, but as the Society could not
operate in the North without the permission of its British equivalent, a
permission that was not forthcoming, other ways had to be found of getting
the money into the areas where it was needed. In one instance, the mechanism was quite straightforward. A body known as the Belfast Refugee

Re-Establishment committee approached Mr Haughey for help, and on his direction £20 000 was paid on 9 October 1969 to the Irish Red Cross Society, which then transferred the money to the committee's account in the Munster and Leinster Bank in Belfast. The account subsequently contained details of every transaction.[68] But other financial transactions were not quite as simple. The same month, Mr Haughey suggested that the Irish Red Cross should transfer £5000 of its own funds to an account to be opened as 'The Belfast Fund for the Relief of Distress' at the Bank of Ireland in the border town of Clones. Mr Haughey then instructed an official in the Department of Finance to pay £10 000 to the Red Cross on the understanding it would be paid into the newly opened account at Clones. The names of three prominent Northern Ireland citizens, two of whom were Stormont Republican MPs, were attached, mysteriously listed in the Public Accounts Committee reports as Messrs F, G and H. These three anonymous individuals were authorized to draw money from the account.

On 10 November 1969, £2500 in cash was drawn and used four days later to open another mysterious account at the Munster and Leinster Bank in Lower Baggot Street, Dublin, under the pseudonym 'Ann O'Brien'. That same day another £4450 from Clones was used as a deposit at the same branch to open a second account under another fictitious name, 'George Dixon'.[69] A third account, 'Relief Committee for the Relief of Distress', had already been put in place a few days earlier, allegedly by Captain Kelly, although he denies responsibility. This became the main working account, with Captain Kelly acting as the intermediary between it and the three individuals authorized to make withdrawals under the pseudonyms 'John White', 'John Loughran' and 'Roger Murphy'. The account was topped up whenever Captain Kelly informed the Department of Finance that specific sums were required. Again, the transfer of these funds was approved by Mr Haughey.[70] Again, they were moved via the Irish Red Cross. Between 12 November 1969 and 9 April 1970, £59 000 of government money was transferred by this route,[71] over £40 000 of it after the IRA had split. The change in the location of the account, from Clones to Dublin, was later explained as 'convenience': it was closer to the paymaster. All these sums were to be used for 'the Relief of Distress' but the Public Accounts Committee, which saw the books, and was horrified at what they revealed, could only tie down the payment of £20 000 to the Belfast Refugee Re-Establishment Committee and £9000 to the signatories to the accounts as sums of money that were used for the purpose for which the payments were intended.[72] The Public Accounts Committee set out its task: to trace what happened to the remaining £76 000 of government money made up chiefly of the following.[73]

Clones account	£8000
Baggot Street main account	£23 150
George Dixon account	£38 249
Ann O'Brien account	£6450

The money which was first investigated was the £31 150 from the Clones and Baggot Street accounts. The committee established that in the twenty-nine weeks between 10 October 1969, the day after the opening of the Clones account, and 28 April 1970, the day of the last withdrawal from Baggot Street, there was a series of twenty withdrawals at, roughly, weekly intervals. There was one gap of seven weeks, which is suspected to have followed the split within the IRA. The committee reached the following disturbing conclusion:

> evidence from other sources concerned with relief in Belfast provided no confirmation of the existence of a relief operation on the scale suggested. Moreover, the destruction of documents has resulted in no corroborative documentary evidence being available to the Committee that this sum of £31 150 was in fact used for the relief of distress.[74]

What, then, was the money used for, and in whose hands did it end up? Paddy Kennedy, the Stormont Republican MP, provided, rather uncomfortably, some insight into how the money was drawn from the Clones and Baggot Street accounts.

> I'm led to believe that individuals came South and collected the money and actually brought it North and distributed it to representatives of the Defence Committees.
> *In cash?*
> In cash.
> *Do you know who those representatives were?*
> Well, I ... I have an idea and certainly certain names have been mentioned but I would prefer not to discuss them.
> *Were you one of them?*
> I would have to answer taking into account the recent Supreme Court decision here in Dublin where Cabinet confidentiality has been confirmed. I don't feel that I'm free to confirm or deny that I was in any way involved.
> *But you know how the money was drawn and distributed?*
> As I say, I have an idea.
> *Was it carried in cash across the border and distributed?*
> Well, I'm led to believe that it was, yes.[75]

One of those to whom the cash was handed over and who did the carrying and distribution was John Kelly, one of the IRA dissidents from Belfast who attended the meeting at which the coup against the leadership in the city was planned. Kelly subsequently became a leading Provisional. He explained that most of the money went to pay the men manning the barricades, at roughly £30–50 a head.

> People at that time couldn't draw the dole who were on the dole because of the situation that existed in Belfast. They had no other means of keeping bread on the table other than getting moneys in that manner.
> *What lump sums of money did you receive to distribute?*
> *You'd be talking in terms of £1000–1500.*
> *How often?*
> Every week.
> *And you'd take that money to Belfast?*
> That's correct, yeah.
> *And to whom would you give it?*
> Well, Billy McMillen was alive at the time. Billy dispersed money to the Lower Falls people. And other moneys then were dispersed to people in the New Lodge area who were manning the barricades. Anyone, in fact, who was on the barricades got paid for their work.
> *Billy McMillen was the Belfast OC?*
> He was.
> *In effect, then, was the money from Dublin going into the hands of the IRA?*
> Well, you would say it was, yeah.[76]

While thousands of pounds were flowing out of these accounts, the IRA finally split. After the fiasco of August 1969, the strains within the organization had become unbearable. It is difficult to establish the precise date, but some time around 18 December 1969 an extraordinary General Army Convention[77] of the IRA was summoned. It is believed to have met in an old mansion-style house at Knockvicar, Boyle, in County Roscommon.[78] The purpose of the gathering was to discuss a proposed change in the IRA's attitude towards 'abstentionism', the traditional policy of refusing to recognize the parliaments in Dublin, Stormont and Westminster on the grounds that they were illegitimate bodies to which no Irish person should give allegiance. The Army Council had decided that if Sinn Fein members were elected to any of these bodies they should take their seats and participate fully. The Army Convention now had to ratify the decision. The vote went against the traditionalists by 39 votes to 12, to the anger of Sean Mac-Stiofain, then the IRA's Director of Intelligence, who allegedly broke down and cried. MacStiofain does confirm it was a highly charged moment. 'During the course of speaking against the motion, I got very emotional, but certainly I didn't burst into tears. No. I was very angry about the whole thing. I passed the remark that this was the end of the IRA as we knew it. The significance of the vote was that they were going to go into all the three Parliaments that fraudulently claimed jurisdiction over various parts of Ireland. It was quite obvious that they were going to get enmeshed in the never-never land of parliamentary politics, which is very laudable in other countries where they have a normal situation, but not for the Republican movement, not for the IRA.'[79]

MacStiofain left the Army Convention with his allies, reconvened elsewhere, and contacted the units who had not been represented at the Convention and the new units that had been organized in recent months. There had been allegations that several units had been deliberately excluded from the Convention. A new IRA leadership was elected and the Provisional IRA was born. MacStiofain became the Provisionals' Chief of Staff. But the formalities of the split were not yet complete. Sinn Fein had to ratify the IRA's vote on abstentionism at its annual conference, the Ard Fheis, to be held at the Intercontinental Hotel in Dublin on 10 January 1970. Apparently the interval between the two gatherings was marked by 'a scramble for delegates that was only equalled by a scramble for [arms] dumps'.[80] Again, Sean MacStiofain was present. 'It was acrimonious. There was great tension. One of Goulding's supporters proposed a vote of allegiance to the old Army Council and I got up and announced that a "Provisional" Army Council had been established. I pledged my allegiance to it and urged all Republicans to leave the conference with me. About 45 per cent of those present walked out with me. The split in the Republican movement was complete.'[81]

The Dublin government would not have been displeased at the news, although it would be wrong to suggest that its machinations had directly brought it about. Certainly the newly created Provisionals had reason to believe that they were likely to find a more sympathetic ear, since their ideology was far more in keeping with that of Fianna Fail. What appears to have happened to the channelling of the covert government funds after the split is instructive. Sean MacStiofain confirms that it changed direction. 'Before the split, the money was going to somebody who was active in the Goulding wing of the movement. Then the money was stopped altogether for a few weeks. When it resumed again it went to somebody who was working with us. That was the way it worked out. The money in Belfast for the Defence Committee was distributed by a person who was one of our leading members.'[82] Dr Garret Fitzgerald was one of the members of the Dail Public Accounts Committee and he confirms that the flow of money changed direction. 'It's not a thing you can easily prove, but the money started coming in the autumn of '69, shortly prior to the split in the IRA, and it does seem to have ended up in the hands of the people who were more Provisional IRA rather than Official IRA. I think that may have been intended by those who passed the money on. I think that there was this concern about the danger of a communist IRA and a concern that it should be influenced more by Nationalist rather than by ideological consider-ations. In retrospect, this may seem curious but there have been periods in every country where anti-communism has taken rather curious forms.'[83]

Remarkably, it appears that the Dublin government, or at the very least some of its senior ministers, had particular plans for the IRA or the newly formed 'Provisional' wing of the organization in the event of a 'Doomsday' situation arising in the North. According to Captain James Kelly, a formal Irish army order was issued on 6 February 1970 to prepare for 'incursions' into Northern Ireland, and to make arms and gas masks available for that purpose.

The role certain senior ministers envisaged for the IRA, according to some Provisionals, was explained to me by John Kelly. 'In the event of a "Doomsday" situation arising again as had happened in August, we would be the Trojan Horse, so to speak: the IRA would be the first line of defence in areas like Derry, Belfast and Newry. We would hold the line until such time as the Irish army got itself in position in Derry, in Newry and in Belfast. That was the crude outline of the strategy.' I said I could see how the Irish army could get to the border towns of Derry and Newry, but how was it expected to get to Belfast? Kelly had an answer. 'This was one of the crux questions that was often discussed. Belfast was the weak link. The strategy was to get Newry first and then drive up the motorway to Belfast. We – the IRA – would hold the line in Belfast until such time as they arrived.' This meant that the Irish army planned to drive up the A1/M1, the motorway from the border to Belfast. I thought John Kelly could not be serious, but he assured me this had been discussed with Captain Kelly. I suggested it sounded like Gilbert and Sullivan. 'Well, perhaps in hindsight it was, but to us at the time it was a very serious matter and was taken very seriously. We believed that was the strategy that the Irish government had worked out.'[84]

Given the continuing tensions in the North, it was not long before Dublin thought that 'Doomsday' had arrived. On the night of 31 March 1970, there was fierce rioting in the Nationalist Ballymurphy estate in West Belfast after a Junior Orange March which had paraded that morning through a predominantly Catholic area on its way to a rally in Bangor. A Catholic crowd awaited its return. There was a sectarian clash and a nearby Protestant estate, New Barnsley, was attacked. The army was called in.

Catholics now saw the soldiers as protectors of the Protestants and attacked them with petrol bombs. Twenty members of the Royal Scots Regiment were injured. It was the first tangible sign that the 'honeymoon' between the Catholics and the British army, which had intervened the previous August to protect them, was coming to an end. The Ballymurphy riots marked the beginning of the process whereby the Provisionals turned from defence to attack.[85] A second night of rioting followed in which more CS gas was used and thirty-eight more soldiers were injured. The next day, the army warned that petrol-bombers could be shot dead.[86] The situation seemed to be getting out of hand. The Irish government acted. The five hundred rifles that had once belonged to the Irish Territorials and had subsequently been retained for just such an emergency were taken out of storage. Captain Kelly, who was abroad at the time, was asked to return to distribute the weapons in the North. 'When the trouble started in Bally-murphy and word came down that these people were under attack and that they were in a bad way and that they might need arms for defence, these arms that had been retained the previous October or November were put on trucks along with the gas masks, and sent to the border. But they only got as far as Dundalk because the trouble blew over.'[87] The consignment was loaded in such haste that the next morning gas masks littered the road to Dundalk. I asked Neil Blaney who would have received the arms had they crossed the border. He puffed on his pipe while he gathered his thoughts. At first, as was his wont, he was evasive.

> They'd have gone into Ballymurphy and to whoever was capable of handling, using and directing their organization, without name, not because I have the name but because I just don't know.
> *But they would have gone presumably to the newly emergent Provisionals?*
> Probably, probably, very probably.
> *Because you say they wouldn't have gone to the Officials?*
> Mmn?
> *You say they wouldn't have gone to the Officials.*
> Oh, no way, no way.[88]

This was the last time that Irish troops roared up to the border. Shortly after the Ballymurphy riots, the scandal of Dublin's dabbling in the North burst. Captain Kelly had not been on the spot to distribute the rifles that were rushed to Dundalk because he had been in Europe with John Kelly buying guns. The money he had used, £32 500 including expenses, had come from the George Dixon account in Lower Baggot Street, Dublin. The arms had been purchased and the money handed over to an arms dealer in West Germany.[89] The whistle was blown when the leader of the Fine Gael opposition, Liam Cosgrave, received an anonymous note, simply signed 'Garda' (the Irish police), and stating: 'a plot to bring in arms from Germany worth £80 000 for the North under the guise of the Department of Defence has been discovered. Those involved are a Captain Kelly, Intelligence Officer, Colonel Hefferon, Director of Intelligence [who was Captain Kelly's boss]. See that this scandal is not hushed up.' The note also apparently referred to Charles Haughey and Neil Blaney.[90] Both denied any involvement in the plan to import arms. Mr Cosgrave told Mr Lynch, and the Taoiseach made a statement which indicated he had already been made aware of the plan.

On Monday 20 April and Tuesday 21 April, the security forces of the country at my disposal brought me information about an alleged attempt to unlawfully import arms from the continent. Prima facie, these reports involved two members of the Government. I decided to interview the two members of the Government, Deputy Blaney . . . and Deputy Haughey. . . . In the meantime I ensured that adequate steps were taken to prevent any unauthorised importation of arms.[91]

Blaney and Haughey were sacked, and Kevin Boland resigned. The Arms Trial opened in Dublin on 7 October 1970. In the dock were Charles Haughey, Captain Kelly, John Kelly and Albert Luykx, a Belgian living in Dublin who was one of Captain Kelly's contacts. They were charged with the illegal importation of arms. The charges against Neil Blaney were dropped. In a sensational verdict, all four were acquitted. The jury decided in less than an hour that the attempted arms importation was *not* illegal because it had been authorized by the Minister of Defence. Dr Garret Fitzgerald summarized the significance of the state's involvement in the arms imbroglio and the encouragement of the Provisional IRA:

Historically, these events were a turning-point because they brought our state up against realities, after a long period when perhaps we were fooling ourselves. The real issue was how this country was to be run democratically by constitutional government, dealing with any group which took up arms in this island. That issue then had to be faced and since then has been faced very firmly indeed by all governments. It provoked very deep emotions and it was a period of great confusion but it came to a head very rapidly at the time of the Arms Trial. And from then on there was a rapid growth of commitment to the concept of no reunification without the consent of a majority in Northern Ireland upon which all Irish policy has since been based and a clear determination to down-face and deal with the IRA – which all governments have pursued since then.[92]

In conclusion, I asked Neil Blaney if what he did helped create the Provisional IRA. He sucked on his pipe even longer as he went through the ritual of stoking and digging it with a match. 'If that is helping to create them, I would say no. We didn't help to create them but we certainly would have accelerated, by what assistance we could have given, their emergence as a force. I don't regret what I did, but I do regret that things have developed in such a way since then that has seen twenty-two years of bloodshed and no end in sight.'[93] It was an admission of partial responsibility.

On 6 February 1971, Gunner Robert Curtis was killed by machine-gun fire in the New Lodge Road in Belfast. He was the Provisional IRA's first military victim and the first British soldier to be killed in action in Ireland since partition. Defence had turned to attack. Joe Cahill welcomed the opportunity to take the offensive. 'It was a turning-point. It was the start of the "War of Independence". Defence had gone out of the window.'[94] To date, over 3000 people have died in the current round of what are euphemistically known as 'the Troubles'. Nearly 1750 of them, including soldiers, policemen and civilians, are estimated to have been victims of the Provisional IRA. Loyalist paramilitaries, too, have taken an equally bloody toll. The Provisionals have now extended their 'war' to Great Britain and Europe, and there is no sign of it ending. Neither the Irish Republic, the state which had a hand in the Provisionals' emergence, nor the United Kingdom, the state whose inactivity helped sow the seeds from which they grew, has proved capable of defeating the enemy each inadvertently helped to create.

8 · A TANGLED WEB

Just after lunch on Tuesday 30 June 1992, there was knock at the door of Mrs Mary Perry's house on the Churchill Park estate in Portadown, Northern Ireland. Churchill Park is a Roman Catholic area and Republican/Nationalist in its political sympathies, although far from every household would support the IRA. The Perry family certainly did not: they had always tried to steer clear of politics, wishing only, like most people in the province, to get on with their lives and survive. The stranger asked whether he should stand on the doorstep or come in. He was neatly dressed with sports jacket, tie, fawn flannels and tan shoes. His cap was fawn too, and he wore it pulled forward to the front of his head. He was nicely spoken and polite. He said he had a message from the Provos but assured Mrs Perry that he was not in any organization himself. Anxiously, Mary asked him in, praying for news of her only daughter, Margaret, who had disappeared a year ago.

The preceding twelve months had been a nightmare for Mary. She had done everything in her power to find her missing daughter, but, as she showed her visitor into her neat, well-ordered lounge, she was no nearer the truth than she had been when she started her quest. It was a year in which Mary felt she had encountered intrigue, obstruction, deceit and lies. A few days earlier, on the anniversary of the day Margaret vanished, 21 June 1991, Mary had written in her diary, 'Margaret disappeared one year ago today. In God's name, what has become of her? I am too sad to think or do anything any more. My life has no meaning.' By now, Mary was utterly distraught. She had been on the phone all that day as on most days during that dreadful year. To find out if there was any news, she had rung the sergeant in charge of the case at Portadown RUC barracks, who was part of at least the third team to handle the case in the course of the year. There was no news. The sergeant said he would be on duty the following month and then would be off to America for a holiday. She then rang Father Denis

Faul, the Dungannon priest who had been such a comfort and support, to discover that he had already gone away on holiday. The sergeant at the Garda station across the border in Monaghan also had no news. By this time, she told her diary, she was 'in the most awful state'.

It was roughly half an hour later that the stranger came to the door. He told Mary that within twelve to twenty-four hours he would have news of Margaret and would call back. She told him to get out of the house if this was some kind of joke. He assured her it was not, said she should trust him and advised her to get in touch with a friend or neighbour to stay beside her. He then left the house. Mary said she had not the strength to follow him to the door to see what direction he took. She thought of calling the police but decided against it lest their presence in the area deterred the caller from returning. Mary rang her best friend, who had stood by her from the beginning. The friend stayed for a while before going home to make tea. Shortly afterwards, a local priest, Father McAnearney, came round and asked if she had had a call during the afternoon. Mary said she had a 'caller'. He then braced her for the bad news: he had received a message that there would soon be word of Margaret and that it 'wasn't good'. Later that evening the news broke. A shallow grave had been discovered by a priest in a forest near Mullaghmore, near Sligo in the Irish Republic, not far from the spot where Lord Mountbatten had been blown up by an IRA remote-control bomb on 27 August 1979. The priest had been directed to the location by a person or persons unknown. The body, it transpired, was that of Margaret Perry.

Just after midnight, Mary received a telephone call from an RUC inspector in Portadown who told her that three bodies had just been found in South Armagh. They had been shot through the head. The inspector told her that both he and she had a good idea who they were but Mary was 'to keep it under her hat until the details came out'. The bodies were found in three separate locations a few miles apart near Bessbrook, Crossmaglen and Newtownhamilton in the wilds of South Armagh. They were naked and covered with black plastic bags. A milk crate, with the bottles still inside, had been placed on the chest of one to stop the plastic from blowing away. The first body was discovered by a motorist driving north across the border who summoned a local priest, Father Aloysius McCourt, to administer the last rites. The bodies were those of three IRA men from the Portadown area: twenty-nine-year-old Aidan Starrs, thirty-two-year-old John Dignam and thirty-three-year-old Gregory Burns. In a statement, the IRA said that Starrs and Dignam had been RUC Special Branch informers and Burns had been an MI5 agent, and that all had been involved in the murder of Margaret Perry. She had been strangled and battered to death with a spade. The RUC, as is standard practice with regard to allegations about informers, made no comment. Comment, however, was plentiful in the media and the House of Commons, where the Prime Minister, John Major, told MPs that 'the discovery of the three bodies in Armagh last night, and the subsequent admission of the Provisional IRA that they were responsible, demonstrates yet again the true nature of terrorism'.[1] The House resounded to a chorus of condemnation.

I was familiar with the names of each of the three. John Dignam I remembered from my work on police interrogation in the late 1970s: at the time, Dignam was a member of the Irish National Liberation Army (INLA) who had been interrogated at Gough Barracks, Armagh, between 22 March and 29 March 1978 and charged with attempted murder after a weekend bomb attack on the Queen's Bar, a Protestant pub in Portadown. The attack was alleged to have been in retaliation for the sectarian killing of two Roman Catholics. His was one of the cases about which the courageous Senior Medical Officer at Gough, Dr Denis Elliott, had expressed concern because of the marks he had observed on his body. Dr Elliott had expressed even greater concern, however, over the bruising that became 'embarrassingly obvious' on the body of Dignam's co-accused, Daniel Joseph Hamill. The Director of Public Prosecutions withdrew the charges against Hamill, presumably because the medical evidence would make his conviction unlikely, but proceeded with the charges against Dignam.[2] Dignam's case came to court more than two years later when he pleaded guilty to lesser charges; on 5 June 1980 he was sentenced to twelve years for kneecapping and causing an explosion.

The name Burns I remembered from my work on the Stalker case in the late 1980s. Gregory Burns's brother Sean was one of the three IRA men killed by the RUC's élite anti-terrorist group, the Headquarters Mobile Support Unit, on 11 November 1982. Sean Burns was travelling in a green Ford Escort along with Eugene Toman and Gervaise McKerr in the Portadown area. Special Branch had received intelligence from a 'mole' within the IRA that they were on their way to kill a member of the security forces. The Escort was intercepted, the police said the occupants opened fire during the pursuit, and Toman, Burns and McKerr were shot dead. None of them was found to be armed.[3] The identity of the 'mole' who provided the intelligence remained a mystery. It was the protection of his identity and the identities of other sources who provided intelligence in the three shooting incidents that John Stalker investigated that led to the insuperable difficulties he encountered. Gregory Burns's claim to Republican fame lay in being the brother of an IRA martyr. He never had any convictions himself.

Aidan Starrs was another name familiar to me from the Stalker era, and he had certainly been under surveillance by the RUC at the time.

I remember reading the press reports of his arrest in a car on 6 January 1983 in possession of four hand-grenades and wondering whether he too had been set up by the same 'mole' who had provided the intelligence that led to the deaths of Toman, Burns and McKerr two months earlier. The RUC maintained that Starrs's arrest was the result of a 'routine search', but I had always had my doubts, since each of the three operations that John Stalker investigated was originally claimed to have been the result of 'routine operations'. On 4 October 1983 Starrs was gaoled for thirteen years, but his sentence was reduced by five years on appeal two months later when his defence counsel argued that he had joined Sinn Fein at the time of the hunger strike in 1981 and fallen under the influence of those who made use of him. Aidan Starrs was released from the Maze prison in 1987, by which time John Dignam had also been released.

John Dignam was buried at the same church on the same day as Margaret Perry, Saturday 4 July 1992. Mary Perry carried Margaret's coffin. Over the headstone lies the inscription 'Sleeping where no shadows fall', words which had come to Mary when Margaret's body was discovered near Mullaghmore. She wrote in her diary, 'We have laid Margaret to rest. The three, S.B.D. [Starrs, Burns and Dignam], have gone as well. Thank God, I won't have to see them again. I feel sorrow for their families and until the day I die, I nor no one, will ever possibly know the *real* truth because this country is corrupt and rotten to the core.... In God's name, why were the three so important to them? Why were they protected all along? The lies and deceit that were handed out to me over the year and two weeks were incredible.' After the funeral, she wrote to the RUC in Portadown, quoting Sir Walter Scott: 'O what a tangled web we weave, / When first we practice to deceive!'

Seemingly hemmed in by what she saw as yet another of Northern Ireland's proverbial 'walls of silence', Mary Perry became resigned to the fact that she would never find out why her daughter died – which was, above all else, what she wished to establish. 'I would like before I die to know that Margaret's name can be clearly and honestly kept apart from the names of those three,' she wrote in her diary. 'I feel sick. I know I will never see or hear Margaret again. It is so hard to bear. I loved her very much.... When I visit Margaret's resting place, I just sit and talk to her and find myself saying, "Margaret, I will have to get to the bottom of this, no matter how long it takes. If I keep chipping away at this mountain, it will crumble some day".' But Mary did not know where to chip or where to begin. The relationship between mother and daughter had not been easy, with disagreements and rows down the years. To Mary's great disappointment and concern Margaret had dropped out of her studies at the University of Ulster, Coleraine, and subsequently been treated for an alcohol problem.

ETA's most spectacular attack: the aftermath of the bomb which killed the Spanish Prime Minister Luis Carrero Blanco in Madrid in 1973.

Hooded ETA leaders at a secret press conference in France after the assassination of Carrero Blanco.

OPPOSITE ABOVE   ETA supporters marching through Ordizia demanding amnesty for members of the *cuadrilla*.

OPPOSITE BELOW   'Koldo' of the Ordizia *cuadrilla* at the block of flats in Pamplona where he was shot by the Spanish police. His fall was broken by the washing line and he survived.

The young Sean MacStiofain (*centre*) and Cathal Goulding (*right*) under arrest following an abortive IRA arms raid on a school armoury in Essex in 1953. Goulding was Chief of Staff of the IRA in the 1960s when the split between the two wings of the IRA developed. MacStiofain became the first Chief of Staff of the Provisional IRA.

OPPOSITE   The Dublin politicians at the centre of the arms scandal, 1969–70: Neil Blaney (*left*), Minister of Agriculture, and Charles Haughey (*right*), Minister of Finance. Blaney was never charged and Haughey was acquitted at the trial in 1970.

TOP Rev. Ian Paisley and supporters demonstrating in Belfast in 1969 against the liberal Unionist Prime Minister, Captain Terence O'Neill.

ABOVE Civil rights leaders, John Hume and Austin Currie, and other Nationalist MPs during a vigil in Derry prior to the abolition of the Stormont Parliament in March 1972.

LEFT Gregory Burns outside Craigavon courthouse on 5 May 1992 where the inquest into his slain IRA brother was being held.

BELOW Gregory Burns's body, covered with bin-liners, was found by the roadside with the corpses of Aidan Starrs and John Dignam on 30 June 1992. The three men had been interrogated and 'executed' by the IRA as alleged informers.

Mrs Mary Perry, carrying the coffin of her daughter Margaret, murdered by Aidan Starrs in June 1991. Her body was discovered in the Irish Republic a year later.

In July 1984, Margaret had written a moving poem to her mother which provides an insight into the way they felt about each other.

The Rose and the Thorn

You gave me life,
You gave me love,
You gave me all that you could give.
And, dear mother, how have I repaid you?
I gave you misery,
I gave you a broken heart.
I gave to you what you did not need.
Never did I mean to be as I am,
Never will I be worthy of you,
For you are goodness itself,
A rose amongst the thorns.
I am the thorn that tears at your heart,
And yet you embrace that thorn and forgive it for hurting you.
How proud and glad I am to call you Mother,
O, if only some day you will be proud and glad to call me Daughter.
I delight not in what I have done to you.
My shame and sadness are my deserving thorn.
I beg that thorn to tear me apart,
And to put me together again as a mirror of my Mother.

Reading the poem, I felt that Mary's determination to find out the truth about what happened to Margaret was driven not just by love but by the debt she felt she owed to her daughter.

I first went to see Mary Perry as 1992 drew to a close. She was nervous and frightened to talk. I explained that we were anxious to unravel the tangled web and establish whether Burns, Starrs and Dignam really were informers, what they did and why they had murdered Margaret Perry. It was certainly one of the most complex and unpleasant stories I had tackled during more than twenty years of reporting on Northern Ireland. Then, just before Christmas 1992, Mary wrote me a letter as a result of my visit.

> I really need to know, why . . . why . . . why this happened to Margaret and why I was never meant to find her and why did the 'powers that be' go to such incredible lengths to deceive me? I would like if you could to find the answers for I'm sure I never will.

I said we would endeavour to do so. I also wanted to discover the truth behind the murkiest of episodes in what has become known as Britain's 'Dirty War'.

From the state's side, the war is conducted by three agencies against the

IRA and their Loyalist equivalents: the RUC's Special Branch, whose priority is to gather 'hot' intelligence that will thwart enemy actions; military intelligence, whose requirement is for both 'hot' and political intelligence that will enable the state to outmanoeuvre its enemy; and the Security Service, MI5, whose quintessential aim is high-level, long-term penetration of both Republican and Loyalist paramilitaries in order to 'read' their tactics, strategy and political direction. These requirements sometimes overlap. The overall policy of the three intelligence agencies is to subvert and destroy the paramilitaries on both sides. The policy of their targets is to survive, which means rooting out, interrogating and 'executing' all suspected informers and agents within their ranks. Such, according to the IRA, was the fate of Burns, Starrs and Dignam. Individuals agree to become players in this most deadly of games for a variety of reasons ranging from altruism and money to blackmail and fear. Those who are uncovered are 'executed' both as punishment for betrayal and as a warning to others. Sometimes the paramilitaries on both sides make mistakes but the innocent do not live to protest. On the Republican side, being a 'tout' is the ultimate disgrace, not just for the 'tout' but for the family from which he comes – which is why many families either do not believe or do not want to believe that their sons were 'executed' in error.

Normal practice is for the IRA to deliver a tape recording of the 'confession' to the family concerned so they can hear the admission from their loved one's own lips. This is invariably done before the bodies are found. The IRA insists that such confessions are only made in strict accordance with its standing orders governing 'courts martial'. The 'court' consists of 'three members of equal rank or higher than the accused' plus an independent Army Council observer either from General Headquarters or appointed by it. When the verdict is reached, it is conveyed to the accused by the Army Council observer who also relays it to the Army Council itself which has to ratify any death sentence passed.[4]

The IRA insists that Burns, Starrs and Dignam were not tortured as alleged but gave their 'confessions' voluntarily during the nine days in which they were held. It is claimed that Dignam broke first, and what he said was used as a lever against Burns and Starrs. Each interrogation was conducted independently which enabled the IRA to cross-check the references. There were doubts raised about the authenticity of the confessions after the bodies were found because the IRA had not sent the families tape-recorded copies as was customary. The IRA said this was because permission had been given to write a last letter home. Extracts from the heart-rending letter that John Dignam apparently wrote to his wife, Clair, a few hours before his 'execution', were read at his funeral:

Dear Clair, love,

I am writing this letter to apologise for all the pain and heartache I have caused you. I have only a matter of hours to live my life. I only wish I could see you and the kids one last time but as you know, this is not possible. I have done nothing but think of you, and Clair, believe me, I've shed some tears for you, Sean and Ruairi, sometimes uncontrollably. You are going to have some bad times ahead of you but never drop your head and keep your chin up. I wish you all the best with our new baby which I'm not going to see. I'll never know if I had a daughter or not. Tears are streaming down my face.

There is only one thing I can say to you now, that I love you and cherish you and the kids until I die, and after if possible. Tell your family and my parents and sister I love them also. Pray for me, look after my grave and visit when you can. Your life is ruined. I hope you can piece it together again. Cherish this lock of hair and letter for the rest of your life. Tell the kids I will always love them and cherish them.
Your loving husband,
John[5]

In another part of the letter, he said he had been well treated by his captors and they were only doing what they had to do under the circumstances. Shortly after his death, Clair Dignam gave birth to a baby girl.

Even by Northern Ireland's grisly standards, the killings of Burns, Starrs and Dignam and the murder of Margaret Perry shook a community long inured to violent death. Never before had three alleged informers been 'executed' at the same time, and the brutal killing of Margaret Perry gave their fate an even more macabre dimension. The question remains: were they informers or did the IRA 'execute' them for other reasons? The families of Burns, Starrs and Dignam found it difficult to believe that their sons were informers and suspected they had been sacrificed to protect British intelligence agents operating at a high level within the IRA. Although such an explanation is the stuff of a Gerry Seymour thriller, it stretches the imagination even in the devious world of the 'Dirty War'. It must be said, however, that in the light of current evidence and in the absence of any proof such an explanation seems highly unlikely. The IRA would see it as preposterous to 'execute' three informers in order to allow other informers to continue within its ranks. On the face of it, the key to the four deaths would appear to lie in the record of the interrogations and the 'confessions' made by the three men. Despite what was originally suspected, these records do exist. I knew that to unravel the tangled web I had to gain access to this evidence. Suffice it to say, it took months, but in the end I succeeded. The following explanation of the four deaths is based on the last words spoken by Gregory Burns, Aidan Starrs and John Dignam prior to their 'execution'. Burns admits he had worked for British intelligence for more than a decade, and Starrs and Dignam say they were 'recruited' by the RUC's Special Branch after the murder of Margaret Perry. But were they speaking the truth throughout their 'confessions'?

Although the IRA always maintained that Gregory Burns was an MI5 agent, it appears that he was not. Nowhere in his confession does he refer to working for the Security Service. He states exactly what he was and what he was not. 'I'm not a Special Branch informant,' he says. 'I'm a British intelligence agent. I've been working for British intelligence since 1980.' By 'British intelligence' Burns means army or military intelligence who, like MI5, run 'agents'. He would be proud of being an 'agent': neither he nor his army handlers would ever use the word 'tout' as a job description.

Burns begins by explaining how he first became involved. He was a painter and decorator by trade. In 1980 he was working as a care assistant at the Coleshill old people's home in Enniskillen (where he lived) with colleagues who were also part-timers in the Ulster Defence Regiment (UDR). Some of their wives worked there too. Burns was only recently married and his wife had 'very expensive tastes' and liked to go out 'two or three times a week'. Part-time work in the UDR was financially attractive. He received an application form and asked the matron of the home and another person, whom he suspected had sent him the form in the first place to give him references. My colleagues Neil Grant and Stephen Walker tracked down the former matron and she confirmed that Burns had asked her to be a referee: she said she had done so but had not recommended him as she did not see Gregory Burns as a UDR officer. Burns' parents were utterly disbelieving that he would ever apply to join, given his Republican political activities which were in the background at the time. The application lay around for two or three weeks, unsigned. Then Burns and his wife had an argument about money and he decided to take the plunge and join. 'I filled it in, signed my name to it and sent it in.' He heard nothing for four or five weeks and then two men came to the house. 'They told me that I couldn't be accepted into the UDR because of my background [presumably his political activities],' he said, 'but they had a thing I could do for them. They explained that they wanted me to start going to meetings, join Sinn Fein, find out what Sinn Fein meetings are all about and report back to them. They left me a contact number to contact them when I'd made up my mind what I wanted to do.' Burns thought about it, and two or three weeks later rang the number and arranged to meet his first 'handlers'. 'They explained what they wanted me to do from start to finish. They said they didn't mind how big the reports were or how small, as long as they were getting what was going on about Sinn Fein activities, meetings, rallies, things like that there. So I started working for them.'

Burns, according to his 'confession', had taken the first step. Money would seem to have been the prime motivation. Soon Gregory Burns became a member of Sinn Fein. When the hunger strike began, he joined the H-Block Committees[6] and the election campaigns of the Republican prisoners who stood *in absentia* in the Irish general election. 'I brought them back reports on the different people who were at meetings.' According to the Republicans who worked with him at the time, Burns was an incredibly hard and dedicated worker. During the hunger strike he moved to Portadown where his family lived. Within a few weeks, he said, his handlers were in touch again, coming to his house and asking him to ring a number. His wife thought they were asking her husband to do some painting and decorating for them. 'So I contacted them and they asked me to start the whole thing all over again in the Portadown area.' Burns also implies that they threatened him if he refused by saying they'd 'make up shortages and I'd end up in gaol'. Precisely what the 'shortages' were was never established. Burns agreed to continue and the thread was picked up again in Portadown where the local IRA unit operated under the overall control of the IRA's 'Northern Command' based just across the border in Monaghan. Having established his credentials during the hunger strike, Burns could be used to further advantage in one of the IRA's most active areas. In the autumn of 1982 the security forces desperately needed the intelligence to combat a ferocious IRA offensive in County Armagh in which five police officers, a former RUC reservist, a serving UDR man and a former member of the UDR had been shot or bombed to death.[7] Burns would have become one of several important informers at the time. He told his IRA interrogators how he operated.

> They'd tell me to come out of Portadown station at the back and head down the back car park. They'd pick me up, put me in the back of a car and put a blanket over me or get me in the back of a van, which was usually an Escort van, and put a sheet over me. In the Escort van, they always had working tools and I could look like I was just going to do a job. They sometimes used the Sherpa van which was fitted out with a two-piece settee, a table, lighting in the inside of the van, which meant we could drive along and have a meeting. . . . They paid me roughly about £200 a month. Sometimes we met monthly, sometimes on a five- to six-week basis.

Burns, according to his 'confession', would feed his handlers with all the information he could. Remarkably and tragically for the Burns family, Gregory says he provided them with a vital piece of intelligence that led to the killing of his brother Sean in 1982 alongside Eugene Toman and Gervaise McKerr when their car was intercepted by the RUC Headquarters Mobile Support Unit. The unit was acting on detailed intelligence, although it appears that Gregory Burns was not the only source. His role in the death of his brother must have been one of the most painful admissions he made. He said he had been warned one night by a local IRA figure to watch himself the next day because there was an operation planned for the area.

> The next morning I rung them [the handlers] and told them. I also saw Starrs and Eugene Toman in the car outside . . . [the location is deliberately deleted in the interrogation record] . . . that morning as well. I rung them and told them it was something going down in the area and these two were in the car park. After I had give the thing about Eugene Toman and the thing being in the car park, I went back to work. I think it was that night that Eugene and my brother and Gervaise McKerr were shot. I didn't at the time think that I had had anything to do with that. I think I realize now that I might have been.

Burns was horrified at the death of his brother and, according to his 'confession', at the gradual realization that he may well have played a part in it by providing his handlers with some of the initial intelligence. For six weeks he kept his distance and then, as he told his interrogators, he made contact with them again.

> We were inside a barracks at Lisburn [British army headquarters in Northern Ireland] where I asked them what the f. . . was going on. Were they responsible for the shooting of my brother? At that time they said they weren't and they'd try and find out for me who set my brother up. I believed that they would. It was probably f. . . . . stupid anyway. They offered me some whisky and I wouldn't take it. I took a drop of coffee and left shortly after that.

Probably thinking that it was best to get their agent out of the way, Burns's handlers, or more likely their superiors, allegedly decided to send him to Holland to infiltrate the Irish community in Amsterdam. The IRA was about to open a European front in its campaign focusing on British military and political targets on the Continent. Amsterdam and the Netherlands were also thought to be a source of weapons and a convenient transit route.

They arranged for me to go from Belfast to London by boat where I was met by an English guy who was very what you call 'hoity-toity'. He was all prim and proper, suit and all. He explained that I'd be meeting someone in Amsterdam the following day from the Dutch authorities.

Amsterdam, from Burns's point of view, was not a great success. He had never really wanted to go there in the first place but may well have thought, in the light of his self-confessed role in the killing of his brother, that he was better out of the way. His handler was allegedly known as 'Dutch', and he was provided with a job at Schipol airport. Burns did as he was told and frequented the Irish bars in the west of the city, keeping his eyes and ears open. Being in Amsterdam had its compensations. 'It was dead on. I was working. I was earning money. There were no ties on me.' It is difficult to assess what value he proved to his handlers, since Burns is surprisingly vague and general in his 'confession' about this brief overseas interlude. He stayed in Amsterdam for around six months, packed in his job at the airport, hung around the city doing decorating jobs and then went off to Greece for a couple of months, presumably on vacation. His handlers picked him up again on his way back to Ireland, where his mother-in-law was ill.

They weren't too happy about the idea of me f. . . . . off completely and more or less told me so. They asked me why I did it: why I didn't stay where I was; they'd gone to a lot of expense to put me in Amsterdam to get me a job and used up a contact within the Dutch authorities. I more or less told them that I got fed up with the whole f. . . . lot. Your man turned round and said, 'Charges are easy picked up again. . . . If you don't start and go back to what you were at, we'll set you up and put you in gaol.'

Although Burns says he was minded to sever his links with his army handlers after Amsterdam, he did not. 'It all started up again.' Burns allegedly picked up where he left off, attending meetings and reporting back on a regular basis. Then the handlers' nightmare happened: Burns says they thought he had been spotted meeting them outside a small village called Gilford. 'They didn't say who or why.' Their agent was at risk, and they took swift but risky action. They told Burns to go to Sinn Fein and say that he had been propositioned by 'the Brits'. From time to time, the Republican Movement gave 'amnesty' to informers if they were prepared to come clean, and Sinn Fein was always ready to publicize the cases of those who had been approached to work for British intelligence. Propaganda is a vital part of the 'Dirty War'. Burns got in touch with Aidan

Starrs, who had just been released from the Maze prison, and Starrs put him in touch with the local Sinn Fein councillor, Brendan Curran. On 9 September 1987 Burns attended a Sinn Fein press conference in Belfast. He said he had been tricked into travelling to Lisburn the previous week and had been forced into a car by armed men who had driven him to an army barracks somewhere in the town. There, he told the press conference, two Englishmen and a Scotsman tried to recruit him:

> They told me it didn't matter how long it took me to get into Sinn Fein, even if it took a couple of years. I was offered £50 plus expenses every time I met these men. It was mentioned that this would be once a fortnight in the beginning. . . . I was also told to stay away from the UDR and RUC – not to get into it with the RUC. They were very definite about that.[8]

It was after the press conference in 1987 that Burns joined the IRA, no doubt to the great satisfaction of his alleged handlers. Successful penetration of the IRA and its Loyalist equivalents can take years. It appears it had taken Burns nearly eight years to progress from the periphery of the Republican Movement to membership of the IRA. And not the slightest suspicion hung over him. The IRA's security checks on its new recruit were nothing more than basic. Was he not from an impeccable Republican family with a brother an IRA martyr? Had he not just publicly rejected the recent attempt by 'the Brits' to recruit him? To the IRA, Gregory Burns was 'sound'. He would have been even 'sounder' to British intelligence. Soon he joined the IRA's Portadown unit at the invitation of Aidan Starrs, who became its 'OC'. Starrs would travel across the border to Monaghan two or three times a week to take his orders from his IRA superiors in the Provisionals' Northern Command who operated from the relative safety of the Republic. By this time John Dignam too had been released from gaol, where he had severed his previous connections with the INLA and joined Sinn Fein. Before long, he too was sworn into the IRA as a member of Starr's Portadown unit. Neither he nor Starrs had the remotest idea that they were working alongside an IRA volunteer who subsequently 'confessed' to being a British agent. Soon, it is claimed, Burns graduated to IRA 'Quartermaster' with responsibility for looking after the unit's weapons and explosives. The title is more grandiose than the reality, since Starrs's unit was never very active or well supplied. Burns says he was asked to look after a 9 mm 'short' and 200 rounds of ammunition which he hid in a 'dump' in the Ballyowen estate. 'I told my handlers I had got the "short" and the ammo. . . . They got me to take photographs on a paper which actually said the date just to prove I had the "short" and the ammo.'

The actions of Burns, Starrs and Dignam were less than heroic. In the eyes of local people they were common criminals who terrorized the community with robberies and extortion that had nothing to do with the IRA's 'cause'. Sometime in 1990 Burns and Dignam robbed a snooker club of around £500 using a replica firearm and a .38 revolver which Dignam was looking after for members of the IRA's East Tyrone Brigade. Around the same time, they also robbed a bookie's runner from the local Gaelic Athletic Association Club of around £70. Burns said that at the time he thought the robberies were being carried out for the 'cause'.

> I thought they were robberies to help the unit in the area, but I soon found out that they were illegal robberies from the start and that they weren't cleared by the army [the IRA]. . . . It wasn't for the Move-ment. It was a personal gain issue, 'cos the money from the snooker club was given to Aidan [Starrs]. We knew he was going to tax and insure the car with it and we knew he used the car for a lot of what he called 'RA business.[9] We didn't mind, but we found out that he used some of it for tax and insurance and also to keep his girlfriend. The money from the bookie's clerk was also give to Aidan. . . . The kick-up came after the snooker club robbery and Aidan told us that, if any-body asked, to say we weren't involved in it.

Prior to the robbery, Burns said he had notified his handlers. 'They just told me to watch myself and make sure that nothing went wrong.' But they knew nothing about the bookie's runner. 'They asked me what was the idea of robbing a bookie's clerk of £70 to £80.' Burns was involved in extortion too. Later on, with the approval of Starrs, he demanded money from a local taxi driver over the phone under the guise of being from a tiny Republican splinter group, the Irish People's Liberation Organization (IPLO). As Starrs told his IRA interrogators:

> The three of us – myself, Gregory Burns and Johnny [Dignam] – decided to extort money from a taxi driver. Gregory rang him and made a few threats against him, like. The taxi driver sent for me and Johnny. We went down and told him we knew nothing about it and that the IRA wouldn't be involved in such things, like. So he'd went to Sinn Fein about it too and then eventually we decided to back off him.

Burns's next target, surprisingly, was a local school-teacher he knew reasonably well. Burns rang him at home saying he was a 'Mr Gilpin' from the UVF (Ulster Volunteer Force) and demanded around £500. Enterpris-ingly, the teacher tape-recorded the phone calls and Burns's ineffectively disguised voice was recognized. He then notified the RUC's anti-racketeer-ing branch and let them hear the tapes. He told them of his suspicions and said that he suspected Starrs and Dignam were behind it too. By then the three were notorious in the area. Despite the nature of the evidence and what would appear to be a golden opportunity for an arrest, nothing transpired. Burns, Starrs and Dignam remained untouched. Before the trio's unsuccessful attempts at extortion, the IRA had become aware of their 'criminal' activities, epitomized by the snooker club hold-up. Shortly after the robbery, the IRA conducted its own inquiry as Starrs recounted in his 'confession'.

> We were sent for and went to a man's house in Monaghan. He was a known Republican and there we met this other guy who we were told was a 'Double O' – 'OO' means 'Operations Officer'. He brought myself into a room and asked me was I involved in the snooker club? I said no. He said, 'Look, if you just tell me the truth, that's it, it's all over with, it's no big deal.' But I was frightened. I'd said no the first time so I stuck to that.

Shortly afterwards, Starrs, Burns and Dignam were 'suspended' by the IRA. That was probably in late 1990.

At this stage, it is important to understand a vital connection in order to follow the events which led to the murder of Margaret Perry. Burns was having an affair with Margaret Perry, and the wife of the school-teacher from whom Burns had tried to extort money, was Margaret's best friend, whom she had known since the age of eleven. I will refer to the teacher as 'Sean' and his wife as 'Roisin'. In his 'confession' all that Burns says about his initial relationship with Margaret Perry is that he lived with her 'for three or four months, maybe more'. That was in 1989. Burns and his wife were separated in November that year.

Margaret's mother was bitterly opposed to the relationship, believing that Gregory Burns was a bad lot and was already married. Margaret was a complex young woman who, according to Mary, had no confidence or faith in herself. After dropping out of university she developed a drink problem for which she received treatment at the Gransha Drug Addition Unit in Belfast in 1985 and subsequently at the Early Treatment Unit at the local Craigavon Hospital a few miles from the Perry home in Portadown. Margaret held down a good job as a civil servant in Lisburn. Gregory Burns was probably her first serious relationship, and she was said to have been infatuated by him. At first, some of her feelings seem to have been reciprocated, but then Burns's interest began to cool. 'Roisin' and Mary Perry both said that Burns simply used Margaret to get his hands on her money because she had assiduously saved for a deposit on a house. At the time she disappeared, Margaret was about to finalize the mortgage arrangements. But there were undoubted tensions. Starrs did not like Margaret. As both Margaret and Starrs's girlfriend liked going out, they started out together to the great displeasure of Starrs. Starrs had been rejected by his girlfriend whom he had constantly ill-treated. He said he wanted to get back with her and he hoped to use Margaret as the intermediary. Margaret refused and her friend told Starrs she wanted nothing more to do with him. Starrs's anger and jealousy grew, as he told his IRA interrogators:

> I had been going steady with this girl for a couple of years and we were going to settle down but then she started running about with Margaret. She started going out at weekends and ended up going with different fellas and things. Margaret was doing more or less the same thing with Greg, like, the time he was going with her. If he was away working weekends, she was having parties and things and going with other men, like. I know it's hard to understand but it was just a genuine personal hate that grew within me. . . . Also she'd started to tell people that Gregory had got money off her under false pretences on a number of occasions and that she was on about we'd robbed the snooker club.

It is impossible to state with certainty the precise nature of Burns's anxiety. By the early summer of 1991, he had left Margaret Perry and moved in with another woman living in Armagh. Margaret was distraught and no doubt jealous. Burns was said to be angry that Margaret continued to pester him. If she had wanted to get her own back, she could have gone to the IRA and told them that Burns, Starrs and Dignam *were* involved in the snooker club robbery despite their previous denials at an IRA formal interview. Lying would have been seen as a serious offence and could have ended in a kneecapping or worse. However, this in itself does not appear to be a strong enough reason for Burns and Starrs to conspire to murder Margaret Perry. The most logical motive for Burns's involvement in the killing would be fear that Margaret might expose him as a British agent. It is certainly possible that she had her suspicions. 'Roisin' told me that one evening after Margaret had been angered by the way she had been treated by Burns, she had said she knew 'one thing that could sink him' but added that she would never tell. Starrs's motive as stated in his confession, 'personal hate', may have been sufficient reason for his part in the murder, given his violent and jealous nature. We only have the record of the 'confessions' to rely on. Perhaps the answer is simple: both Starrs and Burns wanted Margaret Perry out of the way because Starrs hated her and Burns was maddened to distraction by her refusal to let him go when he had taken up with another woman. One thing is clear from piecing the record of the three men's last words together: Starrs was the driving force behind the killing and Burns helped plan it. Since the three were apparently interrogated separately details of their 'confessions' can be cross-referenced with regard to the murder of Margaret Perry. Burns says:

> After a while, Aidan came up with this idea that we had to get rid of Maggie. He turned round and said, 'She knows too much.' I turned round and says, 'Knows about what? We've been doing f. . . all!' So he came up with this, 'She'd been seen', or something to that effect, and at the time I had just agreed with him.

Starrs explains what he meant by being 'seen':

> I told Johnny [Dignam] that I'd killed her because I'd seen her with . . . [he names a prominent Loyalist paramilitary in Portadown] but that was a lie so it was and it wasn't the reason I'd done it at all, like.

Dignam confirms what Starrs said:

> Aidan Starrs said to me that he'd found out that she was working for . . . [he names the same prominent Loyalist in Portadown] that she was giving over our movements to him.

For Mary Perry's peace of mind, these three statements emphatically clear Margaret of any involvement with Loyalist paramilitaries, and she was clearly not connected in any way with the IRA. Tragically, Margaret Perry was an innocent victim.

In his 'confession', Burns says he told his handlers about the plan to murder her.

> About a month before Margaret was murdered, maybe six weeks, I told my handlers about that plot on Maggie. Their attitude was just to try and avoid it, try and stop it, but not to get actually too much involved in stopping it: just come up with simple excuses or things like couldn't get her at home that night or keep her out drinking most of the night or bring her to someone else's house to stay. Eventually, it was their idea that I move her out of the house for a while. . . . They knew exactly from the word go that he was going to kill this girl.

Remarkably, if what Burns alleged is true, the authorities – or at least army intelligence – knew of the murder plot and appear to have done nothing about it. Starrs, it appears, made several attempts to murder Margaret Perry. One weekend he planned to drug her and kill her with tablets. Burns, following his handlers' alleged advice, rang the confidential telephone and said there were drugs in the house, 'and within an hour and half the house was raided'. On another occasion, although this is not referred to in the record of the interrogations, Burns and Starrs allegedly planned to carry out the murder at a beach near Carlingford, a few miles from the border, and then bury the body in the nearby Ravensdale Forest. They apparently invited Margaret out for a day trip but postponed the killing because there were too many people around. Finally, Burns and Starrs decided to kill her while Burns was in hospital. It seemed the perfect alibi, and even more cast-iron because he was in hospital in Monaghan. Around the end of May 1991, he had been admitted to hospital in Craigavon, near Portadown, suffering from a 'cardiac irregularity'. While he was there, he was warned by the RUC that they had intelligence that Loyalists in the town were planning an attempt on his life.[10] Burns asked for a transfer to the Royal Victoria Hospital in Belfast on the grounds that security arrangements at the Craigavon hospital were inadequate, but his request was refused. He therefore signed himself out, crossed the border and was admitted to Monaghan Hospital. Starrs came to visit him and they discussed a plan. Burns was to ring Margaret on Thursday evening, 20 June 1991, and ask her to come and see him. Starrs was to pick her up. Burns rang Margaret at her mother's house around 9.30 p.m. Mary Perry said she was not at home and told Burns to get lost. He then rang her at 'Roisin's' house, where she was, and spoke to her three times. Margaret did not tell 'Roisin' what the calls were about. She then went home to bed. The following morning, Friday 21 June 1991, Margaret left home for the last time. It was 7.30 a.m. Her mother thought she was going to work as usual but Margaret called in sick. At 3.30 p.m. she rang home and said she would be late for her tea. The estate agent had also been trying to contact her. Around 4 p.m. that afternoon Margaret was last seen buying a six-pack of beer at the Craigavon Inn off-licence in Portadown. She then took the train to Dundalk, the first railway station across the border, where she had arranged to meet Starrs, who she had been led to believe would take her to see Burns at some undisclosed location. He had a spade in the boot of the car. It was to be a long journey. Although Margaret knew Burns was in hospital in Monaghan, thirty miles to the west of Dundalk, according to Starrs, 'she was under the impression that Greg had got out of hospital and was on the run and didn't want people knowing where he was'. Starrs told his interrogators the gruesome story of what happened after he picked up Margaret Perry at Dundalk station.

> I wasn't really sure where I was bringing her, like, just I knew in my own mind I was going to kill her but I wasn't sure where or how. . . . I remembered a place up in Mullaghmore which I knew from years ago when we went on holidays there. So I headed in round there, stopped the car and told her we'd meet Greg up this forest. . . . We went into

the forest . . . and it was just then I put the cord around her neck and strangled her. She fell to the ground then. She was still sort of moving. I had tape in my pocket so I taped her hands. I ran back to the car, got the spade which I had in the boot, and when I came back up again she still sort of moved a bit like and in the panic I just hit her over the head with the flat of the spade, twice. Then I dug a hole, dragged her over and buried her. But in the panic I forgot about the tape and forgot that there was a couple of beer cans that she had with her. I had held them while she was getting over the gate.

'Dirty and sweating', Starrs drove back across the border and says he spent the night in Armagh at the house of Burns's new girlfriend. She categorically denies Starrs did any such thing. The following morning, Saturday 22 June 1992, Starrs washed and went home. He had as yet had no contact with Burns. In Portadown, Starrs met Dignam and told him that he had just killed Margaret Perry. This is the point at which he said he had done so because she had been seen with the prominent Loyalist paramilitary in the town. He then told Dignam he wanted him to come to the grave to help tidy up and make sure there were no fingerprints. This is confirmed by Dignam in his 'confession'. He says he met Starrs that Saturday morning in Portadown.

I didn't believe him at the time. He says, 'I'm not joking. I've done her in.' So he says to me, 'I need to go back up to where she was because I've left insulating tape or something behind.' He was afraid of his fingerprints being on it. So I went up with him. To be honest, on the way up, I still didn't believe that he'd done it until I got there. He showed me the place where the girl was buried. What I seen was a bit of leather jacket and a bit of denim sticking out of the ground He [Starrs] found a bit of tape and a beer can. He just proceeded to try and put more dirt over to try and cover her up more. I just put a bush over where the girl was.

Starrs's account is almost identical.

When we got there, you could see a small amount of her coat sticking out of the ground. It wasn't covered properly. A small amount of her jeans was showing too. So we just covered it up and then myself and Johnny just pulled like a log over her, over the grave, lifted the beer cans and the bit of tape. . . . We went into Monaghan Hospital and saw Gregory. Johnny was with me at the time. Gregory says, 'That's great, that's a load off my mind.' He wanted rid of her as much as I did, like.

The details given by Burns also dovetail when he describes Starrs and Dignam visiting the hospital on the Saturday evening after their return visit to Mullaghmore.

> They told me that she was dead. Johnny had went up with him to clear things up. Something about he'd left a beer can or tape or something up there. They didn't tell me where she was buried at the time. Johnny seems more shattered that it actually happened.

The deed had been done. In his 'confession', Burns alleges he rang his handlers the next day, Sunday.

> I told them that the girl was dead. My words was, 'She's f. . . . . . dead now. What the hell's going to happen now?' They said . . . [the reply is unclear from the record]. I hung up at that there and never contacted my handlers from that.

Again, if what Burns says is true, the authorities – or at least army intelligence – knew that Margaret Perry had been murdered and knew who the murderers were. Burns stayed in hospital another four or five weeks and then returned to Portadown to resume a normal life. From time to time he says he saw Mary Perry, who would make 'a sly remark or something. It did eat away at me the girl was dead, every time I seen her mother'.

Within days of her disappearance, Mary's search for her daughter began. It lasted a year. She records she first notified the RUC at 11.30 a.m. on Saturday 29 June 1991, a week after Margaret was last seen. Her case was soon on the local television news. On Tuesday 2 July 1991, 'Roisin' and 'Sean' went to Monaghan to look for Margaret who they suspected was over the border with Burns. They told me they bumped into him in the street, although he was supposed to be in hospital, and he assured them that Margaret was 'alive and well'. 'Sean' also spent hours scouring the river Bann, as indeed did the RUC, looking for her body. Nothing was found. Later that week, Mary Perry, her friend and a local priest went to Monaghan to follow up the recent sighting of Burns. The priest, at Mary's request, had visited Burns's house the day before and had found Starrs and Dignam but nothing else. In Monaghan he went to see Burns in hospital. Burns said he knew nothing about Margaret. Later that month, on 12 July 1991, events took a dramatic turn, if Dignam's 'confession' is to believed. John Dignam was arrested on charges of assault after Orangemen paraded along the edge of the Churchill Park estate in Portadown. He was taken to Banbridge RUC station where he was questioned by the local CID. News videotape of the march shows Dignam being pushed against a Land-Rover by the police, running away and then being hit over the head with a baton. At no time does the tape show Dignam assaulting the police. The killing of

Margaret Perry had rested heavily on his conscience and, according to his 'confession', Dignam suddenly told all.

> During this interview, I broke down and told the police about the killing of Margaret Perry, a local girl who was killed in Portadown. I told them that her body was buried in Drogheda, but I knew it wasn't buried in Drogheda 'cos I had been brought up to where her body was buried the day after she was killed.

According to Dignam, the RUC recruited him as an informer. In his 'confession' to the IRA, Dignam makes no reference to any deal, although then he goes on to say that he gave the police more information.

> I told them names of local members of the IRA, which I was involved with, and people I had been in contact with in Monaghan ... [and] Dundalk. I told them about a weapons dump in Garvaghy Park. There was a number of weapons in. They gave a [Portadown] contact number for them and [told me to] ask for 'Marty'. I think I contacted them about five or six times. . . . I told the police handlers that I was at a weapons training camp in Limerick. I told them what weapons I had been trained in – which was a general-purpose machine-gun and two AK assault rifles. . . . Then I broke off contact. They kept ringing the house to me, and any time I heard their voice on the phone I just put the phone down. I haven't had contact with them since last February [1992 – four months before Dignam was interrogated and 'executed'].

Shortly after Dignam's arrest, Aidan Starrs says in his 'confession' that he was pulled in and interrogated at Portadown Barracks later the same month, July 1991. He says he broke – as he also admitted having done at the time of his original arrest in 1983 for possession of hand-grenades: he said he had been promised a lighter sentence in return for his co-operation, which, indeed, he received on appeal. If what Starrs told the IRA is true, in 1991 he was given immunity for murder in return for becoming a police informer. This is highly improbable. Immunity is sometimes given for minor offences but not for murder. Starrs told the IRA how he claimed he was recruited.

> I was taken to the barracks and the RUC told me that they knew that I'd murdered Margaret Perry. I broke then and I agreed to work for them. I give them the names of all the volunteers that I knew, like. They give me a phone number and told me to ring and ask for 'John' every second Friday. . . . I rang a few times and told them I'd nothing

for them and I'd keep trying. Then one time I rang again and they said if I didn't come up with something soon they'd lift me and charge me with the murder of the girl. So then I got a shotgun and gave it to a fella to mind. Then I rung them and told them that the shotgun was in his house. As far as I know, they raided the house but they never found it.

Starrs also alleged in his IRA 'confession' that his handlers encouraged him to assassinate Loyalists in Portadown. This also seems improbable.

They would supply information on the Loyalists and it would engrace [*sic*] us with the IRA, get us better in til [to] it. On one occasion, the boy I rang actually says that we'd do . . . [he mentions the name of the same prominent Portadown Loyalist] and it'd be seen in the Nationalist community just as good a job as doing Lenny Murphy, like. [Murphy was a Loyalist who was the leader of Belfast's most notorious gang of sectarian killers known as 'the Shankill Butchers'. He was shot dead by the IRA on 16 November 1981, allegedly with Loyalist connivance.]

On 1 August 1991 Mary Perry recorded in her diary that Burns had gone to the barracks to make a 'voluntary statement'. Presumably she had been told this by the police. In fact, Burns was interviewed on 30 July and Starrs on 14 August. Both made witness statements as to when they had last seen Margaret Perry and reportedly said they hoped nothing had happened to her and were worried. It must be recorded, however, that, according to their solicitors' files, Starrs and Dignam continued to be harassed by the security forces, in particular by members of the UDR. Attention on this scale would have been surprising had they been recruited as informers as alleged in their 'confessions'. Mary continued her search throughout that summer. On 21 November 1991 she went to the Garda station in Monaghan. A sergeant showed her the missing persons report, which was identical in its wording to the one she had filled in in Portadown. There was, however, one crucial difference. In her report to the RUC, Mary had stated that Gregory Burns was Margaret's 'boyfriend' and that he was in Monaghan Hospital on 21 June 1991. The Garda report said the 'boyfriend's' name was unknown and he was believed to be working in the Monaghan area. While at the Garda station, Mary also saw a report given to the officers by 'Roisin' and 'Sean', who had described Margaret as 'alcoholic and depressive'. On her return to Portadown, Mary rang the RUC and told them of the discrepancy. They dismissed it as a 'minor hitch'. Mary carried on searching.

The final dramatic twist came on 12 April 1992, when the journalist

Martin O'Hagan of the *Sunday World* ran a remarkable story under the headline 'Missing Woman Driven To Her Death By Ex-Provo'. Margaret Perry, he wrote, had been beaten to death and her battered body was buried in a shallow grave across the border in Monaghan, according to Republican sources. O'Hagan had the location wrong, but the rest of his scoop was remarkably accurate. The article panicked Burns and Starrs. Burns told the IRA what happened next: 'Aidan [Starrs] says we're going to have to go up and destroy the dental records 'cos if they ever found the body there'd still be a murder hunt and we'd be the prime suspects.' According to the alleged record of Burns's interrogation, he allegedly contacted his handlers for the first time in almost a year since the Sunday after the killing when he claimed he had originally told them of the murder. He says he mentioned the plan and maintains that 'they made some suggestions as to what we should do'. Burns did not specify the 'suggestions'. He then describes going to Mullaghmore with Starrs, locating the grave and watching Starrs smash Margaret Perry's skull with a 'lump' or sledge-hammer to render the corpse unidentifiable. Dignam confirms this in his account: 'At a later stage, Aidan Starrs and Gregory Burns told me that they were going back up til [to] the grave. They said they were going to remove any dental traces. . . . After they came back, Aidan told me that he'd hit the skull with a hammer, which I believed he'd done it, you know.'

Even after this, Burns did not choose to lie low. It may have been part of his cover. His parents told me he always enjoyed the limelight. On 5 May 1992, within weeks of watching Starrs smash Margaret Perry's skull, he appeared outside Craigavon courthouse where the inquest on his brother Sean's death was finally being held in the tenth year after the shooting. With some effrontery, Gregory Burns addressed the waiting press and cameras.

> The Burns family had no confidence in the system which give rise to this inquest. We have chosen not to be legally represented as we believe our Sean was deliberately murdered by members of the security forces ... an inquest, given the narrowest of rulings, cannot possibly find out the truth and justice can never be done.[11]

It was Gregory Burns's last public appearance. Mary Perry was now beside herself with grief and frustration. She tried in vain to follow up the *Sunday World* story which had, understandably, caused her great distress. And she gave the RUC little respite. First one, then another officer on the case was replaced. Mary regarded the moves as significant; they may or may not have been. According to her diary, enquiries of the police in Portadown continued to elicit comments like 'a sticky business' and, enigmatically, 'breaking the chain by attacking the weakest link'. On 17 June 1992 she wrote:

I have run out of ideas. Heard rumours of certain inter feuding [within the IRA] or whatever. I am hoping that if there is a fall out, someone will come up with some mention of Margaret. I just cannot believe that all this nightmare has gone on and on with no let up.

The following day contains the simple poignant entry:

Last saw Margaret a year ago today.

A few days later, the stranger came to the door.

The crucial question in trying to unravel 'A Tangled Web' is: were Burns, Starrs and Dignam telling the truth in their 'confessions' to the IRA? Their families certainly think not on the grounds that after being held for nine days of intensive interrogation, they would say anything they were directed to say – in particular if the IRA had promised to spare them. I have little doubt that their account of the murder of Margaret Perry is essentially accurate given the corroborating cross references in the three 'confessions'. The question of whether they were informers is more difficult to answer with certainty. Highly placed security sources categorically deny that Starrs and Dignam were ever recruited by the RUC: furthermore, they say it is inconceivable that they would have been given immunity from prosecution for the murder of Margaret Perry in return for turning informer; nor, they add, did the RUC know about Margaret Perry's murder until her body was found. They insist there was no cover up. In contrast, however, at the time of writing I have been unable to elicit any comment whatsoever from security sources about Gregory Burns, despite almost a year of endeavour. The appropriate authorities have remained tight-lipped. I have no doubt what Mary Perry will think of their silence.

9 · THE AGENT

It took me over two years to get to him. I did not know his name. I did not know where he was. I did not even know which side he had penetrated. All I knew was that he had infiltrated a Republican or Loyalist paramilitary organization to a very high level. 'Steve', I understood, was one of MI5's star agents whose undercover work had saved many lives. Meeting any informer is a rare event. Meeting an MI5 agent is unprecedented. Why would he be willing to talk when, on the face of it, there was nothing in it for him? I assumed there would have to be a motive. Would it be patriotism, vanity or pride? Perhaps he was a seasoned veteran of the 'Dirty War', anxious to prove that not all suspected informers end up as bodies by the wayside like Burns, Starrs and Dignam. 'Steve' had clearly lived to tell the tale, as I have been reliably informed the vast majority of agents do. The problem is they cannot break cover just to prove it. Burns, Starrs and Dignam had clearly brought detection on themselves by openly parading their 'criminal' activities in Portadown. No agent worth his or her salt would ever be so stupid. Perhaps 'Steve' was an unsung hero who wanted to tell an unknowing and sceptical world what he had done – unknowing because it could not know, sceptical because it did not know. I suspected that the frustration of a public impatient with the state's seeming inability to 'beat the terrorists' was matched only by the frustration of the intelligence services unable to tell the public of the successes registered in its name and the sacrifices of those who make them possible. Killings intercepted, bombs never planted, operations thwarted seldom make news. Hooded bodies do. Living agents do not. MI5 is said to have never lost an agent, at least not in Northern Ireland. This the security service would put down not to good luck but to professionalism and 'tradecraft', a notion that is more than just a figment of John le Carré's imagination. Some of the MI5 officers who run agents in Northern Ireland ran agents in the Cold War. These 'handlers' or 'controllers' are veterans in this deadliest of games. The principles of the recruitment and the running of agents are the same, whether the theatre is eastern Europe or Northern Ireland. By the same token, agents are recruited and handled in exactly the same way, whether they are Republicans or Loyalists.

'Steve' finally agreed to meet me. I had long before channelled a message to him explaining my theme: that I wanted to examine how the democratic state responded to terrorism and was anxious to talk to someone who had been involved at its most critical and sensitive interface. Successful penetration of the enemy's ranks by the state is the key to its gaining the upper hand. Baruch Cohen, the Mossad agent, died in the process; Abu Hassan, the 'Red Prince', whom the CIA desperately tried to recruit, died too; dozens of Palestinian collaborators survived in Facma, the depressing informers' village on the West Bank; who knows the fate of the agents and informers who gave the Spanish and German states their leads in debilitating ETA and the Red Army Faction? 'Steve's' different replies to my request took months. At first the answer was 'maybe', then 'no', then 'yes' but only on the strictest of conditions. A filmed interview was out of the question, even in silhouette or disguise. The same applied to a voice interview: even with distortion techniques, the risk was too great. 'Steve' had survived in the jungle for so many years by caution and calculation and was not prepared to risk shortening his years by throwing that caution to the winds. Our conversation, too, was only to be in general terms, since any specifics might give him away.

I finally met 'Steve' outside Northern Ireland. He was not as I had envisaged. He was older than I had anticipated, although I knew he had been an agent for well over a decade, certainly a good deal longer than Gregory Burns appears to have been. Perhaps his years should have seemed even greater given his length of service and the wear and tear on his system. He seemed more relaxed than I had anticipated and displayed an unexpected maturity and poise. It was as if he had become a student late in life and flowered as a late developer. Perhaps he had at MI5's expense, as part of the process of grooming its man. I tried to place his accent, thinking that by now my ear could tell the difference between the Loyalist Shankill and the Republican Falls,[1] but the dialect and intonation seemed to fall somewhere in between. I looked for the tell-tale signs of turn of phrase, local knowledge and even physical characteristics. They were precious few. It was as if he had been meticulously tailored in anonymity. My first instinct was that he was Republican: the way he spoke of his early days was redolent of the way many young IRA men became involved. Then, on reflection, I knew that could apply equally well, given a different perspective, to their Loyalist equivalents. When he spoke of his revulsion at the killing of civilians, I first assumed he was referring to Provisional IRA operations such as 'Bloody Friday' on 21 July 1972 when bombs in Belfast city centre blew nine people apart, or the La Mon restaurant incendiary attack on 17 February 1978 in which twelve people were consumed in a fireball: in both cases, the nature and the timing of the warnings were tragically inadequate. Then I realized that 'Steve' could equally have been referring to the activities of the Loyalist sectarian killer gangs who assassinated eighty-one Catholics in the fevered atmosphere of 1972.[2] Likewise, when he talked of interrogations and hoods over the head, he could have had Loyalists as well as Republicans in mind, although Loyalists are not necessarily wedded to the niceties of an IRA court martial.

'Steve' would not be specific about dates, but I calculated that he must have become involved in his particular paramilitary organization in the very early seventies. It was only at the beginning of 1971 that the Provisional IRA began to be taken seriously as a potential military threat when it took the offensive and killed the first British soldier, and it was in response to that escalating campaign that the Loyalists began to get organized. Recruits poured in to a range of paramilitary groups, from the already existent Ulster Volunteer Force (UVF)[3] to the newly constituted Ulster Defence Association (UDA) which became an element to be reckoned with after the Stormont Parliament was abolished on 24 March 1972 and direct rule from Westminster introduced. Both main Loyalist paramilitary groups had their own separate killer squads, each operating under a flag of convenience designed to separate their activities from the parent body. The Protestant Action Force was to the UVF what the Ulster Freedom Fighters were to the UDA. To complicate matters further, there was a third Loyalist killer squad known as the Red Hand Commandos, apparently loosely affiliated to the UVF. Ironically, both Republican and Loyalist paramilitaries started off at the outset of the current round of 'Troubles' as purely 'defensive' organizations: the Provisional IRA to defend its areas from Loyalist attack and the UVF and UDA to defend their people and, by natural extension, 'Ulster' from the IRA's growing onslaught. It was into this jungle of Republican and Loyalist initials that 'Steve' told me he was originally recruited.

I was approached by men older than myself that I had known for many years and had a lot of respect for. I was asked would I like to be involved in the movement that they were involved in. The reasons that they were in that particular movement and wanted me to join were to help defend the population of the place where I had been brought up. You know the story as well as I. There was persecution. People say there was persecution on both sides. We felt at that particular time that we were on the losing side and a lot of innocent people were getting killed. I was asked would I like to join and help to prevent this from happening. I had a lot of respect for the people who had approached me. They were the sort of men that would have called you as a young boy and said, 'Steve, go and get me a packet of cigarettes.' And you went the message [errand] and came back and they 'clocked' your head. You always respected these men. They were the men that had taken you to matches and lifted you over the fence. These people were there to help you, and, just through respect for them and listening to what they were saying, it was quite easy as a young boy to be recruited into the organization.

'Steve' said, not surprisingly, that he did not regard those who recruited him as 'terrorists' at the time. 'I regarded them as people who were there to protect the community of which we belonged.' It was only later, when he became disillusioned with the tactics used, that he saw the organization in a different light.

'Steve' was ritually sworn in and began his training. Indoctrination came first to ensure that the new recruits became fully conversant with the ideological and political reasons that would be used to justify their subsequent actions. 'This sounded very good for a young man. They seemed very just aims and very just goals that the organization had. They seemed genuine in what they were saying.' Once a firm political base had been established, the military training began. Again, guns and bombs were not just thrust into eager young hands. The process began gently. First they were instructed how to riot and how to take advantage of the ebb and flow of those often vicious engagements. Then they were taught how to make petrol bombs, which amounted to little more than stuffing a lighted rag into a milk bottle of petrol and hurling it at the opposition. Rioting became an art form. Next came the guns and lessons on how to strip, maintain and use basic weapons. Then instruction on how to make simple bombs. All this early training took place within the borders of Northern Ireland. In those days, with minimal security and surveillance, such sessions could be carried out in the fields, mountains and woods of the province with small risk of detection. I asked 'Steve' if he had ever been involved in any 'terrorist' action. I assumed he must have been at some stage, and in a major role, to give him the credibility without which he could not have risen within the organization. He was evasive. He asked me how I would define a 'terrorist' action. I said, that as far as the British Government was concerned, it would be one in which you used a weapon or were involved in the setting up of a 'shoot' or a bombing or any similar type of action.

I'd rather not comment on that. Personally I am happy with myself that what I done at that particular time never cost anyone their lives. That's something I know for a fact, that during the lead-up to working for all the people that I have worked for I hadn't hurt anyone. Now you may say, 'How the hell did you get through the organization without doing that?' By being very careful. Also, I wanted to defend people, not to go out and attack people. I think there is a good distinction between defence and aggression.

I supposed, as I listened to him, that 'Steve' must have become one of the so-called 'Godfathers of Terrorism', beloved of leader writers and commentators in the right-wing press. 'Godfathers' plan and give orders but, like the Corleones in the eponymous movies, keep their hands clean. Their authority is based on fear and respect.

As the campaign escalated, operations were carried out by both Republicans and Loyalists that made some of their supporters distinctly uncomfortable. Civilians were now being killed on both sides. 'Steve' did not keep his concerns to himself, and army intelligence got wind of his unease. He was ripe for recruitment or at least for sounding out. Such approaches are made with enormous care and precision. Like fly fishing, the process requires great patience and skill. The CIA tried to recruit Abu Hassan with less subtle methods such as waving a blank cheque under his nose. It failed. British intelligence belongs to the 'softly, softly' school. Recruitment is like courtship of old; the most difficult step is asking for the first date. 'Steve' told me how he was first propositioned in the early seventies.

The first approach was made by an NCO of the British army, who had obviously noticed how I had reacted to certain incidents in the place where I lived. He'd come along and he'd say to me, 'Steve, what did you think of what happened there?', and I'd say, 'Well, I wasn't very impressed with it.' He said, 'My bosses don't believe that you like this, what's going on round here, and they believe that you're against it.' And I said, 'Well, maybe they're right, maybe they're wrong, but I don't want to know.' That was his first approach.
Were you surprised at what he said?
No, because I had stood up and made my voice clear that I objected to some of the attacks that were taking place. They were counterproductive and we weren't achieving what we were supposed to be achieving. Obviously through the intelligence that the British army had, this had maybe filtered its way back to him. I had over the previous eighteen months seen that it wasn't what I imagined it was going to be. There was no great defence of the community, no great protection for the people. It was rather the opposite. You begin to see that people that you had respect for were being pushed aside and

criminals were moving in. So when I was approached by the army I said, 'Look, let me think about it.'

Once the ice was broken, the follow-up approach was easier. Personal contact and consistency being everything, it was made by the same NCO. A Land-Rover pulled up, soldiers jumped out, and 'Steve' was put up against a wall and given a thorough search. He was on his own at the time. No doubt the 'stop and search' was carefully planned. No suspicion would be aroused at the sight of yet another youth up against a wall, surrounded by soldiers. For the NCO a word in 'Steve's' ear was the easiest thing in the world.

> While I'm against the wall getting rubbed down, he's just talking away. General chat, you know: your name, your address, your date of birth, where you come from, where you are going to. In the middle of this he drops in, 'Would you like to talk to my superior? He would like to talk to you. He knows how frustrated you are about what's going on.' And so I said, 'Yeah, OK, let me think about it.' He gave me a number to phone him.

I asked 'Steve' if he knew he was being approached. He laughed and said of course he did but at this stage he wanted out: he realized it was a big mistake to have got involved. A few days later, a Land-Rover pulled up again. There was the same bit of theatre: name and address and the same NCO. This time, 'Steve' agreed to meet his boss. For the young soldier, presumably in the intelligence corps, it was third time lucky.

'Steve' was not prepared to say where he met the 'boss', who was in plain clothes.

> He introduced himself, his rank and his job and what he was doing. He told me what he would like me to do for them and said there would be rewards in it for me. At first, to be honest with you, that took me back because a reward wasn't why I was going to him. I had come to the part where I had realized that these people weren't fighting for our country. They were ruthless. Life meant nothing to them and I didn't want to be part of them any longer. As far as I was concerned, I was going to do something about it, to stop them just killing innocent people – on both sides.
>
> His role was quite clear. It was his job to get intelligence. He wanted to know if I could point him to specific dumps: if I could let them know what the group of people that I belonged to were planning – what they were going to do, not just their military thinking but also their political thinking; if there was any indication of where bombs were going to be put; if I could let them know about targets. They wanted anything that I could pass on.

At first I used to meet them once a week. Going to meet them was quite difficult because where I lived would have been known. You had to be careful how you set out and how you get to meet them. Even now, as you go to meet people, you've got to realize that the guy I go to meet, his life is in my hands for that few hours. If I'm careless, I can take people to him and cost both of us our lives. What actually developed was that you were having three lives to lead. You were leading the life of the supposed terrorist, you were leading your normal family life and you were leading what probably could have been called your 'real' life doing the actual intelligence work. I took comfort from the fact that if ever I had turned round and said to the wife, 'We have to get out of here', she would have just said, 'Let's go.' I knew our relationship was strong enough for her to accept what I was saying.

'Steve' agreed on the spot to become an army intelligence agent although, of course, he was to carry on with his normal, everyday work – which he would not specify. He had plenty of time to think about it. He would not specify the sums of money he received for his work but insisted they were 'only a small amount'. I asked him if he ever had to sign on receipt. He smiled.

The first time that he [my army handler] gave me money he said, 'Steve, would you sign for it?' I asked him, was his head light? That's an old Irish saying [i.e. was he in charge of his senses?]. I said there was no way I was signing for anything – ever. He said, 'But I need you to sign for it.' I said in that case then you keep the money, forget about it. He just said OK and let it go. I was never asked ever to sign for anything again.

In the early days there was so much happening that I was meeting him once a week and there were good results too. I can't go into details obviously, but it was very rewarding from my point of view because if there was a bullet found or a bomb found, or if you were able to give prior knowledge of a target and that target was told not to be there, or if there was road blocks round that target's house or whatever, then it was very rewarding because you'd have saved a life. I always have drummed into myself that if I can get one bullet, that's one bullet that can't kill somebody.

I wondered whether his handlers had asked 'Steve' to do all he could to rise higher within his organization, because clearly an agent of his calibre was a good long-term investment with the prospect of far higher interest. He said he was not asked: it was just something that happened.

I was popular with the people where I belonged, and some of them might have seen me as a champion of their cause and known that they could depend on me to take their part. So it was a natural progression for me just to come up through the organization. But I must say that, when each promotion was offered to me, I came back to my handler and asked, 'Should I take this?' He usually said, 'Yes that's OK', but it did get to the stage where I was once told to go no higher because if I'd have gone higher I couldn't have kept off certain things.

It was always emphasized to me by both the army and the 'agency' [the Security Service] that anything you do, you must do within the law. If you do break the law, we can't help you. If you're caught out doing something, you needn't turn round, throw your hands up and say, 'I've been doing it for these boys', because we can't cover that. That was always drummed into me.

In other words, agents who transgressed were left to twist in the wind. That would explain why there was little contact between Gregory Burns and his army handlers after the murder of Margaret Perry. Despite his assurance, I found it difficult to believe that 'Steve's' hands were completely clean. Paramilitaries are not stupid. How was it possible to remain in a senior position within the organization and still operate within the law of the land without attracting suspicion? The fact that agents and informers are technically breaking the law because they are, of necessity, members of proscribed organizations, is, I assume, accepted by the state when the balance of public interest lies in doing so. I doubted whether the Israelis or the Spanish would ever have insisted on such operational scruples.

I can tell you categorically that I never went out and shot anyone. I never went out and put a bomb anywhere. But I was still able to rise through the organization because not everyone involved goes out and shoots and bombs. There are hundreds of other things that need to be done like administration and to find out intelligence. My main role was to get information, that's what it's all about, right? For the intelligence services to operate they need to know what the terrorist is thinking and my job was to go and find out what he's thinking and come back and report it. Now you don't have to be a bomber or an assassin to get that sort of information, strange as it may seem.
But how could you rise within the organization without ever having shot or bombed? What's your credibility in the organization?
Credibility? There were times I was asked to go out and do things and I had to come back to my controller and tell him. Meetings with him had to be set up within a few hours, which is hard to do. But I *had* to come back and say, 'Look they want me to go and do this or that.'

Maybe I'd have went to do it, pretending to go through with it, and the place would have been swamped with soldiers or police and you wouldn't have been able to get doing it. Then you come back off it and of course you kicked up hell and said 'Somebody's leaked this', you know, always throwing the ball in the other direction. It becomes a game, if you want to call it a game, that I was pitting my wits against the people around me. You have to build your own defence mechanism. It became a matter of throwing out red herrings all the time, and throwing people off different scents. It might seem incredible that I was able to do this but it did work – and it has worked.

Let's say you're asked to go and take part in a bombing or a shooting. What do you do?

Right, I'm called in and told we're going to hit Joe Bloggs tonight. We'll report back here at a specific time. You leave that meeting and go and contact your 'chum' [handler].

On the telephone?

Yes. You just set up a meeting with him and you go and talk it over. You tell him *exactly* what's going down. What I decided when I was doing this job was that at all times I must tell the truth. There was no way I was going to start telling lies. So I would tell him exactly how much of the operation I knew. We would work something out that would give me credibility. It might be possible to go to pick up what you had to do [I assumed he meant a gun or a bomb from a dump or similar] but you couldn't get to it because the security forces were about the place. You couldn't get near it. This meant that the operation couldn't go on. There were a few times this happened.

But wasn't it risky contacting your 'chum' shortly after you had been told to go and do a job and then have that meeting arranged before the job was done? The time-scale is very fine, isn't it?

Yes. Sometimes you had to make the arrangements by telephone, dangerous and all as it is. We had a codeword system where we could talk round things without coming right out in the open. I don't want to get into great detail on it.

You have to move pretty fast.

They're a pretty good team. It's just not a one-man thing. There's a big organization behind it. You know how hard it is to direct twelve Land-Rovers from one side of the town to the other, set up VCPs [vehicle check points], etc. It was happening day in, day out, so it was no big thing.

You mention teamwork. Did you see yourself as being part of a team?

Oh, very much so, I certainly was not a one-man band. I went out, got the information, brought it back to my 'chum', who would take down what I had said. He would go back, tell the rest of the team, and they would discuss the best way of using this information. They would sometimes come back and say to me, 'Look, Steve, are you covered all right if we do it like this?' We'd talk it all through and at all times my security was a priority. They didn't want to have me finishing up with a hood on my head, you know. But there were times when I knew that to save somebody's life I was going to have to run the risk of maybe having to leave the country if things backfired. And there were times when we were sailing really close to the wind, but we were always able to pull it off and get away clean. But there's no doubt I can tell you in total confidence that between us the team saved many lives – many, many lives.

'Steve' spent roughly a third of his time as a British agent working for army intelligence. As 'Steve' prospered, MI5, working in close co-operation with military intelligence, saw his potential as a rising 'star' with both the individual qualities and the access to the high councils of his organization that the Security Service required. With the full support of army intelligence he was transferred without ceremony. 'Steve' was not one to mind.

I was just handed over. I was told you're moving across and mine wasn't to reason why. I am not being derogatory to the army people by any means, because they were excellent with me, but it was a new ball game.

How was it put? You saw it as promotion presumably?

How was it put to me? 'Steve, here's so and so.' You shook hands. 'You'll be working with this man now.' I was asked would I like to do it; would I like to move over to the other people who would like to have me and would like to take me on? I said, 'Yes, sure, as long as it's continuing to do the work I'm doing.'

When you joined MI5, did your conditions of service change?

They were certainly different. I felt that things changed from my personal point of view. I can't go into great detail to explain, because obviously I don't want to give too much away to the people who will see or read what's being said here. Also, some of the requirements on me were actually harder. I had to try harder to come up with a better grade of intelligence.

But the risks would be greater too, then, surely?

Yes. Or the risks became greater as I progressed because the higher you went in the group the narrower the group of people gets.

Did you get more money?

Yes, I did.

What sort of money did you get?

Let's put it like this, I'll never be a wealthy man, but it made life more comfortable. It didn't increase right away, just over a period of time. It just gradually built up.

How was it paid to you?

Cash.

Did your wife ever say, 'Where's the money coming from?'

No, because I was picking up money here and there doing things, so that to have money was not a problem.

The intelligence agencies are very careful about how their agents are paid. For example, to produce a great wad of notes from the latest pay packet in a Belfast pub might just arouse suspicion. The amount given, certainly in cash, has to be commensurate with the money an individual might be likely to have, even after a successful day at the races. If the agent cannot 'cover' it, the agent does not get it, at least not in cash. There are other methods of payment too. There may be help with a car loan or purchase or some other personal need. Bank accounts may be opened too, although few of them, I suspect, are located in Switzerland. But the agent knows they are there. They may be filled not just with regular payments but with bonus money, too, paid for a particularly vital piece of intelligence or tip-off. Those who authorize the payments see it as being like paying a consultant: the greater the results, the more generous the reward. All this is budgeted for in a typically bureaucratic way. The handler discusses the likely requirements of a particular agent with his superiors and a sum is written into the accounts. MI5 is, after all, part of the Civil Service, and it is public money that agents are paid.

I put it to 'Steve' that when all was said and done he was a 'tout', betraying his comrades for money, as Silke Maier-Witt had done for a shorter sentence. I expected him to rise to the remark. He did not.

Probably everyone who will read your book will regard me as that too. A 'tout' is someone who would do the job for money or vengeance. 'Touts', to me, are motivated by either the money, getting their own back on someone, or else they've been caught and they're being blackmailed. None of those three categories do I fit into. I see myself as an agent working alongside other agents. My controller is just a senior agent to me. I'm going out and doing the spadework, if you like, getting the intelligence and bringing it back to him. But I'm doing this to save lives. The financial thing to me is way down the list of priorities, because I wouldn't risk my life, there isn't enough money for you to risk your life like this. I do it because I'm totally dedicated to trying to save people's lives.

That was clearly what 'Steve' meant by job satisfaction: that was his sense of mission, although he accepts he also has to earn a crust. Being an MI5 agent was a full-time job, although, of necessity, it was not incompatible with his 'normal' job that provided his cover. But few jobs carry such risks and demand such a close relationship with your partner. Agent and handler depend on each other because their lives are in each other's hands. The closer the bond, the greater the fruit and the safer the lives of both. 'Steve' told me he had several handlers in his time and had become very close to them all. All bar one, that is. The chemistry was not there and the handler was moved. To 'Steve', a handler is protector, team-mate and 'chum'. Although it may have seemed somewhat sentimental and overstated at first, I suspected that his description of the relationship was broadly accurate.

From my point of view I have this man who becomes my best friend. After I have done my job gathering intelligence, I come back and relate to him all that I have discovered. Then, after that, we have a time where he becomes my colleague and I will then tell him my domestic problems, if I'm having them. Whatever problems are in my life at the particular time, I bounce them off him. He helps me if he can. If he hasn't got the answers he goes and tries to find out the best way to help me.

You make him sound like an agony aunt.

He becomes my agony aunt as well. You know that might seem strange but who else is there in the North of Ireland that I can go to and tell what's happening to me? If I'm having a problem within the terrorist group that I belong to, that's part of the job obviously, he'll have to be there for this; but it goes much deeper because he becomes very close to me and very aware of my feelings. There's a shoulder to cry on – if you want to put it like that – in times of need, and the relationship becomes a very, very strong bond. He's the only person I can talk to about everything. There's nobody else in my life I can do that to. And it could be about anything. It could be that I'm feeling under threat. They may know that already from somewhere else. We can talk it through, about ways of making my life easier or safer, or whatever. Or it may be simple things, like stresses at home, and we can talk about this. You know there's a million things we can talk about. And if things go wrong it is usually when we don't talk. That's the point: we really are giving each other a great deal of help. And I must never act on my own. That's always been drummed into me. 'My problem is your problem.' I think, if I had been the sort of person who would have tried to sort these things out myself, I probably wouldn't have been able to survive.

From my point of view, I wouldn't like to say how many people have been my handlers, but they've been tremendous people. When their term is up, it's like almost having a bereavement because your best friend goes away. Here's a nice person who comes along and treats you decently and treats you with respect. I was never treated as if I was a 'tout'. I was always treated, not as an equal, obviously not because the controller [handler] always controlled the meetings, but he always treated me with respect. There has always been a warmness between myself and each of the controllers which has been very gratifying. You know that has been a bonus because by helping defeat terrorism you actually make friends in the job and I've fond memories of them. But in some ways it's sad too because many times you're only meeting the one member of the team where you'd love to be brought into the meeting and meet *all* the team, and see all the faces. It would be great but obviously I'm just tied to the one person.

Some of the handlers that come to me, I was able to help a lot in the early days as well as them guiding me. I can't go into specifics, but you know certainly I had a lot of experience and in some ways helped them to adjust. If a new handler comes in, no matter how experienced he is, he's quite likely to be relatively inexperienced with what I've been up to, or the current situation. I train the new guy, in a sense, steer him through the first weeks and months in what is a very fluid situation, training him about personalities, people, situations and so on. It's very much a two-way street in that sense.

Behind all this talk of best friends and 'chums' and close bonds, aren't you really being used, and being used to betray your comrades?

Well the fact is that I'm not being used without my consent. I am being used to do a job that has to be done. As far as betraying my comrades, the people who run the terrorist organization are totally without morals. A life is not important to them, a number of lives are not important to them. They don't care whether they are killing a child, a mother, a grandmother or a father. They would, maybe, after an incident where someone's been killed, go and have a drink and celebrate. If this had happened, if I hadn't been successful, and a life is lost, you feel remorse at this.

The thing is that I would not do this job unless it was within me to do it; that I personally had the commitment to do it; and the only reason I was able to do it as well as I did and survive was because I was totally committed to doing it for the right people. I don't do this just for this 'agency', right. I do it for the people of Northern Ireland, Catholic and Protestant. That's my main motivation.

I asked 'Steve' about his own security. Although he said he had enormous trust in his MI5 'team', he could never be '100 per cent confident'. To take anything for granted was taking a risk. That was how he survived. He certainly never felt 'untouchable' – quite the opposite.

I have to be careful in all things that I do, even in what appears to be the normal life of the man next door. It is not really the normal life, because you always have to be very careful what you do, what you say. Even speaking to you I have to be careful. A phrase could give me away: a saying could give you away. You always have to be on your guard. I am always wary, but I don't run around like a scared deer because to do that would be giving myself away immediately. So what I do is I try to conduct myself as normal as possible. If I have anything that I'm worried about, I come back and I discuss it.

I wondered if 'Steve' had ever come under suspicion. I felt sure he must have. He admitted that he had had a close shave or two but declined to elaborate. Would he ever stop working for MI5? Would he retire? It depended what I meant by 'retire'. 'Stop working as an agent', I said. He measured his words carefully.

Yes, in one sense. Perhaps in the more active sense. But there is bound to be a continuing relationship based on my previous work. My knowledge, of course, will always be useful, and they'll also consult on matters which come up about the years that I was working. There would be a lot of that. I will still be very useful.

Would he get a pension? Under the circumstances, it seemed an inappropriate use of the word. He had been assured that he would be well looked after both when he was 'on active service' and when he 'stopped'. He certainly did not expect to be paid for ever but he said his bosses were grateful for what he had done: they recognized he had put his life on the line and they had assured him their 'gratitude' would continue for as long as possible. They had told him to his face that they were greatly indebted to his bravery and had assured him he would 'not be cast away like an old glove'. To do so, they said, would be immoral. There was no doubt that 'Steve' believed them. I had always assumed that most agents were, to use the intelligence jargon, 'exfiltrated' or resettled outside Northern Ireland when their day was done. 'Steve' told me he had not the slightest wish to be sent abroad but had been assured that, if it were thought necessary for security reasons, it would be done. 'Skilled tradecraft and very, very high security', he had been informed, should keep that necessity at bay. But, 'if it has to happen, it has to happen.' Yet he wondered, 'Would that not be a self-denial of the fact that I have struggled so hard over the years, to try and make Ireland a land where people can live together? Why shouldn't I have the benefits of trying to have as normal as possible life there?'

I concluded by asking 'Steve' the question that I knew he must live with every day, as I suspected most agents and informers do. I was thinking of Burns, Starrs and Dignam. Did he feel the hood over his head? He said there were times when he had 'felt it close' but he had to block it out: 'What you do is you build in a mechanism. You can't be silly about it and say this doesn't exist. Of course it exists, but you must take a respite from it or else you would go crazy.' I knew that Loyalist and Republican paramilitaries trained their recruits in how to resist interrogation by the security forces and wondered whether 'Steve' had received training from the Security Service in how to do the same, should he be lifted by his own side on suspicion of being an agent. 'Steve' assured me that he had. He said he had discussed with his handlers what would happen and what he would say.

It's a topic that we can't run away from. Obviously it's one that we don't wish ever to come to fruition, but we do talk about it sometimes. There isn't really anything very much anybody can do about it, once the net has closed around you. And of course it could close round my 'chum' rather than me. There really is very little you can do. You're in God's hands then, or possibly in the security forces' hands if they have an idea that something's gone wrong. You're out in front a bit there and there isn't a great deal around you, just tradecraft really. If I really was convinced something was going to happen, I'm not stranded, I have methods of contacting my handlers. They haven't just said to me, 'Go away and do this', without telling me that I have certain things that are available to me.

Could you withstand an interrogation?

I don't know. I have made up my mind that I will just have to accept the fact that, once you've been taken for interrogation, you're going to die, and what's the point then admitting anything, or naming anyone, because you're still going to die. Now whether you could do that when the time comes, who knows.

If you are interrogated and you know that you will never leave alive, what do you tell your interrogators? Do you sit there and say nothing, or tell them a pack of lies to put them off the scent?

You sit and deny it totally. What would be the point? Make no mistake about this. This has been a thought that has lived with me, daily. In my mind right down into my subconscious now I have felt it . . . denial . . . denial . . . denial. To admit it would not save my life, but to admit it would cause embarrassment to your family. The last thing you can do for your family and your handler is keep them safe. You might as well go out like a man, because to admit it is just to let these people know that they're right.

People who have been 'executed' invariably are said to have made statements beforehand which appear in print.

Yes, and that's probably because they've been told, 'Well, if you come clean and admit it, we'll let you go. You'll have to leave the country, but we'll let you go.' And the silly people admit it. Then they're dead.

Was that what had happened to Burns, Starrs and Dignam and all the other informers who had been 'executed' on both sides? Was that why 'torture' was always denied? Or had they, as they invariably said, made voluntary confessions? Only those who carried out the interrogations would know.

I put one last question to 'Steve', not just for myself but for all those who might wonder why he carried on taking the risk after surviving for so long.

Some people would say you've done your bit, it's time for you to go elsewhere and be secure for the rest of your life. You're still alive – stay that way.

I love the country, I love the people. It's because I feel like this that I have done the job, and I enjoy the people of my country, both religions. I think they're a great lot, you know, they're the loveliest people in the world, to strangers. It's just sad at the minute that they haven't learnt to tolerate each other, but it will come. I believe it will come and if we can keep putting barriers up in front of evil people perhaps normality will come.

Will you see it?

I don't believe it, but if everyone keeps leaving the country, no one will. What's the good of having a flower pot with no plants in it?

When I left 'Steve' at the end of our two-hour conversation, I still did not know whether he operated within a Republican or Loyalist paramilitary organization. I told myself it was better that way.

EPILOGUE
TODAY AND TOMORROW

The problem of 'terrorism' that confronts the democratic state is resolved either when the insurgents are defeated and give up, or when the state wearies and gives in, or when the political issue that feeds the conflict is finally settled. There is an additional scenario that would be recognized as compromise. This outcome is least satisfactory to both parties because it means each has to accept less than it has been fighting for: the state has to face the fact that it has not defeated terrorism, the goal to which it may have long been publicly committed; and its enemies may have to come to terms with a much diminished goal. Politically, such a settlement has to be acceptable to both the citizens of the state fighting 'terrorism' and the members of the organization opposed to it. Pressure from the body politic and pressure from the paramilitaries may drive both sides to such a conclusion. War-weariness is a powerful propellant. In the process of agreeing such a compromise, there are further dangers for the parties involved: the state may lose credibility if it has promised its citizens it would never give in to terrorism; and its enemy may spawn more militant factions determined never to settle for less than the holy grail of its goal. Any compromise settlement has to include elements that enable both sides to save face: the state proclaims a victory in getting the terrorists to renounce their 'armed struggle'; and the enemy gets its prisoners released, although 'amnesty' is a word unlikely to figure as such in the state's vocabulary and the prison doors are not necessarily opened the same day.

In terms of the conflicts examined in this book, Spain and Germany have driven their enemies to the brink of defeat, whereas Israel and Britain seem driven to compromise. Just as Israel cannot defeat the Palestinians, Britain cannot defeat the IRA. By the same token, both the Palestinians and the IRA recognize that they cannot defeat their enemies. The alternative to compromise is an even more protracted conflict with the same stalemate at the end.

Spain is close to defeating ETA because of all the states under consideration it has pursued the most single-minded and effective counter-terrorist policy. The Spanish state has broken ETA militarily and politically. It has centralized its operations, co-ordinated its intelligence agencies and, crucially, gained 100 per cent political and security support from France in a model of international co-operation against terrorism: there is no shilly-shallying on extradition, to the envy of the British, faced with a history of Irish equivocation on the issue. Politically, Madrid has given the Basques much of the substance of what they want, not least their self-respect as a people now with their own political institutions and police force. Outright independence as relentlessly pursued by ETA is a goal that no longer strikes a chord with the majority of Basques, who recognize the anachronism of Basque independence in an ever closer European community of nations. When we talked informally with senior anti-terrorist chiefs in Madrid, they expressed amazement at the lack of consistency and co-ordination in the British state's responses to the IRA with its roundabout of different Secretaries of State, army chiefs and RUC Chief Constables. In Spain, one man, Rafael Vera, has masterminded the political and military campaign against ETA for the past ten years. When the Spanish Socialist Workers' Party came to power in 1983 and Felipe Gonzalez was elected President, Vera was given a job to do. His work is now almost done. He has almost destroyed ETA militarily and outmanoeuvred it politically. I did not point out to those we met in Madrid than in the process of countering ETA Spain's human rights record was far worse than Britain's in fighting the IRA. I suspected that Spain would have made few apologies, subscribing no doubt to the adage of her ancient Roman conquerors, *salus populi, suprema lex*, 'the security of people is the highest law of the land'. It was the argument made by General Aharon Yariv in defence of Israel's covert assassination of her enemies. Yet, admirably, and despite her draconian security policies, Spain has sat down and talked to ETA and remains in constant touch with its exiled leadership in the hope of bringing the *guerra sucia* to a clean end. If Rafael Vera believes that dialogue will serve the interests of the state, then engage in it he will. He has no scruples about 'talking to terrorists' and he – or his successor – may do so in the months ahead.

Yet it would be mistaken to think that ETA is dead and buried. The organization still has support. Although most members of the *cuadrilla* stated categorically that they would never consider joining ETA if they were young people growing up in Ordizia today, only 'Tanke' said he would. The welcome recently accorded to a young man from Ordizia, who did not wish to be identified, returning home after four years in gaol, was testimony to the emotional loyalty that ETA still commands, however diminished its ranks. Four hundred people turned out to greet him with a fiesta – music, dancing and 'welcome home' speeches. 'Prison simply reinforced all that I had felt before,' he told us. 'They tried to get me to accept the "social reinsertion" [amnesty] programme by signing a document renouncing violence but I refused. They try to burn you out but they never succeeded, nor did they do so with my friends. There will always be young prepared to enter ETA. Now is a low period, but the organization will gain strength again. As long as we do not achieve the right to self-determination, we will always be prepared to struggle. Violence has to be accepted as a legitimate means of struggle, even if it means indiscriminate bombings.' According to him, the state will never win. I felt he was more likely to end up dead than victorious.

The German state finds itself in a similar position, although as much through the force of history as through its own counter-terrorist policies, effective though some of them have been. The disintegration of the Soviet empire and the fall of the Berlin Wall marked the end of the ideology and the state that had nourished the Red Army Faction. With most of its members in gaol, and recognizing that it was finished, the RAF sought to negotiate an honourable end to its twenty-year campaign of terror. The German state was not averse to the proposition, given the prospect of saving lives and, in view of the cost of reunification, saving precious billions of Deutschmarks in security costs. After the 'retirement' of Silke Maier-Witt and her comrades to East Germany, the RAF had regenerated its campaign in the 1980s and carried it through to the 1990s, culminating in the assassination of Detlev Rohwedder on 1 April 1991. Rohwedder was head of the Treuhand, the organization charged with privatizing the former East German industries. He was shot dead at his home in Düsseldorf by an RAF sniper at 11.30 p.m. while working at his desk. The sniper was about 60 yards away.[1] Rohwedder was the first terrorist victim of German reunification.[2] Just over a year later, on 13 April 1992, a four-page statement from the RAF was delivered to the offices of Agence France Presse in Bonn. It offered the state a 'deal' in which it would end its campaign if the state released its prisoners – ironically, the cause that had become the RAF's *raison d'être* after the arrest of its founders, Andreas Baader and Ulrike Meinhof, in June 1972. The statement read:

We will cease our attacks on leading representatives of industry and the state in order to allow the necessary process to begin. . . . We have to face up to the fact that we have not been able to achieve a breakthrough for freedom in our combined international struggle. . . . We are no longer attractive to people here. We have realized that we cannot carry on.

But the RAF concluded with a warning that its members would not just 'sit there and watch' if the state continued to act with what it called 'repression and destruction': 'If you do not let all of us who fight for a humane society live, then you must know that your élites cannot live either. Even if it is not in our interests, war can only be answered with war.'

The statement was a response to overtures made a few months earlier by the then German Minister for Justice, Klaus Kinkel. Kinkel was a liberal and a member of the Free Democrats, partners of the Christian Democrats in Chancellor Helmut Kohl's ruling coalition. Kinkel made it known that he was prepared to release some ailing RAF prisoners and be generous in considering the early release of others. 'Reconciliation is the basis of moral and ethical behaviour,' he said, 'and a principle of Christian thought.' The process became known as the 'Kinkel initiative'. It was shrewd political judgement dressed up in humanitarian clothes. With the RAF's ideological and logistical base in ruins, only the prisoners remained as an issue. If this was defused, the RAF would be finished. To Kinkel, it seemed a small price to pay; but his initiative attracted enormous controversy, especially from his more right-wing colleagues in the coalition Cabinet who railed against 'doing deals with terrorists'. When Kinkel became Minister for Foreign Affairs, however, his initiative seemed to run into the sand. Visiting one of the hard-line leaders of the RAF, Helmut Pohl, in prison near Frankfurt, I was told that the omens were not good. Pohl, who had been one of the leaders of the organization's most recent hunger strike,[3] warned that, unless momentum was recovered, measures would be taken. He did not specify what those 'measures' might be. I suspected it was not an idle threat. On 27 March 1993 four masked and armed members of the RAF blew up a brand-new £100 million prison that was due to open in a few days' time. The damage caused by the 200 kilos of explosive was estimated to be over £40 million. A letter with the RAF logo demanded 'Freedom for all political prisoners'.[4] Little appeared to have changed.

I asked Peter Boock, who had once 'guarded' the kidnapped Hanns-Martin Schleyer and who is still in prison in Hamburg, if he thought the German state had won. 'No,' he said. 'In this kind of underground war, there is no winner at all. The state can crush the group a second time, a third time, but there will be new members afterwards and they will be more fanatical than before. It's a never-ending escalation. I don't think there will be a winner at all. If they don't release the prisoners within a certain time, the fighting will continue. There are still around thirty people [out there] underground.[5] There will be further actions and further dead.'

The words were prophetic, although perhaps not in the way that Boock had intended. On 27 June 1993, Wolfgang Grans, 40, wanted member of the RAF who had been underground since 1984, was shot dead in the former East German town of Bad Kleinen in an undercover operation carried out by the heroes of Mogadishu in 1977, GSG-9. Grams, and his girlfriend, Birgit Hogefeld, 36, also a member of the RAF were thought to have been set up by the third person with them who was believed to be a police informer. Forty-four bullets were fired. At first, Grams was said to have been killed in the fusillade until an eyewitness said that he had been wounded and then finished off by a member of GSG-9 who put a bullet through his head from 'a few centimetres' away. Witnesses described it as 'a real execution' and 'like a scene from a horror film'. There was a public outcry. The Minister of the Interior resigned and the Federal Prosecutor was sacked. Paradoxically, it looked like the RAF had struck the greatest political blow in its history: two of Germany's most senior political figures were removed without the RAF firing a shot.[6]

The German state's current preoccupation is with terrorism from the right rather than the left. But as one extreme breeds another, and as social and political discontent grows at the realization that reunification is not the Promised Land, conditions seem ripe for a new RAF generation in which the 'system', not the prisoners, would be the cause. The terrorist problems of the new German state may be only just beginning.

Despite the confident assertion of General Aharon Yariv that Israel's policy of assassinating her enemies worked, it was never a solution to Israel's 'terrorist' problem; nor was deportation of Palestinian militants from the West Bank and Gaza. Both tactics, one covert and the other highly visible, were security measures of punishment and containment. Arguably, they only made matters worse. When, most recently, Prime Minister Yitzhak Rabin expelled 413 suspected activists and supporters of the Islamic fundamentalist movement Hamas, 'The Islamic Resistance Movement', to the bleak mountainsides of South Lebanon he seemed to create a greater problem than the one he was trying to solve. Far from stopping the violence in the Occupied Territories, the deportations breathed new life into the flagging Intifada and gave even greater credibility to Hamas, the organization the action was designed to cripple after its military wing, Al Qassam,[7] had kidnapped and 'executed' Nissim Toledano, a young member of Israel's border police. The mass deportation also threw a temporary spanner into the complex mechanisms of the 'peace process' to which both the Israeli government and PLO were committed. Both sides recognize, weary after nearly half a century of conflict, that there has to be dialogue and compromise to resolve the world's most enduring and bloody conflict. Israel is prepared to give land for peace and the Palestinians now recognize Israel's right to exist. In practical and oversimplified terms, that means Israel giving up some or all of the West Bank and Gaza, the territories she occupied after the June War of 1967, which would ultimately provide the basis for a Palestinian state. This is the goal to which Yasser Arafat is committed, despite scepticism within his own organization and bitter opposition from Palestinian groups outside it, most notably Abu Nidal's Fatah Revolutionary Council and Ahmed Jibril's PFLP (General Command), who are determined to sabotage the peace process at all costs. In early September 1993, an astonished world suddenly learned that Israel and the PLO stood on the brink of an historic peace agreement, secretly put together in Norway away from the spotlight that attended the apparently inconclusive meetings of the official negotiating teams. On inspection it was not, as far as the Palestinians were concerned, even half a loaf: to some, it was barely a few crumbs. Under the anticipated agreement, Israel was to withdraw from Gaza and the town of Jericho on the West Bank as a first step towards limited Palestinian autonomy: in return, the PLO appeared ready to amend its Charter, eliminating references to 'armed struggle' being 'the only way to liberate Palestine' and 'the establishment of Israel' being 'fundamentally null and void'. But for the hard pressed Arafat, such an agreement would be the first tentative step on the road to Palestine – a road which, at the time of writing, seems unlikely to be free from still further blood. The PLO's political strategy, the foundations of which were laid by Ali Hassan Salameh and the CIA over twenty years ago, is a high-risk endeavour with no guarantee of success, despite the PLO chairman's legendary optimism. Already Arafat has seen his support in the West Bank and Gaza eroded by Hamas as young Palestinians, tired of waiting for the PLO to deliver the political goods, flock to the mosques in the belief that Hamas, not the ageing PLO leadership, will finally secure their liberation and will do so at the point of a gun, the very 'terrorism' that the PLO has rejected. Perhaps that is why on 16 May 1993, in an unprecedented joint operation, the PLO's Fatah joined with Hamas's Qassam in an attack that killed two Israeli soldiers in Gaza.[8] Fatah recognized it had to act to halt the slide in its support.

The Gaza Strip, an hour's drive to the south of Tel Aviv, is currently the brutal interface of the conflict for, while, pursuing peace at the negotiating table with her enemies, Israel has not ceased from using the big stick against them in the Occupied Territories. Gaza, home to 800 000 Palestinians, most of them living in the poverty and squalor of huge refugee camps, is feeling the most savage blows. Not, it must be said, that Israel views its inhabitants as innocent parties. It is from here and from the towns and villages of the West Bank that Palestinians have come to shoot and knife to death Israeli civilians: as a result, on 30 March 1993, Israel sealed the borders of the West Bank and Gaza and kept them closed for forty-three days.[9] Visiting Gaza, you can see the desperation.

We arrived in the Khan Yunis refugee camp early one morning and were surprised to see a crowd gathered for no apparent purpose. Such a congregation seemed unusual so early in the day. They were eager to show us why. The Israelis had just blown up fifteen houses. The soldiers had come at six o'clock the previous morning, they told us, blindfolded and handcuffed all the men, taken them away and evacuated the area. They returned to find their homes in ruins. The Israelis said they had been harbouring terrorists – which, of course, the local people denied. A rocket had been fired straight through the door of one house, leaving concentric arches through several walls and blackened bricks at the end where it had finally exploded. Other homes had been reduced to piles of rubble, with dolls, toys and ornaments strewn like flotsam and jetsam after a storm over great lumps of concrete that twenty-four hours before had been ceilings and walls. A door hung off a fridge, revealing its contents: eggs, cheese and tomatoes, all scrambled and fried. The scenes of devastation were illuminated by a sky that hung where once ceilings had been. The families had lost not only all their possessions but all their savings too, with money burned in the flames and gold melted down by the heat. One family I spoke to had left Kuwait after their home had been destroyed during the Iraqi invasion. They had settled in Khan Yunis and managed to get a house together again. Now it was gone. The mother stood distraught, surrounded by her husband and six children. 'We were sleeping. They came at six o'clock in the morning and ordered us out. They said they wanted to search the house and we didn't object. When we returned we found the house as you see it now. We couldn't retrieve anything. It was completely demolished.' I asked if they had been harbouring any 'terrorists' as the Israelis had said. 'We did nothing. I don't know anything. We didn't see any wanted men. I only care about my family. All that I know is how to wash, cook and feed my children every day. Now we are eight displaced persons. We have nowhere to go.'

The following day, the Israeli Defence Forces announced that troops had captured two Hamas fugitives and two gunmen in an attack on a Qassam stronghold in Khan Yunis. Blowing up the houses, the official statement said, had forced the gunmen to surrender. They were believed to have been involved in an ambush on a Jeep on 30 January 1993 in which two Israeli soldiers were killed.[10] No doubt the informers responsible had been well rewarded for their tip-off. I wondered if their houses had survived. I was familiar with the attack because I had seen photographs of the ambushed Jeep proudly displayed on a huge board at the back of the crowded Khan Yunis mosque. Standing in the rubble, I thought of what I had heard Israelis and others say, 'Grab 'em by the balls, and the hearts and minds will follow.' 'Not in Gaza, they won't,' I thought. Every day seemed to bring more violence and more killings, with younger and younger children apparently the victims as youthful Israeli soldiers, in an admittedly hostile environment, threw caution and training to the winds.

Baruch Cohen's eldest son, Adi, had recently served in Gaza and was horrified at the brutalities he saw and their impact on young Israelis. 'You try to speak with nineteen-year-old "Rambos" – because they walk around with knives twenty centimetres long just like Rambo and they act like Rambo – and you try to explain to them that it's not even a fair fight. I mean, what can a skinny twelve-year-old do against eighty kilograms of soldier? Nothing. They used to hit them when their eyes were closed and their hands were tied behind their back. I used to say, "They can't do anything, they won't see you and they won't see the slap before it comes. Listen, if you want to hit something so much, go to the butcher's shop and find a piece of meat and hit that." I tried to stop them but it didn't work. Once you give them the tool which is violence and the ability to use force, they use it everywhere. You let the animal go.' I asked Adi what he thought Israel's policy of an eye for an eye had achieved. 'I don't know,' he replied sadly. 'And the fact that I don't know means that it maybe hasn't achieved anything. My father is dead, and Ali Hassan Salameh is dead, and everything is the same. There are still bombs, still shooting and still more eyes to take out.' Despite Adi's pessimism, though, I felt that the chances of a settlement, given time, were higher than his gloom suggested, not least because both sides want it and need it.

I wish I could say the same about Ireland. Whereas Israel, Spain and even Germany conduct some sort of dialogue with their enemies, Britain conducts none. It is now over twenty-one years since a British minister last engaged in a face-to-face exchange with the IRA when on 7 July 1972 the first Secretary of State for Northern Ireland, William Whitelaw, courageously met most of the Provisional IRA's Army Council at his colleague Paul Channon's house in London. The Provisionals had declared a ceasefire at the time, so that such an encounter was politically possible. Nothing came of it and hostilities resumed two days later. Except for a second, seven-month IRA ceasefire in 1975 when internment was being brought to an end and a few spasmodic 'cessations' since, both state and 'terrorists' have battled on, with Loyalist paramilitaries taking an increasingly bloody part, to the current security and political stalemate. The IRA says it will prosecute its 'long war' until the British tire and withdraw, and the British say they will pursue the IRA until it finally realizes the futility of terrorism. The 'Troubles' could easily extend well into the twenty-first century, with continuing loss of life on all sides and the strain on our democratic institutions that such conflict brings.

In a domestic conflict that has lasted almost a quarter of a century, the British state has tried most security means of combating IRA and Loyalist 'terrorism'. These include internment, unacceptable methods of interrogation, 'supergrasses' ('converted terrorists' who give evidence against their former comrades), extradition, broadcasting restrictions, RUC anti-terrorist units and SAS ambush teams. Internment, ominously, still remains on the statute books on both sides of the border. Each response has dealt the paramilitaries a blow, some more severely than others, but Loyalist and Republican 'terrorists' have been able to survive and recover. Senior officers in the army, the intelligence services and the police on both sides of the Irish Sea all agree that the most they can do is contain Irish terrorism, not defeat it. The solution, they say with one voice, lies in the hands of politicians, not policemen, soldiers and spies. They recognize the deep roots of Irish political violence and realize that they cannot be severed by security measures alone, however harsh and illiberal they may be. The British state, unlike its Spanish and Israeli counterparts, has drawn the line at deportation and covert assassinations. The three unarmed IRA volunteers shot dead by the SAS in Gibraltar were at least 'on active service'. GAL or the Mossad would have disposed of them in their beds. Despite justifiable criticisms of British security policy and abuses of civil liberties, other states have records far worse than Britain's – which is not to absolve successive Labour and Conservative governments of blame. However, as they would be the first to point out, terrorists are no respectors of human rights, not least of the greatest human right of all, the right to live.

The British state has taken numerous political initiatives, too, in an endeavour to bring stability to Northern Ireland and drain support from the 'terrorists'. So far, it has not succeeded. Madrid has been able to pursue a highly successful political policy in the Basque country because it has only one enemy, ETA, and one side to placate, the Basques. Providing a political framework for the Basque country was relatively easy given the readiness of all parties to comply with what was on offer from Madrid. In a nutshell, the Spanish state, too, may have had a troublesome province, but it did not have a million Protestants to contend with. It is this that makes the Irish question so intractable. The danger for any British government, as it knows to its cost, is that any apparent concession to Nationalists and Republicans invites a backlash in kind from Loyalists and Ulster Unionists. Their paramilitaries settle the score in blood. The Anglo-Irish Agreement, designed in part to drain support from the IRA, has not only *not* done that but has alienated Loyalists still more and made their paramilitaries even more violent. This is the great Irish conundrum: how to devise a settlement that displeases all sides least. To date, attempts at any settlement have always excluded the IRA and Sinn Fein, because to involve them at the negotiating table, the government argues, would not only give legitimacy to terrorism but drive the other side out of the door. It is inconceivable at this stage to imagine the leader of the Democratic Unionists, Dr Ian Paisley, sitting down with the president of Sinn Fein, Gerry Adams, when Unionist politicians will not countenance sitting down and talking with ministers from the Dublin government without preconditions. Yet, if there is to be peace in Ireland and the state of terror that now infects the whole of the United Kingdom is to end, that day will have to come. To leave the IRA out of any settlement, however testing its inclusion may be, is a recipe for continuing conflict. One Loyalist serving several life sentences for murder with whom I spoke in the Maze prison recognized that at some stage everyone would have to sit down and talk: and that included the IRA and the Loyalist paramilitaries too. I suspected he was not alone in those sentiments but he had the courage to express them.

At the time of writing, the IRA is anxious to engage in dialogue with the British government, but, it insists, not from a position of weakness. Its continuing ability to devastate not just the town centres of Belfast, Portadown and Maghereafelt but the City of London as well bears testimony to its strength. In the wake of the heartbreaking deaths of twelve-year-old Tim Parry and three-year-old Johnathan Ball in the IRA bombing of Warrington's shopping centre on 20 March 1993, there were, besides the huge outpourings of public sympathy and anger, indications of a readiness to break the deadlock from both the British government and the IRA's political wing, Sinn Fein – but, of course, on certain conditions. The Prime Minister, John Major, told RUC officers in Strabane:

> I have spoken deliberately . . . of the *constitutional* parties. There are those who stand in the way of that process and our position on them has not changed at all. Those who use violence for political aims exclude themselves by their own actions, and, if they wish to be taken into account, the choice lies entirely in their own hands. They must demonstrate to the satisfaction of people who are rightly sceptical that they turn their backs on violence clearly, unequivocally and irrevocably. They can do that, but only they can do that, and I hope that they will.[11]

In other words, the IRA would have to stop shooting and bombing in order to be 'taken into account'. Four days later, at a commemoration of the 1916 Easter Rising, Sinn Fein's president, Gerry Adams, gave his response to the British Prime Minister and advice to his fellow Nationalists in Ireland.

> Sinn Fein remains committed to building a lasting peace in Ireland but responsibility for this is not ours alone. Both Dublin and the SDLP should join with us in placing this reality before the British government.

The Unionist veto over the future of the Irish people is undemocratic and an obstacle to real talks. It will inevitably come to an end. The challenge for all of us is to make this happen sooner rather than later and in a manner that leads to a peaceful and stable Ireland. Unionist consent on the shape of a new Ireland is clearly desirable, but this cannot entail a veto over our future.

An agreement between London and Dublin to end partition should be the policy objective of the Irish agenda for any future talks. A lasting settlement must seek unity and independence in the shortest possible time, consistent with obtaining maximum consent to the process involved. Any other scenario is doomed to failure.[12]

The British state and the IRA still seem miles apart and the prospect of finding common ground equally remote. But the political geography is changing. Just as history has made all parties to the Irish conflict its prisoner, so history may be now offering an escape. The border dividing Ireland is still a line on the map, but it no longer has any economic significance since the advent of the European Single Market. Britain and Ireland are still sovereign and independent states, but their common interests lie increasingly in the European Community of the twenty-first century in which ancient quarrels and lines on maps dividing one member state from another have less and less place. This is the framework in which the resolution of the conflict may finally take place.

But what of the other 'terrorist' threat that stares the world in the face today and is unlikely to vanish tomorrow? I thought of Hussein Musawi sitting in the shade of his garden in Baalbek with a painting of Ayatollah Khomeini on the wall behind him. He calmly assured me of the ultimate triumph of Islam and the inevitable eclipse of the United States. No doubt Iran would agree. I thought of the giant map of America we had passed on our way into town, smashed through with an Islamic fist. I found it difficult to believe that America would lie down and accede to its own demise; Lebanon had sent Tehran false signals. Hussein Musawi smiled. Conflict was only inevitable, he said, if the United States continued to support Israel and oppress the world's poor. I thought of the captured Israeli armoured personnel carrier a few hundred yards down the road, now covered in Islamic slogans and displayed as a trophy of war. He catalogued those to ᵂʰ⸱⸱⸱ᵐ America gives support in order to impede the march of Islam: the ⸱nt on selling out Palestine by compromising with Israel and ⸱ less than the original goal; the military government in Algeria ⸱d an Islamic Republic by refusing to accept the result of the ⸱iving victory to the Islamic Salvation Front; and President

Hosni Mubarak in Egypt currently trying to destroy the militants of the Islamic Group, who also wish to establish an Islamic republic. America, of course, sees it differently: that is why further conflict is inevitable, since Islam regards politics as inseparable from religion. President Clinton's newly appointed Director of the CIA, R. James Woolsey, has no doubt about the current and long-term threat in the wake of the World Trade Centre bomb. On 21 April 1993 he told the Senate Judiciary Committee:

> Iran is by far the most active and dangerous state sponsor. . . . Tehran supports Lebanese Hizbollah both financially and militarily. In large part because of this support over the past decade, Hizbollah now poses a greater threat to US and Western interests than any other Middle Eastern terrorist group. . . . And senior Iranian officials and Tehran's media organizations are funnelling propaganda to the rest of the Islamic world that the United States is the 'Great Satan' whose policy is to oppress Muslims.[13]

On the eve of New York's 4 July celebrations in 1993, the FBI scored a classic anti-terrorist coup. Acting, literally, on inside information, their agents raided a lock-up garage in the borough of Queens and caught nine Islamic fundamentalists allegedly mixing the 'witches brew' of fuel oil and fertilizer. The garage, which had been under FBI surveillance, was a bomb factory. Eight of the nine were arrested. The ninth was an FBI informer who had guided the agents onto their target. To their horror, New Yorkers were told that the hit list inclded the UN Secretariat, the FBI Building and the two road tunnels under the Hudson river that link Manhattan with New Jersey. The city heaved a collective sigh of relief. The FBI had no doubt they had got their men. the court will decide their guilt.[14]

Gazing at the wall that was once the Marines' bar in Beirut, Colonel Bill Cowan was no more optimistic about the future. Terrorism had won hands down, he said, and America had still not worked out how to respond: rhetoric was no substitute for policy. The American public thought the score had been settled when they 'kicked Saddam's arse' in the Gulf, but nothing could be further from the truth. Saddam was a different matter. The threat from Islamic fundamentalist terrorism was here to stay and the White House ignored it at its peril. The World Trade Centre bomb was only a taste of what was to come. So what should America do, I asked. Accommodate Islam or fight? His answer surprised me. I had expected him to come out with six guns blazing. There was no choice, he said. America had to learn to live with it. The alternative was unthinkable. He looked again at the wall.

NOTES

Chapter 1 Munich

1 The Palestine Liberation Organization was formed in 1964 for the purpose of unifying resistance to what Palestinians see as the Israeli occupation of their land. Its object is the creation of an independent Palestinian state on the territory that is now Israel, including the West Bank of the river Jordan and the Gaza Strip annexed after Israel's victory in the Six Day War of 1967. It sees itself as a government in exile and is now recognized as such by the Arab world. The chairman of the PLO is Yasser Arafat – the leader of Fatah ('Conquest'), the guerrilla group that makes up 40 per cent of the PLO's membership. The guerrilla groups, and the PLO itself, have always been regarded by Israel as terrorist organizations. The other main components of the PLO consist of George Habash's Popular Front for the Liberation of Palestine (PFLP); Nayef Hawatmeh's Marxist Democratic Front for the Liberation of Palestine (DFLP); and various smaller groupings. The Palestinian resistance has always been ridden by bloody, internecine fighting, which causes Israel no dismay. The most prominent 'dissidents' are Abu Nidal's Revolutionary Council of Fatah and Ahmed Jibril's Syrian-based Popular Front for the Liberation of Palestine – General Command (PFLP – GC).

2 In Norway, as we will see in chapters 2 and 3, the Mossad 'hit team' killed the wrong man.

3 On 16 February 1992 the Israelis assassinated Sheikh Abbas Musawi in South Lebanon. (He was the cousin of Hussein Musawi referred to in the prologue 'Men of God'.) His car was hit by a rocket fired from a helicopter gunship. Sheikh Musawi was a leader of the Lebanon's Islamic fundamentalist 'terrorist' group, Hizbollah. There is an even more recent indication: on 5 November 1992 five soldiers believed to belong to Sayeret Maktal were killed while on a training exercise in the Negev desert. Details of the exercise were never revealed. According to the *Miami Herald*, their target was to be Abbas Musawi's successor, Sheikh Nasrallah. Reports of the incident and the proposed target were stifled by Israel's military censor.

4 On 6 September 1970 Leila Khaled and Patrick Arguello of the PFLP tried to hijack an El Al jumbo jet but were foiled by Israeli 'Sky Marshals'. Arguello was fatally wounded and Khaled was imprisoned in London after the jumbo had made an emergency landing at Heathrow. To force her release, other PFLP teams then hijacked a TWA 707 and a Swissair DC-8 and ordered them to land at Dawson's Field, a former RAF desert landing strip near Amman. A British BOAC VC-10 en route from London to Bahrein was also forced to land at the strip. The hostages were released from the aircraft and the planes were spectacularly blown up.

5 Dudley Doust, 'Munich: the gunfire still echoes today', *Telegraph Magazine*, 5 September 1992. This is one of the best and most visually rich accounts of Munich. The precise quotation from Dr George Habash is taken from David Hirst's *The Gun and the Olive Branch* (Faber & Faber, London, 1977), p. 314.

6 Palestine had been ruled by the British under League of Nations (later, United Nations)

mandate since 1920 until the country was officially partitioned into a Jewish state and an Arab state by the United Nations on 30 November 1947. Fierce fighting broke out between Jews and Arabs, since Arabs never accepted partition. The fighting intensified when Britain withdrew on 15 May 1948.

7 The United Nations figure for the total number of Palestinian refugees in 1992 is 2 648 727. This is made up of 1 million in Jordan; 459 000 in the West Bank; 560 000 in Gaza; 319 000 in Lebanon; and 299 207 in Syria. The statistics are taken from a UN chart I found pinned to a wall in Gaza.

8 At the beginning of 1993 a committee of the Israeli parliament, the Knesset, was considering allowing Arabs to return to Birim and Ikrit.

9 It is impossible to establish the authenticity of the 'will' reproduced by the Palestinian News Agency on 11 September 1972, a week after the massacre. Munich may have shocked the world but it exhilarated most Palestinians, who would have been at one with the sentiments expressed in the document. They do undoubtedly illustrate the way Munich was perceived by those on whose behalf Black September operated. It is easy to dismiss it as a piece of *post hoc* propaganda. The imagination is stretched by the idea of the participants sitting down and putting pen to paper for three hours before launching their attack and then sending it at 1 a.m. on the night of 4 September, 'by our secret methods to our secret command'. Nevertheless, sections do have the ring of truth, not least the enclosure with the 'will' of what was left from their expenses – $500 and 37 marks – 'which we want to bequeath to the revolution'.

10 'The "will" of the Munich guerillas', Palestinian News Agency, 11 September 1972.

11 On 30 May 1972 at Lod airport, Tel Aviv, three members of the Japanese Red Army group, acting apparently under contract to the PFLP, opened fire on passengers arriving on an Air France flight from Paris with machine-guns and hand-grenades. Twenty-eight were killed and seventy-six wounded. The PFLP claimed credit for the attack as a response to the failed operation at Dawson's Field and the deaths of two members of the Black September earlier that month in a hijacking of a Sabena plane flying from Vienna to Tel Aviv.

12 The Palestinians had asked the Olympic authorities if they could send a delegation to take part in the Games. The request was refused.

13 Interview with Tuvia Sokolovsky in Israel for *States of Terror* (BBC TV, 1993).

14 Interview with Gad Tzbari in Israel for *States of Terror*.

15 Doust, op. cit.

16 Ibid.

17 Ibid.

18 John W. Amos, *Palestinian Resistance: Organisation of a Nationalist Movement* (Pergamon Press, New York, Oxford, Toronto, Sydney, Paris, Frankfurt, 1980), p. 10.

19 Andrew Gowers and Tony Walker, *Behind the Myth: Yasser Arafat and the Palestinian Revolution* (Corgi, 1991) p. 76.

20 Ibid.

21 Ibid.

22 Ibid. 'Fedayeen' literally means 'those who sacrifice themselves'. It has become a generic term for Palestinian guerrillas, a convenient word which carries none of the judgemental overtones of 'terrorists'.

23 Ibid.

24 The Palestine National Covenant is quoted in full in Amos, op. cit., p. 296. It has never been officially revoked by its authoring body, the Palestinian National Council (PNC), although Yasser Arafat unilaterally declared article 9 *caduc* (a French legal term meaning 'superseded') on a visit to Paris in May 1989. As observers have pointed out, the chances of the PNC revoking the National Covenant are as likely as snow in the Sahara.

25 Gowers and Walker, op. cit., p. 100.

26 Ibid., p. 113.

27 Ibid., p. 121.

28 Amos, op. cit., appendix 8, p. 315.

29 BBC Caversham, Monitoring Short Wave Broadcast (SWB), 1 March 1973, Jordanian TV interview with Abu Daoud, ME/4233/A/1, BBC Caversham, Monitoring Short Wave Broadcast (SWB), 27 March 1973, ME/4255/A/7.

30 In 1991 Abu Iyad was gunned down in his villa outside Tunis, which the PLO had made its base after its forced withdrawal from Lebanon in 1982 when Israel invaded the country to deal a mortal blow to the PLO. His assassin was a young Palestinian who was working, not for the Israelis, but for Abu Nidal. Before his death he published his memoirs (with Eric Rouleau) *My Home, My Land: A Narrative of the Palestinian Struggle* (Times Books, New York, 1978), which is invaluable, although obviously self-pleading, source material.

31 BBC Caversham, Monitoring SWB, 27 March 1973, ME/4255/A/5.

32 Ibid., ME/4255/A/7.

33 Interview with Abu Daoud in Tunis for *States of Terror*. I have taken the liberty of making slight alterations to the wording of this interview so that it reads more easily; I have not altered the meaning of the words.

Chapter 2   Vengeance

1 Interview with General Aharon Yariv in Israel for *States of Terror* (BBC TV, 1993). The other quotations in this chapter attributed to General Yariv are taken from the same interview.

2 The report of the Committee of Inquiry, the Koppel Committee, that censured named officials of the intelligence community for their operational negligence, was never published and even today remains a classified document. The General Security Service is, in Hebrew, Sherut Bitachon Haklali, invariably abbreviated to its acronym 'Shin Bet' or 'Sha'ba'k'.

3 Conversation with Ankie Spitzer in Tel Aviv in 1992.

4 David B. Tinnin with Dag Christensen, *Hit Team* (Weidenfeld & Nicolson, London, 1976), p. 64.

5 Ibid.

6 Interview with Abu Daoud in Tunis for *States of Terror*.

7 Interview with Yariv for *States of Terror*.

8 Tinnin, op. cit., pp. 67–8. See also Samuel M. Katz, *Guards without Frontiers: Israel's War against Terrorism*. (Arms and Armour Press, London, 1990), pp. 40–1.

9 Interview with Yariv for *States of Terror*.

10 Michael Bar-Zohar and Eitan Haber, *The Quest for the Red Prince: the inside story of Israel's relentless manhunt for one of the world's deadliest and most wanted Arab terrorists* (William Morrow, New York, 1983), p. 89.

11 Tinnin, op. cit., p. 75.

12 Katz, op. cit., p. 44.

13 Ibid.

14 Bar-Zohar and Haber, op. cit., p. 189.

15 Quoted in Andrew Gowers and Tony Walker, *Behind the Myth: Yasser Arafat and the Palestinian Revolution* (Corgi, London, 1991), p. 162.

16 Interview with Hannan Jihad in Tunis for *States of Terror*.

17 Interview with Um Jihad in Tunis for *States of Terror*.

18 The subtitle of Bar-Zohar and Haber's book, *The Quest for the Red Prince*. (At the time of writing, Eitan Haber is Press Secretary to Prime Minister Yitzhak Rabin.)

Chapter 3   The Hunted

1 The 'Green Line' delineated the borders of the state of Israel at the armistice in 1949. From the point of Israel's security, the border was unsatisfactory, since it gave her only the narrowest of coastal strips from Tel Aviv to Haifa, always vulnerable to an Arab attack thrusting from the east to the sea and cutting the country in half. Israel's security nightmare was eased after the Six Day War of 1967, when she annexed the West Bank (of the Jordan).

2 The Irgun was the Jewish underground resistance movement that fought both the British and the Arabs. For more details, see Notes to chapter 4, note 1.

3 Michael Bar-Zohar and Eitan Haber, *The Quest for the Red Prince* (William Morrow, New York, 1983) p. 92.

4 Ibid., p. 89.

5 Interview with Um Ali in Beirut for *States of Terror*.

6 The massacre took place under the eyes of the allies of the Phalange, the Israelis, who had entered the city after their invasion of Lebanon in 1982. The world was nauseated by television pictures of bodies piled high and walls bespattered with blood as women bewailed their loved ones. An Israeli commission set up to establish the circumstances of the massacre estimated that between 700 and 800 Palestinians had been wiped out. The onslaught was triggered by the assassination of the Christian warlord-turned-politician, Bashir Gemayel, President-elect of Lebanon. The Falangists believed the Palestinians were behind the death of their leader and took their bloody vengeance.

7 Interview with Abu Tareq in Beirut for *States of Terror*.

8 The PLO involvement in the peace process is, at the time of writing, only indirect because Israel has always refused to talk directly to those whom it regards as members of a terrorist organization. The Palestinian delegation is made up of prominent Palestinians who live on the West Bank. They remain in constant contact with the PLO leadership in Tunis. Israel is therefore talking to the PLO in all but name. The fact that the PLO is involved in the peace process has caused considerable divisions within the Palestinian camp because of fears of a sell-out.

9 Bar-Zohar and Haber, op. cit., p. 46.

10 On 15 July 1958, 1700 US Marines landed in Beirut to aid President Chamoun, who was fighting rebels funded and armed by President Nasser of Egypt.

11 Interview by Nadia Salti Stephan, *Monday Morning Magazine*, 26 April to 2 May 1976, vol. 5, no. 202 (Beirut).

12 Andrew Gowers and Tony Walker, *Behind the Myth: Yasser Arafat and the Palestinian Revolution* (Corgi, London, 1991), p. 50.

13 Ibid., p. 33.

14 Ibid., p. 51.

15 Interview by Nadia Salti Stephan, op. cit.

16 Ibid.

17 Gowers and Walker, op. cit., p. 56.

18 Interview with Abu Daoud for *States of Terror*, 1993. Ibid.

19 Interview by Nadia Salti Stephan, op. cit.

20 Amman radio report of confession by Abu Daoud. BBC Caversham, Short Wave Band (SWB) 27 March 1973. ME/4255/A/7. Ibid.

21 *The Times*, 15 March 1971.

22 *Daily Telegraph*, 16 December 1971.

23 *The Times*, 7 February 1971.

24 *The Times*, 5 August 1971.

25 *Financial Times*, 2 July 1973.

26 *The Times*, 2 July 1973.

27 BBC Caversham, Short Wave Band (SWB). ME/4255/A/7. Ibid.

28 Interview with Um Ali for *States of Terror*.

29 Interview with Nidal for *States of Terror*.

30 Interview with Um Hassan for *States of Terror*.

31 The account of the attempted assassination of Abu Hassan is based on the transcript of the judgement of Eidsivating Criminal Court on 1 February 1974, case no. 182/1973. This is by far the most accurate source, since it is difficult to separate fact from fiction in most writings about the incident.

32 Tinnin, op. cit. Information on the back of the dustjacket.

33 Eidsivating Criminal Court, case no. 182/1973.
34 Interview with Um Hassan for *States of Terror*.
35 Interview by Nadia Salti Stephan, op. cit.
36 Interview with Nidal for *States of Terror*.
37 Interview with Um Ali for *States of Terror*.
38 Interview with Karim Pakradouni in Beirut for *States of Terror*.
39 Bar-Zohar and Haber, op. cit., p. 214.
40 The account of the death of Abu Hassan is based primarily on the report of the official Lebanese investigation into the attack by the Investigating Judge, Mohammed Ali Sadeq, dated 11 February 1980.
41 Bar-Zohar and Haber, op. cit., p. 219.
42 Report of the official Lebanese investigation.
43 Interview with eyewitness, Beirut, February 1993.
44 Interview with Abu Daoud for *States of Terror*.
45 Interview with Nidal for *States of Terror*.
46 Interview with Um Ali for *States of Terror*.
47 Bar-Zohar and Haber, op. cit., p. 221.
48 Conversations with Hassan Salameh in Amman in 1992 and 1993.

Chapter 4   The Hunters

1 Etzel is the acronym from the Hebrew initials of the Irgan Zwai Leumi, the National Military Organization, or Irgun as it is more generally known outside Israel. It was the Israeli underground group that fought to end British rule in Palestine.
2 The storming of Acre prison is taken from Tzadok Offir's own account. For a more detailed description, see Menachem Begin's memoirs, *The Revolt* (Dell, New York, 1977), pp. 360–80.
3 Begin, op. cit., pp. 379–80.
4 Interview with Tzadok Offir in Israel in February 1993 for *States of Terror*.
5 Interview with Norit Cohen in Haifa in December 1992 and January 1993 for *States of Terror*. I have altered the occasional word and phrase in the transcript so that it reads more easily, given the language difficulties.
6 Interview with Meir Cohen in Haifa in November 1992 for *States of Terror*.
7 Dan Raviv and Yossi Melman, *Every Spy a Prince: The Complete History of Israel's Intelligence Community* (Houghton Mifflin, Boston, London, Melbourne, 1991), p. 187.
8 Interview with Norit Cohen for *States of Terror*.
9 Interview with Icki Cohen in Haifa in December 1992 for *States of Terror*.
10 Interview with Adi Cohen in Zephat in February 1993 for *States of Terror*.
11 Abu Iyad was assassinated on 14 January 1991 at a villa in Tunis where he was being entertained by a friend. His killer was a PLO bodyguard who was believed to have been acting for Abu Nidal. Abu Iyad's death, coming three years after the assassination of Abu Jihad, was a heavy blow to Yasser Arafat. He had now lost his two senior commanders who had founded Fatah with him.
12 Abu Iyad (with Eric Rouleau), *My Home, My Land: A Narrative of the Palestinian Struggle* (Time Books, New York 1978), p. 113.
13 Patrick Seale, *Abu Nidal: A Gun for Hire* (Hutchinson, London, 1992), pp. 156–8.
14 Abu Iyad, op. cit., p. 113.

Chapter 5   Betrayal

1 Interview with former Stasi officer in Berlin for *States of Terror*.
2 Translation of forged school report (*Reifezeugnis*), dated 23 June 1967. Courtesy of the BKA, Wiesbaden.
3 Interview with Dirk Buechner of the BKA for *States of Terror*.
4 Interview with Silke Maier-Witt in Vechta prison for *States of Terror*.
5 'The Maze: Enemies Within', *Inside Story* Special, BBC TV, 20 November 1990.
6 Alan Bullock, *Hitler: A Study in Tyranny* (Penguin, Harmondsworth, 1975), pp. 93 and 291.

7 Interview with Ilse Maier-Witt for *States of Terror*.
8 Interview with Sabine Seliger for *States of Terror*.
9 *Political Terrorism*, volume 2: *1974–78*, edited by Lester A. Sobel (Clio Press, Oxford, 1978) p. 252,
10 Sobel, op. cit., p. 251.
11 Interview with Peter-Jürgen Boork in gaol in Hamburg for *States of Terror*.
12 Sobel, op. cit., pp. 248–9.
13 Interview with Hanns-Eberhard Schleyer in Bonn for *States of Terror*.
14 Details from photographs of the flat in possession of the BKA, Wiesbaden.
15 The original set of demands provided by the BKA, Wiesbaden.
16 Sobel, op. cit., p. 254.
17 Ibid., p. 255.
18 Ibid., p. 255.
19 *Daily Telegraph*, 26 June 1979.
20 Interview with General Alexander Haig in Washington for *States of Terror*.
21 Interview with Hans Hooker in Mons for *States of Terror*.
22 Interview with Werner Lotze in gaol in Berlin for *States of Terror*.
23 *Guardian*, 26 June 1979.

Chapter 6   The Village

1 William Butler Yeats wrote of the Irish uprising in his celebrated poem, 'Easter 1916':

   All changed, changed utterly:
   A terrible beauty is born.

2 Herri Batasuna was formed in 1978, partly as a response to its rivals' participation in the electoral process following the death of Franco. Its ideology is Marxist, its structure centralist and its modus operandi collectivist. In the Basque country HB enjoys the support of roughly 20 per cent of the electorate. Those elected now take their seats in the Cortes, the Spanish parliament in Madrid, as well as in the Basques' own parliament in Vitoria and local councils in the municipalities. At the time of writing, HB had thirteen seats in Vitoria and two seats in the Cortes after reverses in the Spanish general election of 6 June 1993 when the party lost two seats. Prior to the election, it had four.
3 The PNV was formed in 1985 by the father of Basque nationalism, Sabino de Arana y Goiri. From the 1930s to the end of the Franco regime, it was the symbol of peaceful Basque resistance to centralist Spanish rule. Its traditional constituency is the urban middle class and rural conservatives. The PNV now has five seats in the Cortes.
4 Euzkadiko Ezkerra (EE), 'Basque Left', was formed in 1977 after a serious split in ETA in which one section decided to renounce violence and follow a political path. Its politics are a mixture of socialism and nationalism. EE has three seats on Ordizia's council.
   Eusko Alkartasuna (EA), 'Basque Solidarity', is a more centrist social democratic party formed after a split in the PNV in 1986. It has two seats on the council.
   The remaining two seats are held by the Partido Socialista Obrero Espanol (the Spanish Socialist Workers' Party), PSOE, currently Spain's ruling socialist party led by the President/Prime Minister, Felipe González.
5 'Commando" is the word used by both ETA and the state.
6 The Tupamaros, or Movimiento de Liberación Nacional, were the left-wing revolutionary group in Uruguay that was founded in 1965 and named after the Inca 'Robin Hood', Tupac Amaru. They once robbed a casino and distributed the money amongst the staff. See George Rosie, *The Dictionary of International Terrorism* (Mainstream Publishing, Edinburgh, 1986), p. 205.
7 *Chronicle of the 20th Century*, ed. Derrik Mercer (Longman, London, 1988), p. 1073.
8 *El Mundo*, 29 April 1993.
9 Peter Taylor, *Families at War* (BBC Books, London, 1989), ch. 2. Mairead Farrell was from a

middle-class home in West Belfast. She was shot dead along with her IRA colleagues Sean Savage and Daniel McCann. The three were part of an active service unit planning an operation in Gibralter to blow up a British army band. None was carrying a gun when killed. The incident triggered fierce controversy over an alleged 'shoot to kill' policy by British undercover forces.

10 The *liberados* were the underground members of ETA. The *legales* were those above ground whose affiliations were not known.

11 'Democracy and the Gun', BBC1 *Panorama*, 3 December 1979.

12 Robert P. Clark, *Negotiating with ETA: Obstacles to Peace in the Basque Country 1975–1988* (University of Nevada Press, Reno, Nevada, 1990), p. 47. This is the best account of ETA written in English. It is both readable and scholarly.

13 Ibid., p. 262. The classic book on GAL, which ranks with Bernstein and Woodward's Watergate epic *All the President' Men*, is *Amedo: El Estado Contra ETA* by the two Spanish journalists who broke the story and made it their own, Melchor Miralles and Ricardo Arques (Plaza y Janés/Cambio 16, Barcelona, 1989).

14 Court statement of Mario Correira da Cunha, 20 July 1988.

15 Legal statement of Paulo Figueredo Fontes in Burdeos, 14 February 1986.

16 Ibid.

17 The Organisation de l'Armée Secrète (OAS) was founded by French settlers in Algeria angry at the prospect of France granting the country her independence during the Algerian war of 1954–62. The OAS waged a bloody terrorist campaign both in Algeria and on the French mainland in the closing stages of the war

18 Miralles and Arques, op. cit., ch. 32, 'Amedo's men in France'.

19 Statement of Jose María Rodríguez Colorado given in Madrid on 29 June 1988.

20 Clark, op. cit., p. 62.

21 Ibid. p. 82.

22 Ibid., p. 82.

23 On 27 February 1987 Txomin was mysteriously killed in a car accident in Algeria just as he was about to begin negotiations with emissaries from Madrid.

24 Statement of José Antonio López Ruiz, undated.

25 Clark, op. cit., p. 55.

26 *Guardian*, 22 June 1993. *Independent*, 22 June 1993.

Chapter 7 The Seeds of Conflict

1 *Belfast Telegraph*, 7 February 1940.

2 *Sunday Times*, 6 July 1969.

3 *Independent on Sunday*, 28 March 1993.

4 *Belfast Telegraph*, 7 February 1940.

5 *Daily Telegraph*, 7 July 1969.

6 Interview with Joe Cahill for *Timewatch*, 'The Sparks that lit the Bonfire', BBC2, 27 January 1992.

7 *The Times*, 26 April 1993.

8 The Plantation (or colonization) of Ulster took place in the early years of the seventeenth century under King James I after the defeat of the rebellious Roman Catholic chieftain, Hugh O'Neill, Earl of Tyrone, at the Battle of Kinsale in 1601. His lands were confiscated by the Crown, and the northern corner of Ireland was colonized with Protestant settlers from Britain, in particular with Presbyterian families from the Scottish Lowlands. The strategic purpose of this Protestant settlement was to keep the province safe for the English Crown and keep any potential Catholic rebellion at bay. The Irish problem of today is the legacy of the Plantation of Ulster.

9 From transcripts of interview with Cathal Goulding conducted by Martin Dillon for *Timewatch*, 'The Sparks that lit the Bonfire'.

10 After partition, the twenty-six counties that had achieved dominion status within the British Empire became known as the 'Irish Free State'. As the link with Britain weakened, the

constitution was revised in 1936 and the name was changed to 'Eire'. In 1949, the Republic of Ireland was proclaimed, and the British government gave its guarantee to Unionists that Northern Ireland would never become part of that entity without the consent of the majority of its people. That majority was, of course, Protestant. Republicans still use the expressions 'Free State' or 'Twenty-Six Counties' because their idea of a thirty-two county Irish Republic as declared in 1916 has still to be realized. Likewise, they never refer to 'Northern Ireland' or to 'Ulster' (only six of the nine counties of the ancient province of Ulster are included in the state of Northern Ireland). To them, the Northern state is 'the North of Ireland' or 'the Six Counties'.

11 Henry Patterson, *The Politics of Illusion: Republicanism and Socialism in Modern Ireland*, Hutchinson Radius, 1989, pp. 90–1.

12 Fianna Fail, 'the Soldiers of Destiny', was the Republican Party founded by Eamon de Valera in the 1920s. It remained committed to ending partition and uniting Ireland. The party is the guardian of the Republican holy grail. De Valera had opposed the Treaty of 1921 that had divided the country and fought the pro-Treaty forces led by Michael Collins in a bloody civil war. The new 'Free State' government executed seventy-seven Republicans and put 3000 in gaol.

13 Interview with Joe Cahill for *Timewatch*.

14 Speech to House of Commons, 14 December 1925, *Parliamentary Debates*, series 5, cxlix, cols 25–49.

15 After partition, there were three 'special' groups within the Royal Ulster Constabulary, the A, B and C 'Specials'. The A and C Specials were abolished after the Boundary Commission reported in 1925 that partition and the separate parliaments in Dublin and Belfast were to remain. But the B Specials were not disbanded and were maintained as a paramilitary police force until they were finally disbanded in 1969. They were replaced by the Ulster Defence Regiment, a part of the British army.

16 Remark made to the author in 1974 for Thames Television's *This Week* Special, 'Five Long Years', transmitted 8 August 1974.

17 *Disturbances in Northern Ireland. Report of the Commission appointed by the Governor of Northern Ireland* (generally referred to as the Cameron Report after the name of its chairman, Lord Cameron), appendix 3, section 3, September 1969, Cmnd 532 (HMSO, Belfast).

18 The name of the city has always been contentious. The Unionists and the British call it Londonderry, the name given by its English merchant founders. Nationalists refer to it by its ancient Irish name of Derry. It is complicated by the fact that many Protestants who live in the city call it Derry.

19 Protestants in the city were besieged by the Catholic King James II in 1689 until they were relieved by the Protestant King William's troops. The following year, King William defeated King James at the battle of the Boyne on 12 July 1690, the most hallowed date in the Protestant calendar, symbolizing the triumph of Protestantism over Roman Catholicism.

20 *Sunday Times* Insight Team, *Ulster*, Penguin Special (Penguin, Harmondsworth, 1972) ch. 2. The following references to discrimination are also taken from this source. Greater detail is contained in chapter 12 of the Cameron Report, op. cit.

21 Cameron Report, op. cit., ch. 12, para. 127.

22 Interview with Paul Rose for *Timewatch*.

23 *Hansard*, 25 October 1967, vol. 751, 5th Series, 1686–7.

24 Interview with Lord Jenkins for *Timewatch*.

25 Interview with Lord Callaghan for *Timewatch* by Martin Dillon.

26 Ibid.

27 Cameron Report, op. cit., ch. 4, paras 35–55.

28 Interview with Cathal Goulding for *Timewatch* by Martin Dillon.

29 Broadly, the main difference between Republicans and Nationalists is that many Republicans (but by no means all) support the use of force to achieve a United Ireland, whereas Nationalists seek to achieve the same goal by peaceful, constitutional means. For example, Gerry Adams,

president of Sinn Fein, is a Republican; John Hume, leader of the Social Democratic and Labour Party (SDLP), is a Nationalist.

30 Cameron Report, op. cit., paras 213–14.

31 *Governing Without Consensus: An Irish Perspective*, Richard Rose (Faber & Faber, London, 1971) pp. 474 ff.

32 Michael Farrell, *The Orange State* (Pluto Press, London, 1976), p. 62.

33 Interview with Cathal Goulding for *Timewatch*.

34 *Violence and Civil Disturbances in Northern Ireland in 1969*, Report of Tribunal of Inquiry, volume I (known as the Scarman Report), Cmnd 566 (HMSO, Belfast, 1972).

35 Ironically, the IRA has always been structured along the lines of the British army, with companies, battalions and brigades. The organization's rank and file are known as 'volunteers'. Although this structure changed in the late seventies in response to penetration by the British intelligence services, the upper echelons remain the same, with an Army Council headed by a Chief of Staff who directs military operations, and a General Headquarters Staff responsible for everything from finance to weapons procurement and training.

36 Interview with Cathal Goulding for *Timewatch*.

37 Harold Wilson, *Memoirs: The Making of a Prime Minister* (Weidenfeld & Nicolson, London, 1986).

38 Interview with Lord Callaghan by Martin Dillon for *Timewatch*.

39 Ibid.

40 Interview with Austin Currie by Martin Dillon for *Timewatch*.

41 Interview with Lord Callaghan for *Timewatch*.

42 Scarman Report, op. cit., para. 1.23, p. 9.

43 Breasal O'Caollai, 'Fianna Fail and the IRA Connection', *New Hibernia* (December/January 1986–7).

44 The word 'idly' was included in Jack Lynch's original draft which he placed before his Cabinet. There was, however, some collective rewriting and the word was dropped on the grounds that 'idly' would create the wrong impression.

45 Interview with Lord Callaghan for *Timewatch*.

46 Interview with Neil Blaney for *Timewatch*.

47 Interview with Joe Cahill for *Timewatch*.

48 Interview with Sean MacStiofain for *Timewatch*.

49 Interview with Kevin Boland for *Timewatch*.

50 Ibid.

51 Captain James Kelly, *Orders for the Captain* (James Kelly, Dublin, 1971), p. 246.

52 Interview with Captain James Kelly for *Timewatch*.

53 Scarman Report, op. cit., para. 2.10, p. 13.

54 Interview with Paddy Kennedy for *Timewatch*.

55 Interview with Jim Sullivan for *Timewatch*.

56 Interview with John Kelly for *Timewatch*.

57 Scarman Report, op. cit., para. 2.5, p. 11.

58 Interview with Captain Kelly for *Timewatch*.

59 Francie Donnelly left the IRA twenty years ago. He is now a senior member of the Workers' Party, the purely political organization into which the 'Official' IRA melted when in 1972 it abandoned the military campaign it had briefly taken up again because of the escalating violence in the North.

60 Interview with Neil Blaney for *Timewatch*.

61 Interviews with Francie Donnelly and Captain Kelly for *Timewatch*.

62 *Fianna Fail and the IRA*, author and date of publication unknown. The author is generally believed to be a member of the Official IRA or its political offshoot, the Workers' Party. This

meeting is also covered in Patrick Bishop and Eamonn Mallie, *The Provisional IRA* (Heinemann, London, 1987), p. 94.

63 The Provisional IRA first went into action at St Matthew's Catholic church in the Nationalist enclave of Short Strand in Protestant East Belfast when the church and the Catholic area around it came under Loyalist attack after a Junior Orange Parade on 14 April 1970.
64 Interview with Joe Cahill for *Timewatch*.
65 Interview with Jim Sullivan for *Timewatch*.
66 *Report of Dail Public Accounts Inquiry. Final Report* (1971–2), para. 20.
67 Ibid.
68 Ibid., para. 32.
69 Ibid., para. 33 and following paras.
70 Ibid.
71 Ibid.
72 Ibid.
73 Ibid.
74 Ibid.
75 Interview with Paddy Kennedy for *Timewatch*.
76 Interview with John Kelly for *Timewatch*.
77 The General Army Convention is the supreme authority within the IRA which is normally scheduled to meet every two years. It is made up of IRA delegates from all thirty-two counties. The Convention elects by ballot an Army Executive of twelve, which in turn elects an Army Council of seven. According to the IRA's constitution, the Army Council should meet once a month. It has the power 'to conclude peace and declare war'. The Army Council also has to ratify any death sentence to be carried out on an informer. The IRA's standing orders are contained in a publication known as 'The Green Book'.
78 O'Callai, op. cit. It has proved impossible to be exact about the precise location of the Army Convention meeting, since Republican lips still remained sealed. This venue, however, seems likely: most sources suggest it took place in a rural area of County Roscommon.
79 Interview with Sean MacStiofain for *Timewatch*.
80 Henry Patterson, *The Politics of Illusion: Republicanism and Socialism in Modern Ireland* (Hutchinson Radius, London, 1989), p. 126.
81 Interview with Sean MacStiofain for *Timewatch*.
82 Ibid.
83 Interview with Dr Garret Fitzgerald for *Timewatch*.
84 Interview with John Kelly for *Timewatch*.
85 The process took about a year. The Lower Falls curfew, imposed for about thirty-six hours from 3 to 5 July 1970 after an arms search by the army, added to Nationalists' growing alienation. Such military miscalculations played right into the Provisionals' hands.
86 Richard Deutsch and Vivien Magowan, *Northern Ireland 1968–73: A Chronology of Events*, volume I: 1968–71 (Blackstaff Press, Belfast, 1973), pp. 62–3.
87 Interview with Captain James Kelly for *Timewatch*.
88 Interview with Neil Blaney for *Timewatch*.
89 Dail Public Accounts Committee Report, para. 50.
90 *Fianna Fail and the IRA*, p. 64.
91 James Kelly, op. cit., p. 48.
92 Interview with Dr Garret Fitzgerald for *Timewatch*.
93 Interview with Neil Blaney for *Timewatch*.
94 Interview with Joe Cahill for *Timewatch*.

Chapter 8   A Tangled Web

1 *Irish Times*, 3 July 1992.
2 Peter Taylor, *Beating the Terrorists? Interrogation in Omagh, Gough and Castlereagh*, Penguin Special (Penguin, Harmondsworth, 1980), pp. 260 ff.

3 Peter Taylor, *Stalker. The Search for the Truth* (Faber & Faber, London, 1987), pp. 62 ff.
4 Details of the IRA's 'court martial' proceedings are taken from the 'Standing Orders' section at the end of what is known as the IRA's 'Green Book'. Added to this is a degree of current updating from Republican sources.
5 *Belfast Telegraph*, 6 July 1992.
6 The H-Blocks were the prison blocks in the shape on an 'H' in which Republican and Loyalist prisoners were held. They marked an end to prison life in the 'compounds' where prisoners on both sides had enjoyed what was known as 'special-category status'. After the abolition of this special status, Republican and Loyalist prisoners were regarded and treated as common criminals, a situation which both sides refused to accept. The 1981 hunger strike in which ten IRA prisoners starved themselves to death was a protest against the removal of special-category status.
7 Taylor, *Stalker. The Search for the Truth*, pp. 30–1.
8 *Republican News*, 10 September 1987.
9 In local parlance, the IRA is most often referred to as simply 'the 'RA'.
10 *Craigavon Echo*, 25 June 1991.
11 *The Times*, 6 May 1992.

Chapter 9 The Agent

1 The Falls Road is the Roman Catholic/Nationalist/Republican area of Belfast next door to the Protestant/Unionist/Loyalist Shankill Road. The two populations are separated by the 'Peace Line', a Berlin-type wall designed to keep the sides apart at times of high sectarian tension.
2 Patrick Bishop and Eamonn Mallie, *The Provisional IRA* (Heinemann, London, 1987), p. 187.
3 The UVF had its roots in the Protestant-Unionist armed force assembled in 1912 under Sir Edward Carson to resist Home Rule for Ireland. The name was dusted down again in 1966 and the organization 're-formed' to oppose the liberal policies of Stormont's Unionist Prime Minister, Captain Terence O'Neill.

Epilogue: Today and Tomorrow

1 Dennis Pluchinsky. 'An Organizational and Operational Analysis of Germany's Red Army Faction Terrorist Group (1972–1991), in *European Terrorism: Today and Tomorrow*, ed. Dennis Pluchinsky and Yonah Alexander (Brassey's (US), Inc., Washington, DC, 1992), p. 78.
2 Ibid., p. 79.
3 The hunger strike as propaganda, tactic and recruiting agent has been used by RAF prisoners eleven times since 1973. Only the IRA has used the hunger-strike weapon more often and more effectively. Ibid., p. 50.
4 *Guardian*, 29 March 1993.
5 This rough estimate was confirmed by the BKA, who share Peter Boork's view that the RAF still remains a threat.
6 *The Independent on Sunday*, 11 July 1993.
7 Named after a Syrian Islamic cleric of the 1920s who saw the potential of religion as a revolutionary tool.
8 *Guardian*, 17 May 1993.
9 *Guardian*, 'The Palestinian Economy', Special Report, 27 May 1993.
10 *The Jerusalem Post*, 12 February 1993.
11 Speech by the Prime Minister, the Right Honourable John Major MP, at RUC station, Strabane, on 7 April 1993.
12 Speech by Gerry Adams, president of Sinn Fein, on Easter Sunday to the Drumbo Martyrs Commemoration in County Donegal, 11 April 1993.
13 Statement by Director of the CIA, R. James Wolsey, on international terrorism before the Committee on The Judiciary, US Senate, 21 April 1993.
14 *The Observer*, 27 June 1993.

BIBLIOGRAPHY

Amos, John W. *Palestinian Resistance: Organization of a Nationalist Movement*. Pergamon Press, Oxford, 1980.

Bar-Zohar, Michael, and Haber, Eitan. *The Quest for the Red Prince: The Inside Story of Israel's Relentless Manhunt for one of the World's Deadliest and Most Wanted Arab Terrorists*. William Morrow, New York, 1983.

Becker, Jillian. *Hitler's Children*. Panther/Granada Publishing, London, 1978.

Bishop, Patrick, and Mallie, Eamonn. *The Provisional IRA*. Heinemann, London, 1987.

Clark, Robert P. *Negotiating with ETA: Obstacles to Peace in the Basque Country 1975–1988*. University of Nevada Press, Reno, Nevada, 1990.

Gowers, Andrew, and Walker, Tony. *Behind the Myth: Yasser Arafat and the Palestinian Revolution*. W. H. Allen, London, 1990; Corgi, London, 1991.

Ignatius, David. *Agents of Innocence*. Headline, London, 1991. (This is an excellent work of 'faction' based on Abu Hassan Salameh's relationship with the CIA. It is a remarkably accurate and readable 'thriller'.)

Katz, Samuel M. *Guards without Frontiers: Israel's War Against Terrorism*. Arms and Armour Press, London, 1990.

Martin, David C., and Walcott, John. *Best laid Plans: The Inside Story of America's War Against Terrorism*. Touchstone, New York, 1988.

Patterson, Henry. *The Politics of Illusion: Republicanism and Socialism in Modern Ireland*, Hutchinson Radius, London, 1989.

Pintak, Larry. *Beirut Outtakes: A TV Correspondent's Portrait of America's Encounter with Terror*. Lexington Books, D. C. Heath and Co., Lexington, Mass., 1988.

Raviv, Dan, and Melman, Yossi. *Every Spy a Prince: The Complete History of Israel's Intelligence Community*, Houghton Mifflin Company, Boston, Mass., 1991.

Tinnin, David, with Christensen, Dag. *Hit Team*. Weidenfeld & Nicolson, London, 1976.

INDEX

Entries in bold face type indicate a chapter/section devoted to a subject entry

Abd el Kader 29
Abu Ali 53
Abu Ammar (*see* Arafat, Yasser)
Abu Daoud 11–14, 17, 19, 36–8,
    48, 53–4, 58
'Abu Hassan' (Ali Hassan
    Salameh) 13, 23–4, 27, 57,
    59, 62, 67, 171, 191, 193
    assassination of **28–49**, 50, 201
    birth and background 34
Abu Iyad (Salah Khalaf) 12–13,
    36–8, 59, 200, 202
Abu Jihad 25–7, 202
Abu Nidal 12–13, 191, 198, 200
Abu Tareq 29, 31–3
Abu Youssef 13, 21–2, 45
Abu Zaiad, Moussa 23
Adams, Gerry x, 137, 195
Adwan, Kamal 21–3, 45
Aerbel, Dan 39–41
agents, intelligence **50–62, 170–85**
Agents of Innocence 42
Aguirre, Karmele Martínez
    attempted murder of 99–100,
    102
Aguirre, Nagore 99, 102
al-Assad, President Hafez 32
Al-Kubaisi, Dr Basil 21
al-Shir, Hussain 21
al-Tal, Prime Minister Wasfi 11
al-Umari, Fakhri 13
al-Wazir, Khalil (Abu Jihad) 25,
    35
Albrecht, Susanne 71, 73–4
Algeria, Islamic fundamentalists
    ix
Ali Ahmed Khair 23
Ali Hassan Salameh (*see* Abu
    Hassan)
Alon, Colonel Yosef 38
Aman (Israeli military
    intelligence) 15
Amedo, Detective
    Superintendent Jose 100–1,
    103

America (*see* United States of)
Ames, Robert 42–4, 46
Ansell, Elsie
    IRA murder of 112–13
Arab League 11
Arab nationalism 35
Arafat, Yasser (*see also* Fatah) x,
    10, 23, 25, 29, 32, 35–7, 41–2,
    46, 48, 57, 191, 198–9, 202
    Black September and 11
    Fatah 10–11, 43
    United Nations speech (1974)
    24, 44
Arguello, Patrick 198
Arnott, John Corbett
    IRA murder of 112–13
Arques, Ricardo 103

Baader, Andreas 7, 66, 70–3, 75,
    77–8, 188
Baader-Meinhof gang 7, 66, 70,
    73
Ball, Johnathan
    IRA murder of 113, 195
Barak, Colonel Ehud 21
Barnes, Peter
    execution of 112–14
    reburial of 129, 137
Basque independence, ETA and
    67, **87–111**, 171, 181, 186–7,
    194, 203
Becker, Verena 77
Begin, Prime Minister Menachem
    x, 41, 50–1, 56
Beirut
    hostages ix, 1
    US Embassy bomb x, 2–3
    US Marine Headquarters bomb
    2–3
Benamane 39–40
Berlin Wall (*see* Germany)
Birim 6, 56, 199
'Bixen' 97–8, 104–5, 107
Black September 6, 11, **15–27**,
    35–7, 42, 56, 58, 60–1, 199

Fatah and 14
Israel's response to **15–27**
Munich massacre **5–14**
Blaney, Neil 128, 130, 132, 134–6,
    144–6
Boland, Kevin 128, 130, 132, 145
bombs ix, 2, 91
    American Embassy (Beirut)
    2–3
    Bir al-Abed car x, 3–4
    Bologna railway station 5
    Bombay blitz 5
    IRA Baltic Exchange 114
    IRA 'Bloody Friday' 171–2
    IRA border campaign 114–15
    IRA City of London ix, 114,
    195
    IRA Coventry 112
    IRA Warrington 112, 195
    Israeli school bus 10
    Iwo Jima 2
    King David Hotel, Jerusalem
    51–2, 56
    La Mon restaurant 172
    Lockerbie 5
    Lod Airport 7, 9, 24
    Madrid rush-hour 110
    Queen's Bar, Portadown 149
    Red Army Faction prison 188
    Sala de Fiestas, Ordizia 91
    Uffizi Gallery ix
    US Marine Headquarters,
    Beirut x, 2–3, 197
    World Trade Centre ix, 197
    Zerama bust 91
Boock, Peter Jürgen 73, 76,
    78–80, 189
Bouchiki, Ahmed 23, 40
Bouchiki, Turil 41
Boudia, Mohammed 23
    assassination of 38
Bring, Dagny 40
Britain
    and IRA **112–46, 147–69**,
    186–7, 193, 196

SAS Gibraltar shootings 95, 194, 203–4
Brown, Janet Venn 19
Buback, Siegfried 73
Buechner, Dirk 65–6, 86
Burgos trial (1970) 90
Burns, Gregory
British Intelligence and 153–61, 177
IRA 'execution' of 148–54, 170, 184–5
Burns, Sean 149, 156

Cahill, Joe 114, 117, 129, 137, 146
Callaghan, Lord 122, 126–8
Cameron, Lord 120
Report 122–3
Carlos of Spain, King Juan 98
Carrero Blanco, Admiral Luis
assassination of 92
Castle, Barbara 120
Catholics and Protestants 67, 112–46, 147–69, 186–7, 193–5, 204–5
Chambers, Erika 47
Channon, Paul 193
Christian Phalangists 32, 45
CIA (American Central Intelligence Agency) 3
Abu Hassan and 42, 171, 174, 191
recruitment of agents 43
Clay, James
IRA murder of 112–13
Clinton, President 197
Cohen, Adi 59, 62, 193
Cohen, Baruch x, 67, 171
assassination of 55–62, 152
Cohen, Icki 59, 61
Cohen, Meir 56
Cohen, Norit 56–8, 60–1
Colorado, José María Rodríguez 103
Cosgrave, Liam 145
Cowan, Lt.-Col. Bill 3, 197
Curran, Brendan 158
Curtis, Gunner Robert murder of 146

da Cunha, Mario Correiro 100–1
da Silva, Rogerio 100–1, 103
de Gaulle, General 58
Dellwo, Karl-Heinz 71, 75, 77
Democratic Front for the Liberation of Palestine (DFLP) 198
Dignam, Clair x, 154
Dignam, John 149–51, 158–62, 165–9
IRA execution of 148, 152–4, 170, 184–5
Direction pour la Surveillance du Territoire (DST) 11

Dixon, George 144
Dominguez, Detective Inspector Michel 100–1, 103
Donnelly, Francie 134–7, 206
Dorf, Michael 40–1
Drumm, Jimmy 137
Drumm, Maire
assassination of 137

Egypt, Islamic fundamentalists ix
Elliott, Dr Denis 149
Ensslin, Gudrun 71–2, 75, 77–8
'Esmith' 95–6, 106
ETA 67, 87–111, 171, 181, 187–8, 194, 203
bombing 87, 91, 88
financial infrastructure 107–8, 110
leadership trial 90–1
'Operation Easo' 109
'Revolutionary Tax' 99, 108–10
Etxebeste, Eugenio ('Antxon') 104
Etzel, the 50

Facma, village of 52–3
Fadlallah, Sheikh Hussein 3
Farrell, Mairead 95, 203–4
Fatah (see also Arafat, Yasser; Palestine) 10–13, 15, 17, 19, 21, 23, 35, 37, 42, 52, 54, 57, 60, 191, 198
Black September and 14
Faul, Father Denis 147–8
'Fermín' 106
Fitzgerald, Dr Garrett 142, 145
Fontes, Paulo 100, 102–3
Franco, Francisco 88–9, 91, 93, 98, 103, 203

GAL (see Grupos Antiterrorists de Liberacion)
García, Jon 94–5
Gehmer, Abraham 39–41
Gemayel, Bashir 46, 201
Gentle, Rex
IRA murder of 112–13
Germany
Berlin Wall 63, 65, 83–4, 188
Munich Olympics massacre 5–14, 15–27, 41–2
Red Army Faction (RAF) 7, 63–4, 66–7, 71–5, 80, 86, 171, 188–9
reunification 188
Stasi (secret police) 63–4, 83
and terrorism 186
Gersbach, Sylvia (see Maier-Witt, Silke)
Gibbons, Jim 130
Gibraltar, SAS shootings 95, 203–4

Gimbernato, Jose Antonio 93
Gladnikoff, Marianne 39–41
Goena, Juan Carlos García 103
González, Felipe 110–11, 187
Goulding, Cathal 115–17, 123–5, 129, 133, 135, 137, 142
Grenzschutzgruppe-9 (GSG-9) 77
Grupos Antiterrorists de Liberación (GAL) 98–104, 194
Gulf War 32

Habash, Dr George 6, 198
Haig, General Alexander
attempted assassination of 66, 80–2
Hamas 190–2
Hamill, Daniel Joseph 149
Hamshari, Dr Mahmoud 20
assassination of 59–60
Hamshari, Marie-Claude 20
Hassan, Abu (Ali Hassan Salameh) see Abu Hassan
Haughey, Charles 128, 130, 132, 138–9, 145
Hawatmeh, Nayef 198
Hefferon, Colonel 145
Hefner, Nora 39–40
hijacks
British BOAC VC-10 198
Lufthansa 9, 76
Dawson's Field, Jordan 6, 198
Sabena 199
Swissair DC-8 198
TWA Flight 847 3
Hitier, Christian 102
Hitler, Adolf 5, 88
Hizbollah (Party of God) 1–4, 197–8
Hooker, Hans 81–2
Hoppe, Werner 77
hunger strikes, 155, 208
Hussain of Jordan, King 10–11, 36
Hussein, Saddam 32, 197

Ignatius, David 42
Ikrit 6, 56, 199
IRA (see also Northern Ireland) 67, 112–46, 158, 186–7, 195
Arms Trial (1970) 145
Britain's means of combating 193
birth of the Provisionals 113–14, 123, 141–3, 146
Citizen Defence Committees (CDCs) 132–3
executions of informers 147–69
financial transactions 138–45
hunger strikes 155, 208
internment 114–15, 193
'Operation Harvest' 114–15, 124
SAS Gibraltar shootings 95, 194

Sinn Fein 114, 117, 141, 155,
   158, 194
split 113–14, 123, 135, 139,
   141–3, 146
structure of 206–7
Iran 196–7
Ireland (*see also* Northern
   Ireland)
partition 115, 117, 204
Irgun 50–2, 201
Islamic fundamentalists ix, **1–4**,
   190, 196–7
Israel ix, 29
   Black September **15–27**
   bombing of PLO bases 9
   eye-for-eye policy 193
   invasion of the Lebanon 2, 201
   Irgun 50–2, 201
   June War of 1967 191
   Mossad assassination
      operations 5, 12–13, **16–17**,
      28–49, 54, 58, 187, 190, 194
   Mossad intelligence agents
      50–62
   Munich massacre **5–14**, **15–27**,
      41–2, 198–200
   Palestinian Intifada 24–5, 27,
      53, 190
   Palestian prisoners 7
   Sayeret Matkal 5, 25
   Shiite prisoners 4
   Six Day War (1967) 9, 15, 198,
      200
   'Springtime of Youth'
      operation 21, 23, 25, 45
   and terrorism 186
   United States and 196
Israeli Defence Forces (IDF) 19,
   21
Italian Communist Party 19
Iturbe, Txomin 106

'Jamal' 53
'James' 39
Japanese Red Army 7, 199
Jauregui, Juan Ramon Basanez
   102
'Jean Louis' 101–2
Jenkins, Roy 120–2
Jibril, Ahmed 191, 198
Jordan 10, 11, 12
'Juanra' 97–8, 104–5

Karameh, battle of 10–11, 15
Kelly, Captain James 131–3,
   135–9, 143–5
Kelly, John 132, 137–9, 143, 145
Kennedy, Paddy 132–3, 140
KGB 21, 23
Khaled, Leila 198
Khalaf, Salah (*see* Abu Iyad)
Khalifah, Mansur Suleiman 11
Khan Yunis refugee camp 191–2

Khartoum atrocity 24
Khomeini, Ayatollah 196
Kinkel, Klaus 189
Kohl, Chancellor Helmut 189
Kolberg, Ronald 47
'Koldo' 89–91, 97, 106
Krabbe, Hanna 77
Kulleh, destruction of 28–9
'Kurt' 63–5

Lebanon 2
   Bir al-Abed car bomb deaths x
   Hizbollah **1–4**, 196
   Islamic Fundamentalists ix,
      1–4, 196
   Israel's invasion of 2, 201
   PLO bases in 9
   Shiites 1–2, 4
   TWA 847 hijack 3
   US Marines invasion 34
Lemass, Prime Minister Sean 121
Lindley, Richard 96
Lloyd-George, Prime Minister
   David 118
Lockerbie bomb 5
Lod Airport massacre, 7, 9, 24
'Loli' 93–4, 96–7, 105
Lorenz, Peter 74–5
Lotze, Werner 81
Luykx, Albert 145
Lynch, Prime Minister Jack
   127–30, 132, 145

McAnearney, Father 148
Macedo, Antonio de 100, 103
McCann, Daniel 204
McCormack (*see* Richards,
   James)
McCourt, Father Aloysius 148
McKee, Billy 137
McKerr, Gervaise 149–50, 156
McMillen, Billy 137–8, 141
MacStiofain, Sean 115, 129, 137,
   141–2
Maier-Witt, Hans-Joachim 67–8,
   70, 72, 84–5
Maier-Witt, Ilse x, 68–70, 72, 84
Maier-Witt, Silke (Gersbach,
   Sylvia) **63–86**, 180, 188
Major, Prime Minister John 195
Mandela, Nelson x
Martin, Leo 137
Marx, Karl 88
Marxism 67, 117, 124
Meinhof, Ulrike 66, 70–3, 188
Meins, Holger 71
Meir, Prime Minister Golda
   15–18, 23, 48, 61
MI5 Northern Ireland agents 152,
   154, **170–85**
Middle East (*see also* individual
   countries)
   peace process 42

terrorism ix-x
'Mike' 40
'Miki' 22–3
Miller, Dr Maurice 120
Miralles, Melchor 103
Mitterand, President François 98
Moeller, Irmgard 77
Mohnhaupt, Brigitte 71
Monday Morning 34
Moravia, Alberto 19
Mossad (*see also* Israel) x
   assassination operations 5,
      12–13, **16–17**, **28–49**, 54, 58,
      187, 190, 194
   intelligence agents **50–62**
Mountbatten, Lord 148
Mousawi, Sheikh Abbas
   assassination of 198
Mubarak, President Hosni 197
Mugabe, Robert x
Munich Olympics massacre **5–14**,
   15–27, 41–2, 198–200
Murphy, Lenny 167
Musawi, Hussein 1–2, 196, 198
Mussolini, Benito 88

Nasser, President Gamal Abdel
   34–5, 45, 201
Nasser, Kamal 21–2
Nidal (sister of Abu Hassan)
   29–30, 38, 45, 47–8
Northern Ireland 115, 126, 204
   (*see also* IRA)
   bombs (*see* bombs)
   Cameron Report and 122–3
   Campaign for Democracy in
      Ulster 120
   civil rights movement 122–4,
      126
   conflict x, **112–46**
   Loyalist terrorism 172, 193
   MI5 and 152, 154
   MI5's star agent in **170–85**
   NICRA (Northern Ireland Civil
      Rights Association) 123
   Royal Ulster Constabulary
      (RUC) 118, 123, 125, 127,
      132, 149, 152, 154, 158, 160,
      163, 193, 205
   Red Hand Commandos 172
   SAS ambush teams 194
   Special Constabulary (B
      Specials) 118
   Special Powers Act (1922) 118
   Ulster Defence Regiment
      (UDR) 154–5, 158, 172, 205
   Ulster Volunteer Force (UVF)
      172, 208

OAS (Organisation de l'Armée
   Secrète) 102, 204
O'Connell, David 137
Offir, Tzadok 50–4, 56–8, 60
   attempted assassination of 55

O'Hagan, Martin 168
Okamoto, Kozo 7
Olympic Games, Munich
    massacre **5–14**, **15–27**, 41–2
O'Neill, Captain Terence 121
Ordizia, cradle of ETA **87–111**,
    187, 203
Orme, Stanley 120
Otegui, Juan Maria
    assassination of 99, 102 104

Paisley, Rev. Dr Ian 121, 194
'Pakito' 91–2, 96–7, 107, 111
Pakradouni, Karim 45–6
Palestine
    (*see also* Fatah; PFLP; PLO)
    British rule of 29, 198–9
    Christian Phalangists and 32
    Israel and 9, 186
    Munich massacre **5–14**, **15–27**,
    41–2, 198–200
    National Covenant 10, 199
    Six Day War (1967) 9
Palestinian
    Intifada 24–5, 27, 53, 190
    prisoners 7, 12
    refugees 199
Panorama ETA programme 96
Parry, Tim
    IRA murder of 113, 195
Perry, Margaret
    murder of x, 147–54, 160–9, 177
Perry, Mary x, 147–8, 150–1,
    160–1, 163–4, 166, 168–9
'Pertur', assassination of 96
PFLP (Popular Front for the
    Liberation of Palestine) 6, 9,
    12, 21, 23, 76, 198
PLO (Palestine Liberation
    Organization) x, 5, 10,
    13–14, 17–18, 21, 24–5, 32,
    35, 42–4, 51, 67, 190–1, 196
Peru, Shining Path ix
Pohl, Helmut 189
Ponto, Jürgen, murder of 74
Protestants, Catholics and 67,
    112–46, **146–69**, 186–7,
    193–5, 204–5

Qassam 192

Rabin, Prime Minister Yitzak 15,
    190
RAF (*see* Red Army Faction)
Rafael, Sylvia 39–41
'Raoul' 39
Raspe, Jan-Karl 71–2, 75, 77–8
Reagan, President Ronald 2–3
Red Army Faction (RAF) 7,
    63–4, 66–7, 71–5, 80, 86, 171,
    188–9
Red Cross 11
Richards, James (McCormack)
    execution of 112–14

reburial of 129, 137
Rifai, Zaid 37
Rizak, Georgina 39, 43, 46–7
Roessner, Bernard 77
Rohwedder, Detlev, assassination
    of 188
'Roisin' 160–1, 163, 167
Romano, Ilana 48
Romano, Yossef 8
Rose, Paul 120
Rowland, Gwilym, IRA murder
    of 112–13
Royal Ulster Constabulary
    (RUC) (*see* Northern
    Ireland)
Ruiz, José Antonio López
    ('Kubati') 106

SAS (Special Air Service) 77–8,
    193
    Gibraltar shootings and 95,
    194, 203–4
Sabra 32
Salameh, Ali Hassan
    see 'Abu Hassan'
Salameh, Sheikh Hassan 29–31,
    35, 37, 40, 43–4, 48
Savage, Sean 204
Sayeret Matkal (*see also* Israel) 5,
    25, 198
Scarman, Lord 125, 127, 132–3
Schleyer, Hanns-Eberhard 75–6,
    78
Schleyer, Hanns-Martin 75, 189
    murder of 66, 77–80
Schmidt, Chancellor Helmut 76
Schriver, Peter 47
Schubert, Ingrid 77
Schumann, Jürgen, murder of 77
Seale, Patrick 60
'Sean' 160, 168
2nd June Movement 74
Seliger, Sabine 69
Sharon, Ariel 15
Shatila 32–3
Shenhav, Eli 50
Shiites, Lebanese 1–2, 4
Shining Path ix
Sri Lanka, Tamil separatists ix
Sievert, Sieglinde 67–8
Sinn Fein (*see* IRA)
Sokolovsky, Tuvia 7
Sonenberg, Guenter 77
Spain 93
    Civil Guard 92–3, 98, 110
    ETA and Basque independence
    67, **87–111**, 171, 181 186–7,
    194
spies (*see* agents)
Spitzer, André 18
Spitzer, Ankie 18
'Springtime of Youth' operation
    21, 23, 25, 45
Stalker, John 149–50
Starrs, Aidan 149–51, 158–70

IRA execution of 148, 152–4,
    184–5
Stasi (secret police) 63–4, 83
Steele, Jimmy 113–14, 129, 137
Steinberg, Zwi 40–1
Stephan, Nadia Salti 34
Stephenson, John (*see*
    MacStiofain, Sean)
Stethem, Robert, murder of 4
'Steve', MI5's Northern Ireland
    agent **170–85**
Stewart, Michael 118
Sukairy, Ahmed 35
Sullivan, Jim 132, 137–8
Syria, PLO bases in 9

'Tamara' 39
Tamil separatists ix
'Tanke' 92–3, 97, 105, 187
terrorism
    compromises with **186–97**
terrorists (*see* individual
    names and groups)
Toman, Eugene 149–50, 156
Tone, Wolfe 116
Twoomey, Seamus 137
'Txinto' 94–5, 97
Tzabari, Gad 8

Ulster Defence Regiment (UDR)
    154–5, 158, 172, 205
Ulster Volunteer Force (UVF)
    172, 208
Um Ali 29–31, 38, 45, 48
Um Hassan 34, 39, 43–4
Um Jihad 25–7, 39
United Nations 12, 24, 44, 93
United States of America
    Beirut Embassy bomb 2–3
    Beirut hostages ix
    Hizbollah and **1–4**
    Marine Headquarters bomb x,
    2–3
    policy in Lebanon 2

Vera, Rafael 187

Wahdat refugee camp 11
'War of the Spooks' 54
Weinberg, Moshe 7
Whitelaw, William 193
Whitely, J. H. 120
Wilson, Prime Minister Harold
    120, 125
Woolsey, R. James 197

Yariv, General Aharon 10, 15–16,
    19–20, 23, 27, 187, 190, 200
'Yoyes' 95, 97
    assassination of x, 106–7

Zamir, Zwicka 'Zvi' 8–9
Zein, Mustafa 42–3
Zwaiter, Wael 18–19
    assassination of 59